In 1995 Helen Percy, a young Church of Scotland minister in an outwardly idyllic rural parish was raped by one of her congregation. But instead of the rapist being put on trial, she was – by fellow Church members, ministers, the media and powerful forces in the Church itself. Everything was done to portray her not as a victim but as a willing participant in an affair that never happened. She was accused of 'scandalous, immoral and improper behaviour'.

Scandalous Immoral and Improper – the trial of Helen Percy is her revealing, remarkable and candid story out of the horror of institutional pressure. If only she could admit culpability where none existed. If only she would agree to turn her back on her house and the spiritual and pastoral work that she felt so committed to. If only she would suffer and conform in silence! With the willing cooperation and collusion of much of the public press and media, this is a real life story of how the victim was hounded into submission.

But having survived an exploitative and almost banally abusive episode of rape and her later treatment, she was able to find strength first in facing her own pain, then in the significant support of others. **Scandalous Immoral and Improper** is a beautifully and powerfully written testament to the strength of the human spirit in the face of adversity. It is a burning indictment of conservative forces in Scotland's national Church and among popularly held attitudes. It is a book that shakes to the core our sense of ourselves as compassionate beings.

SCANDALOUS
IMMORAL
and IMPROPER

the trial
of Helen Percy

HELEN PERCY

ARGYLL✣PUBLISHING

© Helen Percy 2011

First edition published in 2011
Argyll Publishing
Glendaruel
Argyll PA22 3AE
Scotland
www.argyllpublishing.co.uk

The author has asserted her moral rights.

British Library Cataloguing-in-Publication Data.
A catalogue record for this book is available from
the British Library.

ISBN 978 1 906134 74 7

Printing: Bell & Bain Ltd, Glasgow

To the memories of

Herbert Whyte, Joe Ritchie, Dennis Leadbeatter,
Hamish and Elizabeth McIntosh, and Steven Mackie
who loved me, believed in the gifts I had to offer,
and never ceased to be proud of me.

Two elderly men had been selected from the people to act as judges that year. . . At midday Susanna used to take a walk in her husband's garden. Two elders who used to watch her every day gradually began to desire her. One day Susanna came as usual. The day was hot and she wanted to bathe in the garden. There was no-one about except the two elders, spying on her from their hiding place.

'Look,' they said, 'the garden door is shut. No-one can see us. We want to have you, so give in and let us! Refuse, and we'll both give evidence that a young man was with you.' Then she cried out as loud as she could.

Next day a meeting was held at the house of her husband Joakim. The two elders arrived, in their vindictiveness determined to have her put to death. . . Susanna was very graceful and beautiful to look at; she was veiled, so the wretches made her unveil in order to feast their eyes on her beauty. All her own people were weeping. The elders then spoke, 'A young man went over to her and they lay down together. From the end of the garden where we were, we saw this crime taking place. . .'

Since they were elders of the people, and judges, the assembly took their word. Susanna was condemned to death.

Daniel began to shout, 'Are you so stupid as to condemn a daughter of Israel unheard, and without troubling to find out the truth? Go back to the scene of the trial.' When the men had been separated, Daniel had one of them brought to him. 'Now then, since you saw her so clearly, tell me what tree you saw them lying under?'

He replied, 'Under a mastic tree.'

Daniel dismissed the man, ordered the other to be brought and said to him, 'Tell me what tree you surprised them under.'

He replied, 'Under a holm oak.'

(Daniel 13 vv 5-58, Jerusalem Bible)

Contents

PART I
SIN

Branding Day At Kilry

March 2011

Her nostrils are filled with the reek of burning horn and she trembles with fear. She is young yet; a maiden ewe, unused to handling by men.

The branding iron is lifted from the side of her head and set back down in the heat of the flame. She is marked now. The letter 'D', seared into her horn, will tie her to this hill farm in the Parish of Kilry for the rest of her life. Whether she strays, breaks through fences, or is lost on the moor, she will always be known by it.

I stroke her speckled brow before releasing her. Momentarily, I see my own reflection in her bronze eye. My virgin flesh was once ripped open by the use of a metal implement. And, like this little sheep, I will be associated with an event in the Parish of Kilry, whether I stay or leave, until the day I die.

I, too, have been branded.

I have been scorched with shame.

Thrift

MY RIGHT HAND is reaching up to grasp the mud-guard of the pram. This morning I was wheeled out to the potato field. This afternoon I am walking home, for the first time, steadying myself by holding on to the side of the vehicle that has transported me since birth.

I have to learn to walk because it is October. The gypsies and their ill-tempered piebald ponies have moved on with their covered wagons and rangy dogs. The harvest is over and we are gleaning what is left. My mother needs to load my black 'Royale' pram with the tubers she picks up from the abandoned drills. Tonight, and many other nights during the winter, we'll bake them in the embers of the open fire. The hard outer shells, encrusted with ash, taste even better than the yellow innards.

In a couple of years, when I'm old enough to go to school, I am enlisted to work, which I enjoy. I come home before dusk, run into the porch to change out of my school shoes and go straight out to the field to glean, until it's quite dark. If the ground is frosted, my fingers are numb with cold and the tatties are as hard as the stones that are upturned from the earth with them. It is impossible to tell stones from potatoes in the gloaming.

I do not think we are poor. It is rather that my mother grew up with the deprivations of the Second World War and is accustomed to practising thrift in all things. She writes out all her weekly housekeeping lists by reciting the items in the same order as they appeared in the ration books of her childhood: *butter, marg, lard, cheese, tea, sugar, bacon. . .* She shows us her own prim school needlework samples of patching and darning and is scathing of my cobbling together the holes in the elbows of my shirts and jumpers. She makes us unplug the iron while there is enough heat left in the plate to press the last garment: we must not waste electricity.

I do not suffer any complex arising from my mother's idiosyncrasies, and I do not remember ever wanting anything. I don't mind that my friends are horrified by the wizened, pitted apples that I eat at dinner-time. The old-fashioned varieties from my grandparents' garden have far more taste than unblemished supermarket French Golden Delicious, so I'm not caring. My older sister is more fashion-conscious, or perhaps more subject to peer pressure, than I am. I trail around the shops behind her as she searches for the 'in' style of school clothing the week before term begins. She has her hair permed. She has new horse-riding boots and jodhpurs. If I ask for anything I don't suppose it will be refused, though it may well be grudged. It's just that I can never think of anything I'd like.

For my fifth birthday I am given a three-legged tortoise and I call him Fred. My summers are spent picking masses of yellow buttercups for him and watching him devour them like a lion at the kill. I also waste hours, sometimes days, searching the herbaceous borders and hedgerows for my sprinting three-legged reptile. Put Fred down in the middle of a great lawn and take your eyes off him for thirty seconds and he will maraud purposefully in his selected direction and vanish into the undergrowth. In the winter Fred is packed in a box of hay and put into the loft to hibernate.

I declare that I will marry Fred when I grow up.

It is during this year that my mother, my big sister, my aunt, my cousin and I visit a small zoo. My mother goes to the ticket booth to pay for the tickets. She must have asked for two adults, two children and one 'under five: entry free'. I am not listening because I can already see the long-necked llamas behind the fence and I'm excited. The ticket man leans right out of the booth and, smiling, asks me cheerfully, 'How old are you, lass?'

I turn my head and beam up at him, pronouncing proudly, 'I'm FIVE!'

My mother is furious with me and I cannot understand why because I have only told the truth.

On Saturday mornings my mother looks in the local paper to find out where there is a jumble sale and off the three of us set on an adventure to one or other small town or village. We join the queue and fall in through the doors at 10 o'clock and make for the tables heaped high with second-hand clothing. People begin churning through the piles, pulling out from the bottom a corner of any material that catches their eye. My mother teaches us all her best bargaining tactics. Always put together a bundle before asking for a price – the stall-holders will charge more for individual items. Hold out one shilling and he will probably not ask for another. Check on the floor to see what has fallen down in the fray, because the rag-and-bone men will take everything that's left. Don't let the big sweaty women elbow you out of the way. Haggle. It is not as if we can't afford to pay two shillings – a pittance – for a second-hand coat. It's just that my mother relishes half-price satisfaction. It's part of the sport.

We have a two-seater Mini pick-up van with an open back. My mother and my big sister sit in the cab. I clamber over the tailgate, on top of the heap of our recent acquisitions. I love travelling in that pick-up. I like to lie on my back watching the canopy of the trees passing above me. It's all the better if it rains, especially splashing along through puddles.

We spend the afternoon having a 'trying on' session and the house is filled with gales of laughter. A skirt, a pair of trousers, is rejected by one and tossed to another to try for size. We are immensely pleased with our better buys, some of which are almost new. Sometimes, I sneak in one thing that is totally ridiculous, just for fun. I never spend more than a few pennies on it. It could be a puce pink blouse with a flouncy collar, or a pair of trousers made for a man with the vastest waistline imaginable. My sister climbs into one leg and I climb into the other and we parade around the room screeching with amusement until we fall over.

I am happy at the little village primary school. I'm confident, competitive, a born ringleader, and I don't stand for unfairness. I trip up the rumbuctious boys if they try to overtake in the dinner queue. I befriend the shyest and the poorest children. There is a family from one of the outlying hamlets who are always dressed shabbily. They come on the school bus unwashed, with matted hair, and the stench of their soiled pants incurs cruel rhymes: '*Cabbages make you stink, beans make you fart. . .*' The names of the victimized children are inserted here, and the ditty ends ungrammatically, '*What a pooh-ey lot you art.*' I make a point of going to sit cross-legged on the floor beside the older boy at story time and I don't hold my nose. I do take care not to brush against him though, because everyone knows he has nits, and my solidarity with the beleaguered doesn't quite stretch to risking contagion. I make sure the youngest, a girl who never speaks, is included in our games of hop-scotch. I push her pebble into the next square with my toe, defying anyone to call it cheating. I don't permit anyone to be teased and I'm not above giving a sharp kick in the shins to sort out a bully. Once, I stage a walk-out from a class in which a teacher is mocking a boy who is dyslexic, and I tell on the teacher to the headmaster.

14

If it was not for my Robin Hood tendency to defend the weak and favour the outcast, I would be classed as a thug. I don't know where this social consciousness comes from! Certainly not from my parents, who are believers in each one doing the best for themselves – even though for my mother the idea of 'enterprise' only includes entering the cut-throat world of jumble sales. She is racially intolerant and disparaging of those she considers 'common'. We're not exactly bourgeois: one of my grandfathers was a baker, the other worked on a pig farm. As for my father, he left school when he was twelve. He's a salesman. He is made redundant from different firms a dozen times, but I never remember him being out of work for long. We're cock-a-hoop if he's working for a biscuit company, as boxes reaching their sell-by date come our way. The samples from the tobacco industry, clockmakers, or tinned soup manufacturers are less popular.

I like our coal-merchant. His kind eyes sparkle in his round sooty face. I don't like having to go and play with his daughter, though. She has callipers on her legs, like a locomotive engine, and she makes scary growls instead of proper words. Another house I don't like going to visit is my best friend's. Her brother threatened to put me in the mincing machine and feed me to the pigs. The animals go berserk when the swill is poured into their troughs at feeding time and the squealing terrifies me.

My big sister is horse-daft and spends all her time at the local livery stables. She tries to teach me to ride on an abominable little grey pony that dives out of the unfenced corner of the sand-school every time we circle round, gallops full-pelt across the paddock, and tips me over his shoulder unceremoniously twenty times during each lesson. I only get back on him because it never occurs to me that I could actually refuse to do something my sister tells me.

I prefer to stay in the stable-yard grooming one particular horse, a Lipizzaner stallion, with which I have developed a bond. Maestoso is seldom ridden as he is old and has earned his retirement. I take him out on the end of a rope to graze the grass verges. I lean against his neck and I tell him he is beautiful. Once or twice, his owner has me fetch a blanket from the tack-room, which he folds and places on Maestoso's back. Then he lifts me up and lets Maestoso and me trot around the sand-school. There's no girth or roller holding the blanket in place. Every time that horse feels the blanket slipping, he stops until I right myself. He never lets me fall.

My big sister is going to the stables to watch the stallion 'cover' a mare and I want to go, too. My mother is very peculiar about it. She's upset, in fact. She doesn't want me to go. She thinks it's dangerous, for some reason. I promise I'll stay behind the fence, well away from the horses' feet. They won't be able to kick me. My mother doesn't say much more – she can utter a whole battery of disapproval in one emphatic, 'Hmmpf!' – but in the end she does let me go.

I am enthralled by the stallion's magnificence, and the change in him. His nostrils flare scarlet. He bares his teeth as he screams, rending the sky with the sound. He prances like a powerful warrior-chieftain, his skin glistening, darkened with sweat. The men use a twitch to hold onto him, otherwise he would drag them – insignificant dwarves – across the ground. He flings himself mightily onto the mare's quarters, biting her neck fiercely, scraping her flanks with his fore-hooves. She wets herself with fright.

My mother need not have worried. I know that the mare will produce a foal in eleven months' time but, strangely, I don't connect this with how humans conceive. This is a question I don't ask. Even at secondary school, I divorce the scene of the mare's service – and other experiences – from the flat diagrams in our biology text-book. We copy out into our jotters the teacher's words from the blackboard: 'The male gamete enters the fallopian tube and unites with the female gamete and a zygote is formed.' I learn it by rote. I don't want it to mean anything to me.

The Ghost of Christmas Past

EVERYONE in our house hates Christmas, except my father. He wants to put up the Christmas tree early and fiddles for hours unravelling the fairy lights. That's when the tempers begin to fray. The lights were put back in the box in working order last January, but it only takes one bulb to have been knocked and the whole circuit's affected. The trouble is, he never knows which one has blown and has to test each one until he finds it.

The fairy that perches uncomfortably at the top of the tree with a spike of pine needles up her frock is scarily ugly. I think she's really a witch. She has a tonsure of lank black hair but her crown has moulted. Her dress is yellowed with age like a rat's teeth, as if she has lived with smokers all her life, and not just for two weeks in each year.

The same things happen December in, December out. The same disjaskit robin on a decaying piece of bark, the same pair of white plastic reindeer with fading improbable ribbons around their necks, the same baubles on the tree (only a few less each year as they

17

tinkle to their grave) and the same figures on the Christmas cake. Jolly Santa Claus lives in a jar at the back of the kitchen cupboard with small sprigs of plastic holly and some inch-high snowmen. A few days before Christmas my mother unscrews the lid of that jar, and tips them out onto the formica kitchen work surface we have always called 'the bluetop'. Out they tumble like the contents of Pandora's box. They hold a horror for me I cannot explain.

The arguments don't change, either. Visitors come to the door with parcels for my sister and me. My father offers round the mince pies and my mother is seething because now she will have to set to and make more.

My father's mother will be here and the first thing she will notice will be some cobweb on the ceiling – and she *will* remark on it. Nanny is obsessed with cleanliness and she has no tact. My mother is tight-lipped and more than usually terse the whole week before her arrival. My father absents himself to go and play with car engines and open a can of beer in next door's garage and is harangued when he returns. My sister, goody two-shoes, helps to prepare a sink full of Brussels sprouts. I have to be nice to nanny, who comments on my acne.

'Haven't you got a lot of spots!'

'Yes, Nanny.'

I am not very fond of nanny.

We have chicken. A fat capon with crisp brown skin. My mother dislikes cooking and lets it be known, though she does it well. My father carves. War only breaks out when the Christmas pudding arrives. Every year without fail, it is precisely as he lifts the handle of the cream jug that, knowing the answer full well, he asks pretentiously, 'Is this single cream or double?' My mother explodes over his criticism of her little economies.

'You *know* it's only single cream!'

'I'm only asking,' he ripostes. 'I'm not complaining; just commenting.'

'You bastard!' puts in my sister. That really ignites the gun-powder, as my father is hyper-sensitive about his ancestry. His father was illegitimate. The cream is thrown across the table. Cutlery flies back.

I cry.

The script was written years ago, although my sister only learns the meaning of the word 'bastard' when she goes to secondary school. Thereafter she uses it as an incendiary device.

I don't know why he always asks about the cream. Each time I will him not to say anything, but he always does.

My father doesn't like my mother being so thrifty with the housekeeping, but he doesn't know all of her tricks. He maintains that certain brand names of products are superior. Kellogg's cornflakes, for example. For over a year now my mother has had a Kellogg's box on the shelf, which she is re-filling surreptitiously with the Co-op's own variety.

We've barely recovered from the double or single cream issue and it's time for the Christmas tea. Tiny sausage rolls heated on a blackened metal tray, followed by tinned fruit and ice cream. Leaning on the bluetop, my mother instructs me to open a tin of sand-textured cubes of white pear, shrivelled anaemic grapes, and bits of peach. I struggle to use that tin-opener. It is the old-fashioned kind, where you have to jab hard with the pointy bit to puncture a hole in the lid and then lever the nose of it around the rim, down and up, down and up. If the point goes in slightly skewhiff it rips up the metal, so you have to make further incisions until they join up. Failing that, you prise up the part of the lid you've lifted, and knife out the contents as best you can. Somehow I never learn to use the tin-opener properly. My mother scolds me for being cack-handed and making dents, rather than holes, in the lids. I cannot explain, even to myself, why this implement is so difficult for me to manage.

My father's birthday is on Twelfth Night and he wants the tree to stay up until then and is stroppy if my mother takes it down any sooner. On his birthday he receives the same royal blue box of handkerchiefs with his initial embroidered on them that was given him at Christmas twelve days earlier. It is also the same box that has sat in the bottom of his sock drawer unopened since January last year. He never appears to notice. This I don't understand about my father; that he will cause ructions over something as paltry as the thickness of the cream, and never comment on something over which he has legitimate cause to grumble – like being given the same box of handkerchiefs twice every year. The corners of that handkerchief box are scuffed and torn, it has been around so long.

Sometimes, I feel sorry for him.

That's Christmas over. Only two more months of dark home-comings from school, mittens threaded on elastic through both sleeves of my coat so I won't lose them, hand-knitted Balaclava helmets, and ribbed green tights that won't stay up, so the crotch is always somewhere down between my knees. Then it will be spring.

The Pea-Green Coat

IN my last year at primary school there is a single incident that I am to shut out of my mind for the next twenty years. For the time being, I remember only the dramatic effect on my psyche. There is a shift in my personality, a turning upside down and a shaking of all that I am.

The confident, outgoing child who has starred in school plays, loving an audience, suddenly becomes withdrawn, shaky and uncommunicative. I won't go into the village shop to buy a packet of sweets. I sit cross-legged for an hour rather than ask to go to the toilet. The school bus arrives and I burst into tears and feel sick. My mother's friend visits for coffee and I hide in the wardrobe. This goes on for weeks. I cannot tell the family doctor what is wrong. He advises forcing me to attend school. So I sit near the classroom door in case I need to be sick. The primary school teacher takes me aside at playtime. I make up an excuse that I miss my best friend, who has moved to Wales.

How can I ever explain to my teacher the horror of what has been done to me? I don't have the vocabulary, even if I could overcome my self-disgust. I dare not bring it to the surface of my memory again. It is better to shut it away. One day I am a child, the next a grown-up. And there are some things about being grown up that have to be borne alone.

I have very few new clothes as a child. Where does the pea-green coat come from? Who gives my mother that coat? Unlike most things, it hasn't been handed down from my older sister. The coat is tailored beautifully, but I hate it. It is gaudy and I do not want to stand out. Nevertheless I am made to wear it. 'Why are you so pig-headed, child? It's a lovely coat!'

I am ten and I make up my mind to run away. If I leave home on the school bus and disappear before the register is taken, I'll have all day to cover a distance. The teacher will assume I am sick until my mother phones to ask why I'm not back at four o'clock. There's only one problem: my coat, pea-green, will make me visible a mile away. But the weather's too cold to do without it.

I bundle up the coat and stuff it under my arm until I've circumvented the village. Along a lonely farm track, I put it on. I don't know how far I've run when I hear a tractor coming and I crawl down into the bottom of a ditch. The farm-hand slows up as he levels with me and shouts above the great roar of the engine, 'You'll need to get rid o' that coat if y'want to hide!'

The pea-green coat is not the only garment my mother forces me to wear against my will. She insists that my sister and I have enormous thick-hemmed knickers that come up almost to our armpits. 'You'll get cold in your kidneys otherwise,' she pronounces. It's no good arguing with her that our kidneys aren't between our shoulder-blades. Anatomy and biology are not my mother's strongest subjects.

I run away because my father hugs me. I hate being touched. I try to push him away or wriggle out of his grasp. The harder I resist, the tighter he squeezes me. I feel revulsion towards him, but he fails to sense my repugnance. His own need is too awful.

Every evening, after I have gone to bed, he comes to say goodnight. I hear him, panther-like, padding down the passageway. He stops at my bedroom door and moves the handle up and down four times to announce his arrival.

I remember nothing else. . . But sometimes I wake up fighting for breath, with a great weight on top of my chest, suffocating me.

The pea-green coat has blown my cover and my feeble attempt at escape is foiled. But I have invented a place where I can go. There are mountains in the clouds. I marvel at them, towering rose-pink over the dawn horizon. I stare at them. How strange that they don't seem to be moving but, subtly, they change in every moment. New peaks appear. Rose becomes amber and then is tinged with flame. This is my cloud-mountain kingdom, my Promised Land. This is where my mind is when you lie beside my body and wish me goodnight. You think I am on the bed. I am not. I am a figment of your imagination. I have gone.

The woman who taught me to look at the clouds works at our primary school. She isn't actually a teacher but perhaps she just can't stand looking at our ignorant paintings any more. She hovers behind me, looking at the grey-white sheet of paper on my easel. There's a thick green line of grass at the bottom, a blue stripe at the top, and a big space in the middle. I have also drawn a house. A square house with a red door and four windows and a pointy red roof. No-one in our village has a house like that but that's how all of us draw them. She takes my arm and guides me out of the class-room to look at the cloud-line and the grass. 'There!' she points. 'There's no gap between the earth and the sky, is there? Go back and look at your picture and tell me what's wrong with it!'

She's right. There is no void. You can pass easily from dirt to oblivion if you really need to.

He hefts himself onto my narrow bed but only my shell lies

there. I notice for myself that clouds are not white. Clouds are blue. Or violet. Or yellow. Or the colour of flamingos in the zoo. Even crimson, if you're lucky. The only colour clouds can never be is green.

At secondary school, I skulk in the boiler rooms all afternoon rather than mouth the word 'period' to the swimming teacher, whereas other girls reach the age of fertility and proclaim it with pride. They laugh when the boys ping their bras on the bus, but I wear a thick jersey right through the blazing heat of June so that no-one will see the straps through my blouse. The bra problem is exacerbated by one more of my mother's parsimonious practices: she has acquired a grey – once upon a time blue – second-hand 28AA for me, not wanting to spend money on an item I may outgrow quickly. It would be fine if the elastic had not already 'gone' with over-washing and if I had enough of a chest to keep the garment in its place. As it is, every time I reach up my arms during netball practice, the diminutive piece of lingerie ends up around my neck.

My mother casts an appraising eye over my breasts, still as flat as fried eggs beneath my school blouse. 'You're getting bigger. You may see a little blood one day.' So I carry on wearing the detested bra and keep watch for my nipples to start bleeding.

When it happens – not from my breasts – my sense of embarrassment is so acute that I am almost crippled with self-consciousness. I hate my body. I want to vanish; to be camouflaged. I have a terror of standing out or being noticed. Eventually I starve myself until I lose enough weight for the monthly bleeding to cease and I no longer have to contend with the shame and mess of being a woman.

My class teacher calls me to her desk. I stand beside her, shaking with nervousness, wondering what I have done. She only asks if anything is worrying me. I am more sensitive than the rest of the class put together, she says. I tell her nothing is wrong. She knows it is a lie. I want to confide in her, but I don't have the words, and my shame is too brilliant a hue.

The headmistress has my parents brought into the school because other teachers have noticed that I am very thin and I tremble all the time, like a cornered rabbit. She summons me to her office and leads an inquisition from the throne-like seat behind her desk. She asks outright why I shake. I won't tell her. This is the worst action she could have taken. I am terrified of the headmistress and now my mother is accusing me of drawing attention to our family. Letting people think there could be something not right in our house is the ultimate disloyalty in her eyes. I have broken the commandment. 'The Bible says, "Honour thy father and mother." This means you must never tell anyone outside what happens behind closed doors.'

My mother is paranoid about 'Stranger Danger'. She never stops reminding us of an incident reported in the newspapers, in which a schoolgirl named April Fab was abducted when she was out on her bicycle not a mile from her home. Once, doubtless thinking of April Fab, my mother tracks me for hours when I visit a bird reserve. She is but a few hundred yards behind me, without my knowledge, the whole day. Eventually I find her sitting on a wooden bench in tears. My mother is terrified lest a man jump out at me from the bushes. She is so solicitous of me outside, but deaf to things that may happen through thin walls.

Hornbeam Wood

You can reach the big wood of hornbeam trees by running up
the grassy lane where so many primroses grow, as far as the
blackthorn copse, where you can stop to swing on the vines
of Old Man's Beard, but don't touch the Lords and Ladies
because they're poisonous. Then on to the Big Manure Heap
of muck, dug out of the winter cow-byre, that's used to
fertilise the land for growing crops. Take the track that leads
between two unfenced fields. A quarter of the way down on
the right hand side there's a slight rise in the banking. You
must lie belly down in the grass to smell the sweet violets
there. Be careful crossing the mossy bridge over the ditch at
the bottom because the planks are rotten.

The hornbeam wood is the refuge to which I flee to be alone,
and daydream. Wild hyacinths flood the place. I let all my
hurts be drowned in purple-blue. Sometimes I pick a bunch
of the hyacinths for my granny. One or two of the stems do
not snap near the bottom but come up with the white parts
from under the ground. The bulbs will never produce flowers
again if this happens. There must be billions of bulbs in the
wood, but the thought that I've wounded one makes me
weep with remorse.

Dusk after dusk I watch the sun turn a particular tree, a wych-
elm, yellow. I am at once transfixed by its glowing leaves, and
poignantly aware of decaying bark and wind-ripped branches.
The wood speaks to me of death as well as transcendence. I
glimpse heaven through coils of barbed wire.

University

HIGHER education has not been an option for previous generations of my family. My cousin is the first to go to university, and I am the second. But I am still a child. I am un-streetwise for my years. I have been brought up in a rural community: I've rarely even travelled alone by bus. I've never been inside a bar or a bank and only once seen a film at a cinema. I've never had a proper boyfriend, never bought an alcoholic drink, never been offered drugs. And I've chosen to go to a university as far away from home as possible.

Why is it theology that I decide to study? Is it because I discovered a sense of spiritual destiny in the hornbeam wood? Do I feel an imperative to warn the world of some kind of evil? Perhaps I just need to interpret these spiritual experiences, which are peculiar in someone so young.

I am at St Mary's College, St Andrews, for a couple of weeks before the first tutorials are arranged. I'm part of a group detailed to meet in the 'annexe classroom', but I don't know where that is.

I'm afraid to speak to the professor, but it will be worse facing his wrath if I fail to find the class, so I dare to ask him.

'It's the room above the ladies' loo.'

'Please, Sir, I don't know where that is either,' I whisper. I've been walking a mile back to the students' residence whenever I need to go; too shy to ask where the toilet is in the college buildings.

'The ladies' loo? That's *far* more important! I'll show you.' He endears himself to me from that moment, because he understands that I am wearing pea-green.

St Mary's is a small faculty within the university and students here and in the hall of residence reach out to me in spite of my shyness. I do my best to merge into the background and hide my homesickness (for where?) and my terror; but in small tutorials or groups where I feel safe, the contradictory side of my personality sometimes emerges. I say little, but when I do interject it is to 'pierce to the heart' as one lecturer observes, at times flooring people unused to such honesty. He also comments that, most students finding university a maturing experience, I grow and blossom quite remarkably.

I don't do well in the first year exams, partly because I am too timid to ask how to take books out of the library. It takes so much energy just to survive, when so many everyday things are unfamiliar to me. I am crippled by my sense of pea-green conspicuousness.

I remain dangerously naive. The first Christmas after I start university, I help in a London charity project, de-lousing vagrants. On Christmas Eve I have nowhere to sleep and I accept floor-space from a male volunteer whom I meet on the shift. He is not going in on Christmas Day and I walk several miles from the Elephant and Castle with an A to Z in my hand, oblivious to my foolhardiness.

At one point I myself have lived in a hostel for the homeless. I am hungry and it is food that lures me into accepting the friendship of a retired bus driver in the next room. He goes out all day, leaving a stew in his slow cooker and invites me to share his supper when he returns. I possess three teabags and a small tin of curried beans, donated from the parish 'poor' cupboard, as I am ineligible for the dole, being too young. The bus driver never touches me, but I could be overworking my guardian angel.

There is a middle-aged Roman Catholic priest tutoring in college. He is shy to the point of being socially inadequate, and desperately unattractive. I've been selected as a volunteer with The Samaritans, in the city of Dundee across the Firth. My first shift is on a windy night when the Tay Bridge is closed to buses. This priest offers to drive me to Dundee in his car. He stops in a dark street and puts his arms around me. I am baffled about what to do, so I make no movement at all. The expression on his ruddy, pockmarked face is that of a mistreated dog. I am intensely aware of his loneliness, his need simply for human comfort. He just holds me, no worse. I sit as still as a statue, wishing the time to be over.

On the train at the beginning and end of each term, passengers with peculiar mannerisms always – without fail – sit next to me. Once it is a transvestite ex-priest who has been in psychiatric care. Another time, a man with a severe speech impediment on the Scotrail Express engages my attention, loudly. The other occupants of the carriage nurse their briefcases and pretend not to notice. People with special needs latch on to me, too. I make friends from every age and background imaginable. Some have university degrees and some cannot even write their names.

No social misfit ever harms me. Rather it is the grandfatherly professor who does so, mainly through unintended rejection. I lose count of the number of times my absent-minded mentor offers to meet me at the station and forgets, or promises to visit and doesn't. At first his memory lapses amuse me, but several times I prepare meals for him, and after I've waited in all day I ring his home number. 'It slipped my mind,' he says.

There is a part of me that, despite the horror of showing up in pea-green, is extrovert. I seldom go to pubs and parties, but when

I do I can play the fool or entertain the company with a wild performance, quite without aid of alcohol. Here I am entering a Cossack-dancing contest at a wedding: my partner is the rotund Trinidadian father of the bride. Everyone else clears the floor to watch our antics. He is almost helpless with mirth and finally plumps himself down with his arms folded in front of him and shoogles his ankles in the air. I am kicking out my legs and turning ridiculous circles, balancing on one hand and then the other. We claim the prize.

Now I am at the College Dinner, donning a white surplice and standing on a table, miming an infant school nativity angel, doing my best to keep up my heavy winged arms, and unselfconsciously adjusting my itchy halo.

I put on an even brighter, more lurid jacket over the top of the one I am trying to hide.

I learn so much more at university than theology. I meet people of different nationalities. I become accepting and tolerant of diverse cultures. My parents have tried to inculcate in me racism, homophobia and Thatcherite values. I broaden my contacts, confirming my suspicion that my parents' attitudes were not always reasonable. My mother washed every piece of fruit she bought, cackling, 'You don't know what dirty old black man's had his paws over that!'

I shall not see my parents again; for this, and other reasons.

Lindisfarne

ONLY once am I 'in love'. Perhaps it is with the island backdrop itself that I begin a romance, rather than with the boy.

It is the university recess. I am working on Lindisfarne for the summer. The sand-dunes are spangled with Northern marsh helleborines and pearl-white grass of Parnassus, as if flakes of snow have just begun to settle – in July. The boy and I, liking but not yet loving, reach the shore as the sun is sinking and lie side-by-side on a flat rock, listening to the melodious moaning of the seals. We gaze out to sea as the horizon catches fire, scarcely able to breathe because of the beauty of it. The air becomes chillier. I have a sweater with me which I have pulled on over my t-shirt, but my legs are bare and I shiver slightly. My companion places his leg over my shin, to warm me.

All at once the spell of the singing seals is broken. I am a wild bream in the river. The rim of the net is being dropped over me. I panic, and flip. Inconceivably, he fails to notice as I tense up in fear

31

and gasp for breath. He begins to run his big toe up and down the sole of my right foot, like the poacher playing the fish. I am hauled out of the water, drowning in air.

Already it is late September, and the weather hot. The boy gives me a rose from the garden, this last day before I go back to St Andrews and tells me hesitantly that he has fallen in love with me. Did I not realise it, in those weeks since our dark walk back from the rocks where the seals were chanting? I am less certain of what I feel for him. This is so new to me. It is true that my heart almost stops beating when he comes into a room, but entrancement is intertwined with an unnamed dread.

We talk late into the night. The boy is confused by his feelings, too. He does not tell me now, but only later, that he has been in love before – with another young male. He has had a number of sexual encounters since the age of fifteen, and all of them with men. He does not know how his orientation would have been defined if he had not been in a religious institution at this turbulent age, and attracted so much attention from homosexuals there. He is in his early twenties now, but still looks an angelic fourteen. The dark eyes, the dimpled cheeks, the shy manner, have been his misfortune.

His room is tiny. Only a single bed, a bookcase, and a bedside table. We sit side by side on the bed, like a pair of bewildered newly-fledged birds perched on a ledge. I am getting up to go back to the female accommodation when the boy puts an arm around my shoulders and makes as if to kiss me. I feel his breath on my neck, his tongue at my ear.

In my last year at primary school there is a single incident that I am to shut out of my mind for the next twenty years. . . *There was something that happened, a decade ago now. I do not yet know what it was.*

He brushed my ear-lobe, that's all.

I dive for the waste-paper bin and retch.

Several hours later, my face still swollen with crying, it is too late to return to my own room. My housemates will have locked up. I stay with the boy, but I wear all of my clothes, as well as his long winter coat from the back of his bedroom door. On this hot summer night.

We write to each other – I from St Andrews University, and he from his job south of the border – two emotionally vulnerable young people. Our care for each other is suffused with all the bittersweet agony of a fated love-story. He copies out poetry for me and sends pressed wild flowers and grasses from the machair. I freeze in draughty public telephone boxes all that winter, pushing coins into the slot, and standing one foot on top of the other on the cold concrete.

The boy is still torn between his attraction to his male lover and his emotional need for me. He is also toying with the idea of returning to the friary, this time as one of the religious brothers. I hold all this in my heart, a loyal Heloise to my vacillating Abelard.

I think my heart will break when he enters the friary, but unwittingly he eases the parting for me in a chance conversation that sheds a new light on him entirely. I have already begun to think that giving up his girlfriend is not going to be so difficult for him. Sacrificing me is a means of gaining the applause of less devotional mortals. I am a character in his tragic drama; part of the line he reels out, to anyone who will listen, about how noble it is to submit one's life to God.

We are sheltering from the wind behind the castle wall, a fortnight before he is to begin his noviciate. It is the last time I am to visit him and I have been crying at night for weeks. I ask how his boyfriend has taken their final goodbyes. 'Oh,' he says, casually. 'I'll still be able to see him. I'll have holidays, you know. Many of the friars have sex with several other men. Celibacy only applies to nuns.'

'Why? Why should it be different for women?'

'It's the act of penetration that makes it count as promiscuity.'

So that's it! A woman becomes a man's possession, his chattel, which he can choose to keep or discard, by penetrating her? He impales her on the end of his spear and then she becomes his prize? He 'scores', as they say, but she is labeled a slut and is classed as used goods? I cannot believe my ears: that I am hearing this in the 1980s from a male who is not, supposedly, a savage.

Winchester Farm, Boarhills

THE Final Examinations are over. The students are leaving and the halls of residence are being prepared for the use of summer tourists. I have nowhere to go. I visit college friends who have been renting a farm cottage outside the town, which is cheaper than university accommodation.

Jumping down from the coastal route bus at the farm road end, I see the elderly farmer striding towards me across the field. I tear down the quarter of a mile to the semi-detached cottages. After tea, the same old man brings a bucket of windfall apples and collects the rent. Glancing at me for the first time he soothes, 'You need never run away from me, my dear.'

I do not, indeed, need to be afraid of Herbert Whyte. For his size and for all his shoulders are as broad as those of a bull, there is a gentleness of spirit, almost a tenderness about him. He is the Session Clerk at Boarhills Kirk, a bachelor living with his spinster sister.

Herbert Whyte interviews me in the big farm kitchen before agreeing to my taking over the tenancy of the cottage when my friends leave. He asks direct questions. Will I keep the garden tidy? Do I have a boyfriend? No, I answer, I won't have anyone staying with me. I assume Mr Whyte wishes to be sure of my 'moral fitness' to occupy the premises. In fact, he requires only honesty.

Herbert Whyte teaches me how to plant and hoe and keep straight the top pole for the runner beans by lining it up with the horizon.

I haunt the cliffs. Kyttock's Den in May is awash with wild hyacinths, an indigo foretaste of the ocean at its foot.

At dusk I enter the byre where the sheepdog is chained. The white tip of Jay's tail, flicking welcome, is all I can see in the darkness.

One night when he comes out to feed her, Herbert finds me curled up in the straw beside Jay and invites me into the farmhouse kitchen for cocoa. We sit either side of the fire hugging the warm mugs, and Herb begins to relate tales from his time in a German POW camp. They passed the long hours in the flea-ridden huts after labour by holding informal classes: one man teaching a foreign language, perhaps, or some other subject of which he had knowledge. There was a common dread, unspoken, that armistice would never come. Some had already starved to death. Herb describes the time they enticed a cat through the wire, with promises of affection and a titbit saved from their meagre rations, then strangled and ate it. The tabby farm feline twists itself around Herb's legs, hoping for milk, as he is speaking.

'I can tell you these things, my dear, because you've suffered too.' How can he know this? I've never spoken of it. He has no idea of the nature of my hurt, but he senses that I am attuned to pain because I have borne it.

Winchester Farm is a haven for me and for a number of mice determined to over-winter in the saucepan cupboard. I eat healthily for once, as the garden yields peas, neeps and such an abundance of beetroot that I am searching for recipes for beetroot jelly and beetroot biscuits! Beetroot pie? Cake?

Today I'm graduating as Master of Theology with Honours. I've won the Samuel Rutherford Prize in Practical Theology and Christian Ethics and the N.H.G. Robinson Prize in Divinity. I want someone to be proud of me, someone to be here in the place of my parents today. My lecturers and professors are present, including the Adviser of Studies who, two years ago, declared I was 'on the slow side'. I don't hold it against him. There was so much keeping me back.

Slowly, my confidence has crept out from underneath the hem of the pea-green coat.

Voluble Mrs Drummond-With-The-Cats, in the adjoining cottage to mine at Winchester, is calling in her cosseted pussies with strips of turkey breast. I'm living on a shoe-string and open my mouth before I can stop myself. 'I've never tasted turkey,' I hear myself saying. My neighbour gives me some of the cats' dinner, and I am embarrassed.

I do have turkey this Christmas: Peter Douglas, the jolly, balding, kilted minister with cartoon-character tufts of white hair above each ear, jalouses that I shall be alone. 'You'll come to the manse for your dinner tomorrow. Pick you up at twelve.'

I think their table will break under the weight of the biggest bird I've ever seen. I've never had brandy butter, nor seen real candles on a Christmas tree. I always anticipated Christmas with dread as a child. Now, as an adult, for the first time I am round-eyed with wonder.

It is to Peter Douglas, the minister at Boarhills, that I first verbalise my sense of 'calling'. I know I'm going to end up following the same path he has taken. I experience it as a nagging, a gnawing, a knowledge that I am being pulled up a path I have not chosen for myself. I try to resist it and explore more attractive career possibilities, but I can never shake off my earlier sense of 'prophetic' purpose that I felt so strongly in the hornbeam wood as a child. I'm hardly destined to be a famous martyr, like Joan of Arc and Saint Bernadette who were my girlhood heroines. Nevertheless, the sense that there is something I must do, and cannot avoid, festers in me like a wound that won't be ignored.

I help paint the window frames for Peter's house. He's only just brought them across from the glazier, but I lean too heavily on the heel of my hand and shatter a pane. I anticipate anger, but Peter laughs. My mother has always damned me for breaking things, even though I never drop them on purpose. Fear makes me clumsy. If someone shouts instructions at me I become dithery and incapable of taking action.

It is months before the son of Mrs Drummond-With-The-Cats utters a word to me, or even raises his sun-visor when scuttling up the path running between our two gardens. He is as taciturn as she is talkative. He and I only ever have three conversations in as many years – about motorbikes, or rare wild plants we've found in Kyttock's Den or along the shore. In the third year he asks me to be his girlfriend. Rather, Sandy Drummond asks his mother to ask me to be his girlfriend! I blame myself if he has mistaken my friendliness for something more than that. My refusal will hurt. I write a letter, circumventing his go-between mother, and tell him I think I have been abused sexually and this has left me too afraid to countenance a relationship with any man. I write this to soften the blow of rejection for him, not because I am looking for any sympathy.

Sandy Drummond's reply is genuine, surprising, and without rancour or self-interest. He wants me to find help and to be released from fear. He has seen me working with children with disabilities. I shed my fear of the coal-merchant's daughter and her leg-callipers long since, and now spend any spare time I have teaching such children to ride ponies. Sandy Drummond sees me setting off uphill on my bicycle on Saturdays, to help at the Riding for the Disabled.

I'm very slight in weight, so I can sit on a small pony and hold a child in front of me. Isn't it time I was as gentle with myself? My healing is more important to him than any disappointment over being turned down.

I summon the courage to take Sandy Drummond's advice and find the number of a telephone help-line for survivors of sexual abuse, based in London. The man who answers my call has a gift for drawing people out to speak about what has happened to them. He talks about his own experience in such a matter-of-fact fashion that it is possible to say absolutely anything to him. He tells me I should buy a teddy bear, of all things! I may be grown up now, but I must allow myself to be the child I was never given the chance to be. He asks if I had an eating disorder as a teenager. There's a strong correlation between anorexia, bulimia and sexual abuse, he says. It's true, I was anorectic for several years in my teens, because I hated my body and the womanhood it represented. I wanted to punish it because I felt dirty. By starving myself, I was exercising control over my body, when someone else – whose features are a blur – had stolen that control.

The man on the help-line also guesses that I am terrified of anything to do with sex. I don't need to tell him much; he seems to know everything about me. 'Some of us become promiscuous because of premature sexual sensitising. For others, like you, sex becomes repulsive,' he explains. 'But even though you are afraid, you can behave in ways that some predatory men will choose to misinterpret as sexually provocative. We've been propelled into adulthood, you see, but bits of us are still childlike. That makes us vulnerable. It invites exploitation. You are totally without guile. Quite unguarded. Most adults are wrapped around with many layers of pretence and the pretence protects them. You are still open, like a child.'

'Why is it all so foggy?' I ask. I am thinking of the incident on the seal rocks on Lindisfarne, when I wanted to slip underneath the waves because the air was drowning me. 'It's as if my body recalls every minute detail, but in my mind there's a trip-switch. Something happened, but I don't remember what it was.'

'It's called dissociation. It's a coping mechanism. If you can't remove yourself from danger physically, you absent yourself mentally. You go somewhere else in your head. If the trauma is repeated many times, eventually you become almost too good at this disappearing trick: it's like, there's something that triggers it, and your brain short-wires itself. PING! You're in China, or Outer Mongolia.'

My kingdom in the clouds. It's easy to go there. The difficult part is bringing myself back.

'In your case, whatever it was that happened, the noise of the alarm became so shrill and terrible that you had to sabotage the fuse box to silence it.'

I never see Sandy Drummond again but I respect his selflessness and his integrity. I sense he must harbour some private agony, too. He could not be as reclusive, nor as sensitive to another's hurt, without bearing a wound of his own.

Sandy Drummond's secret is buried with him. He is found murdered the following year. His strangled corpse has been dragged along a track not far from the farm. His killer has never been found. If I had been as good a confidante to Sandy Drummond as he was to me, perhaps he would have entrusted me with some clue to what was going on in his life. Perhaps his death could have been avoided.

I am shell-shocked.

I find it hard to trust. I am secretive. I catch myself prevaricating, even when friends ask where I've been on holiday. It's not as if there's any reason for them not to know. I just can't throw off my family's injunction 'not to tell what happens in our house'.

I meet Paul, a veterinary surgeon, when a friend in England is on holiday and I am looking after her few sheep. Paul asks me out on a date. I agree but, really, it is his job that is the appeal. I try to visit on weekends he is 'on call' so that I can be there when there's a difficult cow calving or assist in the surgery in an emergency. If Paul is doing routine tests on a herd I check the animals' ear-tags and label the test-tubes. My friendship with Paul is an antidote: it is as phlegmatic as the Lindisfarne one was emotionally charged. We live a long way apart and he signs off his letters, 'Best wishes, Paul.'

I am surprised when Paul soon suggests we become engaged. Panicking, wanting to warn him off, I blurt out what has happened to me. He replies laconically, 'I suppose at my age I'd be lucky to find a wife who's untouched. At least you don't smoke.'

His remark makes me feel tarnished, but I don't write off the idea of marrying him altogether, because he does not push me towards sleeping with him. He says he never will, even if we wed. I am unlikely to meet another man like him, I think. There is no spark between us, but he is decent and kind.

The fear does not go away. A few months after our tentative engagement we visit my cousins on their farm in the New Forest. I stayed several summers with them when I was at school, relieved to escape from home and happy to spend hours grooming and stroking the horses and feeding the cows. The father, Dick, used to tease me constantly. He thought me a strange, serious little creature. His own children were so much more confident and robust. I adored Dick. Despite his ribbing I sensed he was safe. I seldom wanted to be close to any man, but I craved affection from the two or three who did earn my trust: safe, uncomplicated, innocent affection. A two-second hug. A friendly cuff over the head. An arm steadying me as I climb down a ladder. Then, let go of me! Never prolong it. Never foist it on me.

Dick and Muriel wonder why, after a gap of ten years, I am bringing Paul to meet them.

'Is there anything you'd like to ask old married folk then? Anything you need to know? Everything all right?' ventures Dick.

I throw a glance at Paul, feel tears coming, and run upstairs.

It is some time before Dick appears at the door of my room. Paul has obviously told them why I can rarely bring myself even to hold hands with him and why we've made no actual plans for a wedding. They are shocked. They don't want to believe it, but they see it all falls into place.

Eventually I ask my doctor if anyone can help me overcome the terror. I tell him how my only previous boyfriend once licked my earlobe and I threw up in a waste-paper bin and sobbed uncontrollably for several hours.

My doctor believes that sexual abuse is the key. Child abuse is only just beginning to be discussed publicly. Specialist clinics are few; waiting lists full. It takes five months for a referral to Dr Ballinger, a recognised expert in this field. I have only one half-hour appointment in which to trawl the depths of my fears. It worries me that I have few clear memories, even though I display all the typical symptoms of having survived sexual violation. 'If there's something you don't remember, something happened,' is Dr Ballinger's helpful riposte.

I feel guilty about taking up limited resources, having in any case ended my engagement to Paul while my name was on the waiting list. I had to set him free.

Marrying Paul would have been a huge mistake but this has been the relationship least tainted with tragedy since Fred the Three-Legged Tortoise.

Annebeth Mackie, whose husband Steven is one of my lecturers, has asked me to help her string redcurrants. We are sitting at the kitchen table and she is speaking about her neighbour's difficulties following a sexual assault.

'Like me?' Why do I choose this moment to hint at what is hidden by my pea- green coat?

'Oh!' She draws in her breath, silent for a few seconds. 'Shall I tell Steven?' I am not convinced that, just because he is ordained, her husband will handle the information better than she can.

I am wrong. Steven phones at tea-time and asks if I will walk back to their house. He shows me into his study and offers me a chair across the room. He doesn't know what to say, but it is not awkward. He sits in silence, watching me, for a while. He holds my pain. I don't need him to have advice and ready answers. I need someone who dares to be powerless in the face of my utter darkness. So few ministers or priests possess that kenotic quality. They do not understand the significance of renouncing strength, as the crucified God.

Only when I apply to become a minister myself does Steven suggest that I should say to anyone what was done to me as a child. He tells me I should hide nothing from the Church of Scotland selection panel, including the psychologist. They will be dubious about anything 'mysterious' in my past. I follow his advice, and the panel does not see it as an obstruction to my being ordained. I am accepted on my first application, surprised, and over the moon.

I have only to return to college to obtain a Postgraduate Diploma in Pastoral Theology, which is for the most part a practical course, with a day each week in the college reflecting on the hands-on experience.

Ordination

'If it wasn't for that black sheath, you'd be like any one of
us. I saw that at first glance'

George Bernanos: *The Diary of a Country Priest*

STEVEN Mackie has lent me an old-fashioned little book, set in a
parish which is lent a fictional name of Crainie. It's not on the
required reading list for the diploma course and Steven has not
recommended it to other students, but he sees that I have an
iconoclastic approach to pastoral care and he thinks I will understand what is at the heart of this simple story. In it, the minister's
compassion and his self-understanding deepen through his
involvement in the lives of his parishioners. He learns the true
nature of sin and of redemption. It is a beautiful book and its lessons
will remain with me throughout my ministry.

12th December 1991

The day of my Ordination. I've been 'called to a charge' as a fully-fledged minister in the town – technically a city since it has a university – of Paisley. I wear the cassock bought for me by members of the congregation where I finished my apprenticeship in Edinburgh. I particularly had not wanted standard funereal black, nor bog-standard boring 'Church of Scotland blue'. My first choice is a rich green – jade, not pea. This is jettisoned, however, in view of the significance of certain colours in the more sectarian western regions of Scotland. All my training having been in the east of the country, this factor had not entered my head, but I am persuaded to choose instead a lovely shade of paler-than-sky-blue. A friend has stitched me a jade frock to wear after the formal ceremony is over and the 'party' begins.

Greenlaw Church is a cavernous building, all in dark wood, originally built to seat eight hundred people. It's pretty much full tonight because bus-loads of my friends have come from St Andrews, Edinburgh, and The Borders. The hymns are rousing and we come to the part where I answer the set questions and make my vows of obedience to the laws and government of the Church of Scotland. Then I kneel in the centre of the chancel as all the clergy present crowd around me as if in a rugby scrum. The Moderator of the Presbytery places one hand on my head and reads a pronouncement from a book held in his other hand. Those who have dived forward first put their hands on my head too and the bees on the edge of the swarm put hands on each other's shoulders. This is supposed to be a solemn moment. I'm being crushed by the weight of them. I wonder if, when they all draw back, I'll be no more than a pale blue rag flattened on the flagstones.

During the 'social' half of the evening, former colleagues introduce me to my new congregants with much light-hearted slagging, as is the custom on these occasions. One tells them I am an excellent minister but a rotten cook. A second protests that I am a very good cook – as long as you like it burnt or lumpy! They are well prepared, then, for the 'sponge' cakes I shall bake them on church cleaning days – solid, and flat enough to use as car wheel discs!

I am desolate when my friends go home, leaving me alone in the manse on a new estate on the far side of the large unfamiliar town. A far cry from the fields and woods that are my natural environment. I am trapped by a pavement atoll, my inadequate pen bounded by concrete.

This is the first time I have lived in such a place. St Andrews, perched among ragged rocks where clumps of sea-campion cling, hardly counted as a town. Half a mile to the east are meadows that sweep down to the sea, sun-bright with kingcups. It is only a brisk walk inland, past turreted stone houses and gardens azure with scilla and spring squill, to rolling farmland. To the west, unspoiled sands stretch out as far as the River Eden and the pine forest beyond.

The fields that used to lie between Paisley and Glasgow have long since been swallowed up by a busy motorway, housing schemes and industrial outlets. The town centre boasts a magnificent historic Abbey, but this has to compete for space with a monstrosity of a modern police station and a run-down shopping centre. The old cotton mills have closed down, with the result that unemployment statistics are high. Several of the outlying housing estates are notorious for drug dealing, and glass from broken windows mingles with discarded needles on the grass below the flats.

Leabank Avenue has an odd social make-up because it is a new cul-de-sac built on waste ground between two contrasting areas. It opens off Potterhill Avenue, a 'desirable' location for professional families. On the other side, as the residents prefer to forget, only a thin strand of wire divides them from the council houses of the Glenburn scheme. A patch of grass between the two avenues is the favoured toilet area for poodles and Tibetan terriers. A row of six red brick semis footing the banking are definitely contemptible in the eyes of the 'villa' owners. These detached dwellings are of a standard design and architecturally unattractive, but vastly over-priced because technically in the salubrious Potterhill area.

No.5 Leabank Avenue – the manse for Greenlaw Church – is unique in being detached but not owner-occupied. Thus it ranks in neither camp. It is also the most exposed dwelling, on a corner with a road running round three sides of the property. It is built slightly lower than street level and large patio doors open onto the pavement. Pedestrians and drivers reversing at that corner see straight into the sitting-room. Several tiers of houses up the bank look right into the bedroom. At the back, every house in Crestlea Avenue overlooks my treeless patch. There's not an inch of privacy in house or garden and I hate it.

Lace curtains. I just won't have them. I overcome the problem of the glass doors opening onto the public thoroughfare by creating a display of foliage. The centrepiece is a monstrous Swiss cheese plant that will be an invaluable source of branches for Palm Sunday processions, and serves as a jungle through which passers-by have to peer if they want to know what I am having for tea. Spider plants trail from the curtain rail and ivies thread up to meet them through a red-veined begonia. I am proud of my artistry, but one neighbour feels the need to apologise to her visitors for the veils of greenery next-door, explaining, 'It's a Lady Who Lives On Her Own.'

A 'Lady Who Lives On Her Own': an unacceptable oddity in a street where two cars must be washed, waxed and polished on Sundays and immaculate lawns must be fringed by regimented alyssum, salvia, lobelia. . . . alyssum, salvia. . .

Just as at university I have been long in throwing off my childlike naiveté, so in those first years of my ministry I retain many of the traits of a student's existence: my fellows acquire yuppie houses, business suits and shiny cars. They decorate their rooms with fashionable striped wallpaper, contrasting borders, tiebacks and pelmets. I acquire second-hand curtains that don't quite meet in the middle, and a fiendish cat that strews gall bladders of mice in the hallway and, spitting, pins visitors to the bathroom wall.

My kitchen will always be a gathering-place with the open welcome of a student-type flat. Letters and cards littering the table will be shoved aside to clear space for a tea-pot.

The postman for Leabank Avenue passes on what my 'wannabe' neighbours are saying about my open house policy. It is less than complimentary. At best I am running some kind of women's refuge: 'All Sorts of Women go in and out, all hours of the day and night.' (The postie chuckles, because his wife's best friend is one of my temporary lodgers: having left her husband, she has nowhere to stay, and does, when on call, occasionally leave the house at odd hours.)

At worst, I must be a lesbian. Some of my visitors are 'butch women with short haircuts', apparently. Julia and Monica, both elfin and feminine, are highly amused by the inference, solely on the basis of their cropped hairstyles!

What has immediately precipitated the comment however is the night when an elder from Edinburgh stays with me in order to catch an early flight from Glasgow Airport. She orders a taxi and the driver beeps his horn in the street. Wendy, at all times elegantly dressed, leaves at five in the morning when curtains are twitching. 'All Sorts of Women' indeed!

In an attempt to bring normality to an existence devoid of cabbage-patches and trees and backyard hens, I buy a pig at the livestock market. It is not a happy episode. My porcist neighbours, in their ignorance condemning pigs as slovenly creatures, force me to put her away to a smallholding/ farm shop. She is a hit with customers, who I fear will kill her with kindness. She devours packets of jammie dodger biscuits on a daily basis. 'Grace' is becoming grossly overweight. I weep whenever I go to visit her.

Fortunately, I am happy in the less well-off parish where my church is. I have a long list of house-bound folk to whom I take Communion, and each time we celebrate the Sacrament it is special.

The elder who assists fries me a piece of fish most Tuesdays and we leave the radio on for his budgie and set out on our rounds of the tenements. He carries the sherry bottle – 'to save your reputation!' I adapt the service to suit the six-second concentration span of a woman suffering from Alzheimer's. But those six seconds are precious. Another parishioner rehearses the gory details of her bowel disorder in between the Bread (which tiny square she informs us will play havoc with her innards) and the Wine. The elder and I dare not look at each other until we are outside, when we crease up with laughter on the pavement.

When I baptize my very first infant I feel, with sudden inexplicable force, the full significance of my Ordination. The same sense of fulfilment I felt when I pulled out a live calf from a cow and tickled his nostrils with straw until he spluttered his first breath.

One eighty-four year-old confides in me that she has been attending Communion for years, but was never baptised on account of being illegitimate. The stigma in her generation is such that she's never told her family. A fuss being made on a Sunday morning will embarrass her. We hold a private midweek ceremony. I ask her to make her vow before Christ. She looks up at me and answers, 'Yes,' in such natural fashion. My eyes well up.

Most of all, I am enjoying working with teenagers. I am amused that adolescents confide in me as someone older than themselves, but not in the same category as their mothers. I am privy to their secrets, worries, and love-lives. One of their favourite pranks is to make me laugh just as I'm about to process ceremoniously into the church behind the Beadle, who bears the huge pulpit Bible like a coronation crown. The choir is piping up with the *Introit*, and young Andrew McPhee will whisper:

> 'Mary had a little lamb.
> She tied it to a pylon.
> A thousand volts shot up its arse
> And turned its wool to nylon!'

At other times the little devils are at pains to defend me. I take them all to Ayr the weekend after Easter and, having promised not to make them attend church, have them take pots and pans out of the Youth Hostel early on Sunday morning and follow me to the empty beach. There they must remove the wheels from my car and rope them to tattie boxes to make a raft. Some set out to sea with a fishing net. The rest build a driftwood fire. Jim shouts out to the fishermen the Resurrection story from the end of John's Gospel. I simultaneously direct the catching of crab sticks (in a packet) and the stripping (not naked) and plunging of 'Peter' into the shallow water. We all help pull the raft ashore, and dry out as we scoff porridge and fish from the fire – just as in the real story. Several weeks later they ask me, very earnestly, if the story we dramatised really was from the Bible. They are writing an account of the weekend for the parish newsletter and don't want to get me into trouble!

They consult me about things they would never do, were I a parent or teacher. One fifteen-year-old asks me to go with her to a Family Planning Clinic. I tell her she doesn't have to sleep with the laddie; but it is better for her to have one adult she can trust with her secret, rather than feel I am just one more person who disapproves of her. Her description of what is happening to her is not pretty: 'If I won't have sex with him he just wanks on me. It makes me feel like I'm filthy. He asks if I'm doing it with someone else. I tell him it's not that. I don't want to do it with him because my Dad just died and I can't think of anything else. But he doesn't understand.'

Lassie, o lassie! You deserve a thousand times better than this! How can I ever make you know your worth? A million women have been where you are, all of us demeaned and beaten into believing we are so much dirt. Not for this did Christ become incarnate, being born of one of us, with our blood and with the pangs of our labour! This he came to redeem!

One member of my congregation says, 'Church has never been boring since you came. We never know what you're going to say next. If you send "disciples" round to the vestry door and tell them, "There you will find a colt, the foal of an ass. Untie it and bring it to me," there really is a live donkey outside, and you mean them to bring it into the sanctuary!'

By the same token, they are not averse to surprising me: I cry when the Sunday School children bring in a birthday cake for me during the last hymn. Another time I can't work out why the birds are cheeping so loudly during the Easter Morning prayers, when Johnnie Watson walks in with a box of chicks from his work at the city farm. . .

They astound me, too, with their resilience. Six months into the job, I find out that the treasurer is embezzling their hard-won funds, culminating in the disappearance of a legacy that was to save us from axing by the Presbytery. They rise to face the crisis and consider selling the cherished side-street church building to developers. They'll then have the funds to convert their hall, half a mile away on the main Glasgow Road, in the heart of the community. The hall can combine as a place of worship and a much-needed weekday child-care facility. We can have a meeting-place for older folk, too – offer them broth and some company. An architect draws up plans for a flat upstairs, so No.5 Leabank Avenue can also be sold. I shall live among the people, not the other side of town. This is how a church is meant to be. Services will be at unconventional times. Youngsters can come when the bars close after midnight. . . Surprisingly, the oldest folk in the congregation are enthusiastic for change. It's some of those in their forties who are the die-hards.

It is an unusual idea, but it will work. It is all about taking the church out to the people, rather than expecting the people to come to the building that many regard as irrelevant to their lives. Beautiful old stones that have echoed praise for generations, drawing us to the sublime, are a luxury this parish cannot afford.

The Powers-That-Be in the Church do not support our plan. The project is too imaginative. A future minister may not want to live among his people, in a flat. We are not entitled to funds from the sale of our own properties. We shall face years of bureaucratic complications and be milked dry before we begin. . .

The only answer is for me to look for another post, and for Greenlaw to unite with another congregation. It tears my heart to go. I may be miserable in the manse at No.5 Leabank Avenue, but I love my parishioners. Scotland's working classes are known for their warmth and sense of humour, especially in the west. Paisley is no exception.

I've been here for three years, and I am still easily the right side of thirty.

Kilry

June 1994

I am to share the ministry of six rural parishes with the Reverend Robert Ramsay. We were at St Mary's College at the same time. I haven't come across him since then and have been warned that he's become 'rather pompous' and 'puffed up with self-pride', but I'm looking forward to being part of a team. Besides, we'll also have independent spheres: Robert is the Presbytery Clerk, and I am to be Senior Chaplain at a penal institution twenty-five miles away. Half my salary will be paid by the Scottish Prison Service.

The Induction takes place in the village of Kilry on a hot June evening. Reverend Joe Ritchie, stooped, diminutive with age, and with a thick shock of white hair, is in the clergy procession, and comes to stand by my side. I look down on his hoary halo. I knew Joe in Edinburgh, where he was supposed to be enjoying retirement, but he still went out in wintry squalls to pastor to folk younger and healthier than he.

Another minister of Joe's ilk introduces himself to me after the service: 'Dennis Leadbeatter. Oldest working minister in Angus Presbytery. You're the youngest. I understand you keep a porker? When can I come and enjoy a grilled chop?'

'She's not being turned into bacon, Mr Leadbeatter, but you're welcome to bring her an apple and scratch behind her ears!'

This is another world from Paisley. The six parishes take in part of the glens of Angus. The northernmost point is a pile of rocks at the top of a mountain, where the snow remains in deep crevices year-long, and the crags echo with the bark of October rutting stags. Deep in the hills are hidden silent lochs, where lone larch trees lean away from the prevailing wind. For a few weeks in August when the heather blossoms, purples and pinks predominate, followed by the tans and russets of autumn. High up is the haunt of red deer, mountain hare, and ptarmigan. Hardy sheep graze the lower slopes and clusters of Scots pines are quickened by the twin-toned exultation of tomtits. From there, the snow-melt tumbles down the course of the River Isla into tamer ground that is worth being tilled. This time of year, the hedgerows are spangled with dog-roses and the scent of honeysuckle wafts through open windows. Centurions of foxgloves patrol the frontiers of the midsummer woods, but for the duration of winter the fields will alternate between frost-hardened and mist-sodden.

The only shop in the whole glen is the tiny post office at Glenisla, which is open for a couple of hours most mornings and sells such sundries as sweets and tins of soup, pencils, and picture postcards. It's ten or twelve miles from there to the Co-op in the diminutive town of Alyth, which also boasts a bank, a butcher, a hairdresser's and a hardware store. There are secondary schools in the slightly larger towns of Blairgowrie and Kirriemuir, but many of the farmers travel on to Forfar, where there is a livestock market. You'd have to go to Dundee or Perth to find a chain-store or a cinema.

Kilry has a small primary school with about twenty pupils, a post-box and a village hall. It used to have a petrol-pump, but it never had a pub. There's no actual manse at Kilry, so the church has rented me a cottage. 'The Faulds', as it's known, has a stone-built byre and half an acre for me to keep a pig and begin the smallholding I've always wanted. Long ago, there were 'faulds' or 'folds' here for penning sheep overnight as they were driven on foot from the glen to the market towns. The drovers would have boarded in the end room of the cottage, probably, and so it is the closest Kilry ever came to having an inn.

The first sound I hear when I wake is the bleating of today's sheep. Then a cuckoo. I am already in love with the cottage. It is the first time since fleeing from home as a teenager that I feel I belong in a particular place and want to stay in it for ever. I count the number of flats, hostels, and box-rooms in which I've slept since leaving my parents' house. Fifty-seven. And some forgotten.

July 1994

Grace Pig arrives, ferried in a trailer by a minister and friend from Glasgow whose tow-bar more often pulls his holiday caravan. Grace waddles down the ramp, grumbles about the rough journey and buries her head in the sweet cicely.

I bury my head in work, discovering the whereabouts of hundreds of farms and dwellings in the six parishes and visiting older folk who've moved into the small towns.

Unlike the manse in Paisley, The Faulds wraps itself around my animals and me. Grace, in season, breaks out, goes on the randan, and becomes lost. Parishioners spot her in a field. She is glad to be found and hurries up to the gate with a relieved expression on her wrinkled face. The day's escapades have been too much, however. We 'wheelbarrow' her back along the lane, using her back legs as handles. I collapse every few yards: she is weighty and I am breathless with mirth.

The second time she escapes I am out. Neighbours round up the escapee, mend the fence and leave a note and a pot of jam on the kitchen table.

I have acquired two more pigs. They have ripped up several wellies and left me with two for the same foot. I find a note stuck in each: 'Left?' and 'Right?' It's Kenny the gas man. After that I have some peculiar invoices: my computer-generated address becomes:

> Reverend Helen Percy Three Friendly Pigs Please Shut the Gate,
> The Faulds,
> Kilry.

As Kenny meets my growing menagerie he carries news back to the office staff at MacGas. The address labels are updated:

> Reverend Helen Percy Three Friendly Pigs a Goat and a Cockerel
> Please Shut the Gate,
> The Faulds,
> Kilry.

Later:

> Reverend Helen Percy Three Friendly Pigs, a Goat,
> Cockerel Likes Digestive Biscuits
> Please Shut the Gate,
> The Faulds,
> Kilry.

August 1994

I have written to Joe Ritchie telling him how happy I am ministering in a farming community where I can don overalls, feed calves and bale hay. His wise pastoral letter arrives the following week: 'Strive to be a better minister than a farmer, my dear. It is that to which you are called.' It is such a gentle remonstration, but a few days later he writes again, remorseful for having been 'too severe' on me. Joe could not be harsh if he tried! If only I could be one fraction more like Joe in my ministry. Old man, the depths of his compassion and human understanding are unfathomable. If you told Joe you had committed the most heinous offence, the knowledge of absolution would be complete.

Mindful of Joe's mild 'reprimand', I don't 'play farms' all the time, though my parishioners seem to appreciate my interest in their way of life and labour.

Kilry church seems to be controlled by the landowners. Traditionally the Minister has been in their pockets. Hardly any agricultural workers attend the kirk and many express surprise that I am as apt to visit the cottar houses as the mansions, and mix with folk who don't go to church. I show no favour to the 'rulers'. Perhaps they find I preach an uncomfortable gospel, and are taken aback by the way I treat everyone equally. I'm not suitably reserved and detached, as male ministers they've known.

Most are kind folk. If I ask for toys for prisoners' children, or hospitality for convicts after a special service, they give without asking the nature of the crimes. They impress me, the way they support the other half of my work. The jail is another world to them.

Conviction

I ENJOY my chaplaincy work at Noranside Prison. I'm glad my first parish was in Paisley, where I learned how to 'give as good as I got' in the friendly sparring that went on. A number of inmates originate from Paisley and Glasgow and their humour is quite different from the east coast variety.

'Open' prisons are a half-way house preparing prisoners for release. All of them have 'done time' in 'closed conditions' first – some for months, most for years – but as long as they have earned a 'C' category (meaning that they are not, or are no longer, regarded as high risk to the public) they can apply to be drafted to Noranside. Here, they will be phased back into life on the 'outside'. The convicts work on the prison estate, or are taken by mini-bus to outside placements or college. They are locked into the accommodation blocks at night, and also during the day if there are staff shortages or security alerts, but there are no fences or coils of razor wire around the prison perimeter. It would be easy enough to run through the trees and away, although Noranside is miles from anywhere and there is no public transport.

After a few weeks, the men are allowed to go home for their first weekend leave. A fair number fail to return from that first weekend. The test is too difficult. If they don't report back, they are soon picked up by the police and returned to a medium security establishment – or occasionally to maximum security if they have committed a heinous offence in the meantime. Remaining absent without leave, or returning in possession of drugs or alcohol, will affect the length of their sentence and the likelihood of early parole. It's probably difficult for someone who's never been incarcerated to understand how terrifying that initial taste of freedom is, or how nervous a man becomes at the prospect of seeing his kids again, for the first time since he let them down. How will things be with his girlfriend? He is certain she will have another man by now. How will she react? He looks forward to all the beers his mates will stand him, thinking they are doing him a favour. He's had access to drugs in the jail, but probably not to alcohol, so he'll be pissed pretty quickly. This may help him cope with the social strangeness of it all – seeing his pals, his wife, his wee gran . . . It may make him feel eased back into his role in the household and neighbourhood, but he has to be sober enough to get back on that prison bus at 4pm on Sunday afternoon. That, in fact, is the hardest part of all. A sword is hanging over him. This crossing over to his old life will be over almost before it has begun. He will be torn apart from his wife and his children, all over again, in less than two days. He has been at home just long enough to be unsettled himself, and to unsettle them.

The 'cons' don't reserve any politeness for me on account of my gender or title. The prison officers ask if I'm not afraid of venturing down to the cells unescorted, but I've never been threatened by a con. The language and the jokes are explicit, but never directed at me. On the rare occasion that one goes a bit too far, his mates soon sort him out. They are very protective of me.

There are some sex offenders, who are not segregated in this prison. Certain crimes are detestable to other prisoners, but privileges would be forfeited if one of the 'beasts', as they call them, is 'done over' here.

Tonight as I leave the building and go to let my dog out of the car, I come face to chest with a large man who's been convicted of a string of gruesome crimes. He strangled his female victims to death. Last time he was lifted by the police, a woman's bitten-off nipples were found in his coat pocket. Whenever this particular prisoner meets me, he insists on shaking my hand with one of his shovel-like paws. He is always polite; even affable. Anyone who didn't know his story would think him an avuncular gentle giant. If you met him on the street, you'd have no sense of evil. Just one of those huge hands, however, could squeeze my throat and choke the life from me in less than a minute, I can't help thinking. He engages me in conversation now. I'm not worried: it would be more than his parole is worth to do anything daft at this stage in his sentence. It does occur to me, though, that he has an extraordinarily disturbed mind. If his killer instinct did come upon him in an instant, no-one would hear a commotion. No windows overlook this part of the car-park and it is a dark night. Suddenly, from within the trees, I hear someone calling to my dog. My uncomfortable acquaintance stops talking and slopes off towards the building, as two other prisoners make their presence known. These men are both life-sentenced prisoners, too, but they are not serial killers.

Ironically, the majority of murderers are unlikely ever to re-offend, whereas most of those who have been put away for lesser crimes will slip up again within seventy-two hours of release. Murder is seldom pre-meditated. It is a split-second act, often under extreme provocation or after excessive use of alcohol. These two 'lifers' come over to speak to me now. They tell me they saw 'that psycho' heading for the car-park area. Knowing it to be about the time I usually let out my dog, they decided to tail him. In such ways as this, the cons watch out for me. I am protected by a hundred and thirty body-guards.

Gigha, my dog, is an asset. Some lads, newly arrived from closed conditions, haven't seen an animal for years. They talk to her and, through her, to me. They tell her about their own pets, their children, their worries past and future. Then one of the screws bans me from bringing her. Prison is a place where many rules are necessary, but some are imposed just because they give the rule-makers the satisfaction of exercising control. There is a conflict between those who believe the purpose of incarceration is to dehumanise, and those who believe it is to re-humanise.

Most of the prison officers – the 'screws' – are fine. It's easy to tell the ones who enjoy wearing a uniform, though, just as it's easy to spot a minister who fears he'll be mistaken for an ordinary human being if he takes off his clerical collar.

The first time I witness unnecessary force being used to 'ship' a prisoner who has broken the rules, I am shaken. The atmosphere among the officers down the block is tense. They won't tell me what is about to occur. Then they pounce. Does it really require six men to frog-march one inmate along the corridor, now he's already handcuffed?

My face is white when I go into a 'peter' further up, where five of the lads are sitting on their bunks. They realise then that I am not part of 'The System', because they can see the shock on my face. The previous chaplain had new prisoners brought to his office so he could punch their details into his computer; and there he sat all day. I have no office. I eat with the inmates in their dining-room, and spend my hours down in the cell-blocks. I sit on top of the washing machines and talk to the lads while they do the laundry, and help fold the linen. I pick tomatoes with them in the poly-tunnels. I stand rubbing the forehead of one of the cows while I listen to the prison farm-manager telling me about his family. People open up more easily if they don't have to make direct eye-contact. I go everywhere in this prison, except the men's toilets. I see what happens around me.

Wednesday night is Chaplains' Night, when we hold a discussion group on a variety of issues. The Roman Catholic priest stuns me with the answers he gives. He is so simple and so profound. One night, I see light dawning in prisoners' eyes such as I have never seen among those who sit in the Sunday pews. They've been asking about Jesus; about why he had to die. 'He upset the Establishment,' I explain. 'He was too outspoken against authority. A rebel. They stripped him of everything that gave him any identity, used violence against him, spat on him . . .'

'Like us?' interjects one. It is not a question so much as an expression of wonderment. So Christ had been with him when his own clothes were removed and he was issued with the standard prison brown ribbed jersey and was given a number for a name. And Christ had been there with him, when three screws held him down and took it in turns to bugger him.

There is a period when there never seems to be a room available for Chaplains' Night. We are given space in the foyer one week, in a corridor another. For several weeks we seem to be settled in a corner of the painting and decorating workshop. A garden gnome sits on one of the work surfaces and in high spirits a couple of cons decide to 'kidnap' the elf and leave a ransom note, hiding him behind rolls of wallpaper. Subsequently we are banned from using the area because someone disapproves of the joke. I cannot believe innocent fun has elicited reprisals. 'When we reach Heaven's gates,' I exclaim, 'there'll be some surprises as to who gets in! I don't believe we'll be judged on our righteousness. It will all depend on our capacity for compassion – and maybe a little on our sense of humour.'

'Are there other ministers like you?' the prisoners ask, bemused.

I make mistakes in dealing with volatile people, as anyone might from time to time. To someone who has been in an impersonal institution for years on end, genuine concern can grow into a fantasy of exclusive affection. Once, a prisoner declares ridiculous love for me. I've sat at his table at mealtimes a few times, and he's confided in me his worries about his children, but he knows nothing about me at all. When, aghast, I point out that I cannot reciprocate, he becomes cold and moody, and retaliates by putting round imposs-ible stories. The inmates can't be bothered with mindless gossip, however. Prison is not like a small village. Real life throws enough problems at them, without them having to invent dramas.

I am called as a witness at an inquest regarding the suicide of an inmate. The penultimate to be called, I am left in the waiting room with an odd little man who claims to have been the last to have spoken with the deceased and to have been responsible for his 'finding the Lord'. Zealous for Jesus's work among guests of Her Majesty, my companion is effervescent when he learns I am a chaplain. He wants to know if I've made many converts. This isn't language I use readily. I tell a Jewish prisoner about it afterwards. 'I hope you told him, "No. They just like my tits,"' comments Abraham dryly. The remark is not meant to be offensive. I laugh. There are just some Christians who make Abraham want to puke. He is an intelligent man who has reflected long on religion, sin, redemption. He has come very close to Christ; closer than I. And he is right: certainly men speak to me initially because they see so few women, but then they discover there is more to me than my bust.

It is the honesty of many prisoners that impresses me. They know they are criminals. They do not pretend to be more virtuous than they are.

December 1994
I learn that a couple of the prisoners are to be sleeping in the Care and Resettlement of Offenders hostel in Dundee over the festive

period, when the 'open' prison is 'shut'! While most of the cons are cock-a-hoop about having a whole week's leave to be with their families, there are two or three lifers and long-termers who no longer have any contact with relatives and who are, if the truth be told, dreading the morning the prison bus puts them out on the pavement. They have to give the hostel as their home-leave address and although they must be there at night, they'll have all day to wander the city streets watching other people spending money on last minute gifts for loved ones. The officers tell me these men will spend their week's pocket money the first day, drink themselves into oblivion, and hope that oblivion will see them through. Lifers have been known to turn up at police stations at Christmas begging to be taken back to a 'closed' prison.

I check the backgrounds of the affected individuals with the social workers and Governors and am given permission to work with them at home. If they make their way out as far as possible by bus, bring no alcohol, and do not expect me to cook, they are welcome in Kilry any day until the prison re-opens. I don't put up any decorations in the cottage, but most prisoners don't want to be reminded it's Christmas anyway. Several of them join in a Christingle service in one of the parishes, but it's the everyday normality of my life they like. Bread toasted on my fire and buttered could be a slap-up dinner for the pleasure it affords them. It is so easy to give to those who have nothing.

After the Christmas Morning service, because there is no bus service to Alyth, I run my wee car into Dundee to pick up the three prisoners and return them early in the evening.

A couple of days after Christmas, church members Angus and Evelyn Hood invite me to join their family for a meal. I thank them, but explain that I have promised my own home will be open, and that a life-sentenced prisoner has taken up my offer that day. They insist that I should bring him along with me to their house.

The Hoods do not skimp on entertainment. There are half a

dozen silver forks and spoons at each place set on the damask cloth that covers a mahogany table. There is a whole Stilton cheese, a round moon ten inches deep. The prisoner's eyes grow to take it in. Brought up in a council flat in the industrial belt, and having spent all his adult life at Her Majesty's Pleasure, he has never dreamed of anything quite like the lavishness of this household. He thinks Evelyn the kindest, most genuine person he has ever met.

Why does she have to ruin the magic for him? When spite takes over from Christianity, Evelyn Hood makes the most of her 'Murderers in the Manse' story. She works in the local media as a journalist and so she knows what to say to whom and how it can be twisted to advantage. The gutter newspapers make out as if I have been 'entertaining' (in the worst sense) dangerous killers who have gone AWOL and that poor Evelyn had no choice but to have my despicable 'house guest' at her table.

The Prison Governors, in a way that the Church never once does, defend me against misrepresentation. They knew of the convicts' whereabouts and affirm there has 'never been any suggestion of impropriety' in my work.

But I am more angered at the shattering of the prisoner's belief in Evelyn's benevolence than at the integrity of my own actions being queried.

Betrayal

January 1995

Some friends are staying at The Faulds for Hogmanay. It is fine that the house is not empty for once when I come back from prison. There has been a power cut for over twenty-four hours. Mine is almost the only house in the village without an oil-fired cooking range and consequently has no hot water and no heat. We sit in one room in front of the open fire wearing overcoats and scarves, reading by candlelight.

I have good neighbours. The Ogilvies give us hot soup from their Aga, and Moyra Nicoll offers to fill our hotties if we go down to Easter Craig Farm before bedtime. I happen to mention to the Nicolls that my grandfather died two days after Christmas, but that I am not going to attend the funeral. Mr Nicoll follows me into his kitchen when I go to boil the kettles.

'Are you sure you don't want to go to your granddad's funeral? I'd come with you if it helped.'

I do not know the Nicolls very well, have told them nothing about my family, and am surprised at Sandy Nicoll's perceptiveness. I am taken aback by his kindness in offering to go with me, without even knowing where my granddad lived or how far it will be to travel. I owe him an honest explanation of why I don't want to be at the funeral. I tell him in one short sentence why I have no desire to meet certain relatives there.

His expression is one of pain, but he says only, 'Oh. That's why.'

Then he begins to speak of his own father, of the manner of his dying, and how his mother in her grief precluded him from expressing his own.

February 1995

It is a week or two before I am back at the farm and, as it happens, Sandy Nicoll is alone. He says I'll always be welcome at Easter Craig Farm. I may treat it as second home. He apologises for his reaction to my disclosure. He had wanted just to hug me but feared it would be the wrong thing to do. He has told his wife, Moyra, and she does hug me when she comes in. She gives me a posy of winter flowers, and sends me away up to Cramie with Sandy and a load of hay on the tractor.

June 1995

She has a soft heart, sometimes, Moyra. At other times she can be terse. You just never know. I am often at Easter Craig. I tell her one afternoon that I plan going to the Western Isles in October. 'I wish I could come,' she says.

'Well why don't you? I'd love you to. Sandy could surely make his own dinner for a few days. Your children are all adults. They're my age! It won't hurt them to cook for themselves when they come home from work, will it?'

'What! And leave here in the middle of the hairst!' I am shaken by the sudden sharpness of her tone and quite frightened of her – hurt enough to mention it to one of her friends: 'Moyra was always that way. Even as a teenager she took the face off the postie for being late with the mail. Don't fuss yourself.'

As it happens, the harvest is over by the end of August this year, and Moyra does come away with me.

November 1995

I come across a tiny tumbledown cottage for sale on a back road from Alyth. I have felt the insecurity of living in a tied house. Against the enforced vagabond existence of my youth, my dream is to have a roof over my head that I can call my own. I tell Moyra Nicoll about my find and she wants to drive over to have a look at it straightaway. 'Oh, it's sweet!' she exclaims, peering in the windows. 'My friend in London would love it!'

Bids are made, her friend puts in a higher offer than I can and buys it as a summer holiday cottage.

At the time, the sense of betrayal of trust is awful, although I realise later that the place required renovations I could not have afforded to carry out.

Few people have guessed that the Nicoll marriage is over because farm marriages simply do not end. Too much of the estate is tied up in land and livestock and half a farm is no use to anyone. Socially, the Nicolls put on a good front. It is only now that their children are leaving home and setting up families of their own that Moyra allows friends to know that she and Sandy are living in separate wings of the big farmhouse and using different staircases. The first hint I am given that all is not as it seems is when Sandy, distraught, confesses to me he once ended up in bed with one of Moyra's relatives – though he says nothing 'happened' because they'd both been drinking. He also alludes to physical violence being used against him over the years. I am a little reluctant to believe him, as men are so much more commonly the perpetrators of domestic abuse. I am also alarmed that the physical affection I've shown him, though always in the presence of his family and not in any way secretive or furtive, could be misconstrued. I tell him I hope he has never, and will never, misinterpret my feelings towards him. He is the same age as my father.

'You mean you hope I'm not attracted to you? It's all right, Helen. I know you just want a bit of safe affection, that's all. A dad you can trust.'

I am relieved. So relieved. But actions can belie words.

1st December 1995

I am feverish. My head hurts if I turn on the pillow, and my bones ache.

I've left the door undone since crawling out to throw food to the animals. You couldn't do that in a town. Here, neighbours know just to come in. Gigha barks if someone knocks first, but wags her tail if they let themselves in.

I don't want the soup Moyra has sent up with Sandy. I call out to leave the pot on the cooker. He puts his head round the bedroom door to see if there is anything else I need.

'Just boiled water, please.'

Sandy puts down the mug of water.

Then, unbidden, he sinks down on the side of the bed.

Resisting, or leaping away from him, is no more an option than it was when I was a child. I do what I learned to do then: hold my breath and black out.

All I ever recall of those early incidents was 'waking up' with a great weight on top of me, struggling to breathe again. I absented myself mentally until it was all over. Afterwards, I couldn't remember what had happened. It was as if I hadn't been there. I had leapt into another horizon, where there were dark thunder-clouds, and no green grass at the bottom of the canvas.

Now I experience the same dissociation between mind, sensation, and memory. I am paralysed. I can neither move nor feel. A switch trips in my brain. It is the reaction of the deer at the moment its predator seizes it. From then on it feels no pain. It isn't dead but it seems so. The lion tears at its flesh but it does not quiver.

Sandy goes to the door. 'That was just a bit of rape, wasn't it?' Strange words and an embarrassed apology. I don't answer.

I should feel anger. I am numb.

Something happened, a long time back. Suddenly, the barbs of memory arrow through me.

The tin-opener. It was twenty years ago. I remember it now with absolute clarity. That time, there was no Promised Land of clouds; no colours. Only blackness. I hadn't learned about jumping into horizons then.

For a week afterwards I scream each time I have to pee. . .

I think not even my cloud mountains are safe anymore.

What has just taken place with Sandy Nicoll is not in the same league as the time with the tin-opener. Was I raped? There was no violence. But there was violation. There is not a bruise on my body, and yet the dynamics of power between us were unequal. I believed our relationship was 'safe'. I held affection for him and trusted him. He has experience of life. I am a young woman, still peculiarly childlike at times. He is old enough to be my father and is a 'ruling elder' in the church. Though a minister, I have not taken up the authority generally associated with that role.

Conversations with dozens of women come back to me: 'It's not the first time I've had sex when I didn't want it,' I hear one friend saying, 'but I could hardly go to the police and say I was raped.'

Another, 'There's nothing different about me from millions of women. You don't even have to have been abused in the past in order for this to happen. Most of us have had the spirit knocked out of us some way: all of us as girl children have been brought up to be obliging and nice to people and say, "Yes" to whatever's wanted of us.'

A third. 'He was my husband. Rape within marrtiage was still legal in the last decade.'

A terrible keening sound rises from the depths of my being.

'The result is paralysis of action, judgement, feeling and voice. This can last for minutes, days and sometimes years. . . At this point a woman can completely shut down her feelings, dissociating herself from the body. This split creates a state called 'psychic numbing'. . . the effect on people who are completely powerless in the face of overwhelming catastrophe.'

Peter Rutter: *Sex In The Forbidden Zone*

Cankered Blossom

Christmas 1995

The first night of the insufferable carol singing. The temperature has dropped to –9 degrees. My throat is rasping and I know I am coming down with a second dose of flu. I sit squashed into the back of a car with a woman who's just moved into the village, who witters on incessantly about her ancestry. If I did not feel so cold I'd take off my scarf, wrap it around her neck and pull both ends.

Aucharroch Farm. Our last stop. Colin McLean is pouring drams for the men. Young Jinty McLean stands on her step with her arms around me while I shiver gratitude for her warmth, and mouth the final *Hark! The Herald.* Afterwards I wait in the kitchen until Colin puts a glass in my hand, only then joining the women in the front room. I seldom drink whisky, but tonight my throat has shards in it.

I couldn't have flu at a better time. I escape the next three nights of parish carol-singing and am excused the marathon of lessons and carols on Christmas Eve, in order to save my voice for the midnight service. Then, between eight o'clock and ten, God sends a blizzard wild enough to deliver me from that, too. By daybreak there are drifts so deep that even Land Rovers are thwarted: no Christmas Morning service either.

The little *mille-fleurs* bantam cockerel, with his spangled apparel, does not want to set foot in the snow. He descends from his roost to land on my head and is thus transported about the yard until all the other creatures are fed, then he comes indoors for his own special breakfast. He perches on the handle of the porridge pot and inspects for lumps while I stir. Today, Boxing Day, he flies across the kitchen, splat-plop in my bowl, spattering cream all over the table. I scold him and hoist him out of the dish. His feathered feet are clagged with porridge. I wash it off before flinging him out of the window, else it would freeze and set like concrete blocks round his ankles.

I am permitted to be miserable because I am ill. The hardest part about Christmas is the obligation to feign cheerfulness. I cannot seem to throw off the memories of childhood Christmases, when my father was off work for a fortnight. The inevitable family arguments, and it too cold to hide outside in the wood-shed. . .

Since the incident with Sandy Nicoll three weeks ago I have been experiencing flashbacks. There is a recovered memory from an event at Christmas twenty years ago: suddenly I know that it is not just because of our family's misery that I dread these festivities. There was another person involved. The 'Ghost of Christmas Past' again:

Christmas 1975

It is the primary school Christmas party in the village hall. 'Simon Says', 'Musical Chairs', 'Pass the Parcel'. Tea has been laid in the back room. Robert Mackie is told off for wolfing into the crisps before the minister has given thanks. Sandwiches are eaten, the crusts left, iced gem biscuits devoured. Who likes jelly, who just wants ice cream? Then we are told to hush and listen for reindeer bells.

I know who Santa is. It is always Tom West who owns the Big Manure Heap. I am not stupid. Even in the years when I believed the real Santa filled my sock on Christmas Eve, I was not taken in by the premature impostors in the shopping malls. I've gone up to receive my tissue-wrapped book from Tom West at all the previous parties and peered at him philosophically through the stupid cotton wool disguise.

The infants are called up first, their expectant faces bright. Each one sits on Santa's knee and is asked for a kiss, which is given with awed and affectionate coyness. I too go forward, but stop short of the stage steps: this year, it isn't Mr West. Behind the hood and beard I recognise the watery blue eyes. This is the man whose gaze makes me feel prickly and uncomfortable. He has this magic way of staring at my dress, as if he can see my body through it somehow. I feel horror. I have been lured up to a few feet from Santa only to find that the man who made me suck his 'pink lolly' is waiting for me to sit in his lap and kiss him. My limbs won't carry me. The parcel is proffered, the knee patted. Everyone waits. I still stand, like a mesmerised rabbit.

I feel the hot wetness trickle down my leg and a puddle begins to finger its way along the seams of the wooden floorboards.

It was not my father who mutilated me with the tin-opener.

It is fuchsia-pink that he wears. Never scarlet. My sister ices his face on a sponge one Christmas. She keeps tipping up the bottle of cochineal, trying to make up true red. All she produces is puce. And tears and a bad mood. And a cake no-one can eat.

He isn't wearing a Santa outfit the day he opens me up. The association is always with me, however, and in my mind he is dressed in fuchsia – the colour a Bishop would wear – and his face is disguised under a long false beard. I am the one who grants him this cover. I cannot hold in my head this cruelty, together with the man I have looked up to and adored. This is how a child does rationalise incongruous adult behaviour, I suppose. One man becomes two. One is the man I still need to be able to love. The other is Santa Claus, in a fuchsia-pink cloak. One man cuts up the food on a little girl's plate for her because she cannot use a knife properly yet. The other pushes tangerines into the toe of her Christmas stocking and takes up a blade to carve the flesh between her legs.

Twenty years on, I still cannot abide tangerines.

Christmas 1995

The religious festival is worse, being a minister. I'm 'theologically compromised' during a season when sentimentality reigns. The Incarnation has less to do with cute donkeys and a blue-frocked virgin crooning over a sleeping baby in a crocheted shawl, and more to do with God's total identification with a vagrant teenage girl terrified by an unplanned pregnancy, sweat and blood running down her legs, and only dank straw in the corner of a rat-infested cowshed on which to nurse her bawling, naked infant. But people want to be patted on the head and encouraged to indulge themselves. They certainly don't want to hear the gospel imperative to live in solidarity with the poor.

This Christmas, I am spared because of the snowfall. However, I am about to learn more of Mary's dread than I imagine.

January 1996

The bout of influenza leaves me, but I still feel washed out and unwell. Workmen have been treating woodworm in the loft and I put my queasiness down to the fumes from that. It is only when I wake one morning and start retching, with nothing in my stomach but grey-green bile, that I realise with horror that I am pregnant.

The roads are lethal with all the impacted snow and I am too afraid to drive to a chemist. My closest friend, whom I could have told, has gone to Australia. I am a sole maimed goose on a frozen loch, trapped in the ice, paddling desperately to keep a clear circle around me; but exhaustion is giving way to fast encroaching and constricting glass.

I finally telephone another friend, Freya. She is a GP, her husband Douglas the Head of Church History at Glasgow University. Freya has worked in family planning. She'll know what to do.

I tell Freya what Sandy Nicoll has done and the even more dreadful result. She asks if I have thought of going to the police after the rape, but she cautions that since my reaction was to freeze they will be unlikely to take such a complaint further. 'I didn't fight, Freya. He didn't force me. But I was paralysed. I didn't stop him.'

'No, you wouldn't. With your background, you wouldn't have resisted.' Freya already knows my childhood history. 'You could go to the police in the city. There'd be female officers there. They might give him a warning. You know these things can happen again. . .'

'Their marriage is already fragile. I suppose that's the reason he did it. I don't want his family to be broken by the knowledge of it.'

'No. . . What do you want to do about the second problem – the pregnancy? Your GP would be difficult, being local. There's Family Planning in Dundee. . . Or will you come here and we'll look after you?'

I didn't expect Freya to be able to do more than tell me where to go for help. I am daunted, ill, and in shock. The relief, finding someone practical, is immense.

I feel sick most of the time, not only when I wake up in the mornings. There is a thaw and the brightness of bejewelled snow and blue skies changes to a drizzling greyness. The sun does not break through for days. I lie late in the mornings, my room never becoming light. A neighbour has given me an indigo hyacinth in a pot. It started to bloom but has rotted for want of warmth and light.

It is five weeks since Sandy brought me the soup. I have agreed, reluctantly, to have a termination. In another two weeks the sickness will be taken away from me, but the budding flower within me will also be uprooted.

I am in the very early stages and yet the powerful mystery of biochemical changes has already begun and they have an effect on me I have not foreseen. I never wanted babies. The physical damage incurred in my own childhood made intercourse and pregnancy as an adult unthinkable. Now it is real, and I want the child I cannot have. I am convinced in my head that it is female because I cannot cope with the thought of a boy. As long as I believe it is a little girl, I feel an overwhelming protectiveness towards her, sick and frightened as I am. I give her a name: *Heather*. She should have been born when the hills will be mauve and purple with ling and bellheather.

One of these awful, precious, mornings I lie tracing the line of my still flat stomach with my fingers and sense that this time is magical. These few days I have left will never be repeated, and I have to treasure them. It is the only time I have ever felt there is anything of worth or loveliness about my body. Defiled, I have regarded my body as an object to be starved or punished, and certainly never to be enjoyed. But for this short time, it is a sanctuary. Within it, I hold this tiny undefended thing, safe. Enshrined.

I have visitors in the cottage when Sandy drops in with a church notice. I find a minute alone with him in the kitchen to tell him what he has done to me. He says he knew, even before Christmas, just by looking at my face. Told I have arranged to have a termination, he looks stricken, and asks if I'm sure that is what I want to do. A few days later, however, when I tell him I've changed my mind and cannot go through with it, he is angry.

I have no choice. There'd be no support from him, and I'd lose my job and my home. I'd never survive in an anonymous bed-sit where the council places single mothers. I picture pushing a pram along grey pavements to a soulless shopping centre. I hear traffic rattling along the street outside. Imprisoned within a concrete apartment block, I know that I would kill myself and the child. If I couldn't see trees and hills. . .

I resent Sandy for allowing me to carry all this alone – I drive myself to the hospital two hours away in Glasgow, stopping in several lay-bys to vomit.

Freya, knowing my background and that I could not bear for anyone to touch me or look at me, has written to the consultant asking for the process to be carried out under anaesthetic. Normal practice, so early on, is simply for pessaries to be used. The doctors, who treat me with utmost sensitivity, realise that such an intrusive procedure will be too traumatic for me, and in the circumstances anaesthesia is agreed.

Several members of the staff team advise me to go on 'the pill', because a man who forces himself on a woman usually does so more than once. 'This kind of lightning does strike twice,' they warn. I am certain, however, that I shall not let him do this to me again.

On the morning the surgery is to take place another health worker appears, cheery and matter-of-fact, to inform me about contraception. She suggests I have a coil or intra-uterine device inserted. I refuse. Next she tries to foist on me condoms, pulling a handful from her pocket in a matter-of-fact fashion. I gaze at her, shake my head slowly, and whisper, 'I was raped. I'm never going to have sex with anyone again. I don't need them.' Now she is apologetic. She's been on holiday and has not been told my case history.

It is two o'clock in the afternoon before they come for me. The tears begin to run down the sides of my face as I am wheeled into the theatre. It is the first time I've cried.

Freya comes to collect me from the hospital late in the day. I've been told I'll be kept in overnight unless I manage to sit up and drink and eat a biscuit. The threat of not being allowed to go with Freya is enough to force me out of the overwhelming misery in which I have lain motionless since being returned to the ward.

Douglas, her husband, is already home from the university when Freya takes me back to their apartment. He is as affable as always, and I manage to eat with them. For that one night I permit myself the luxury of the vast softness of cream bed linen folding around me. I'd stay longer but don't feel I deserve it. I return to The Faulds. It is cold and damp and I am alone.

I don't hear anything from Sandy. Guilt, perhaps, keeps him away when in fact I need to talk to him. I've never needed him before, but I do now. He is the only other person who could possibly acknowledge and share the hurt and the grief. There have been times in the past when he's bugged me with incessant phone calls, but during this long wet month, before the shafts of the snowdrops have even lanced the dead earth, he never calls.

February 1996

A tractor towing a trailer laden with hay is ahead of me on the back road from Kingoldrum to Noranside Prison. Its passage is slow, as the road is narrow and twisty, but I'm not in any great hurry. I'm going to pull off the road at Pearsie in any case, as I often walk my dog in the woods here, to make up for her patient wait in my car while I work in the jail. We seldom see anyone. There are only rabbits, chaffinches, and sometimes roe deer. Today it seems we are to have company: the hay-wagon draws into the next lay-by ahead of us and the driver jumps down from the tractor while I am sorting out a rope for Gigha, in case she disturbs game-birds. I look up and see that it is Sandy. I had not known it was his tractor because all I could see was hay, but he must have recognised my car in his large wing mirrors some distance back. He is walking towards us.

'How are you, Helen?'

I just look at the ground.

'Please, talk to me. Let me walk with you and Gigha for just a minute?'

There's a crumbling disused church in the clearing, a dozen yards from the single-track road, and easily visible to passing traffic. It's little more than a hut with a corrugated tin roof. A few items of game-keeping equipment are locked inside it – some barley, and some sticks for beating the undergrowth to put up the pheasants for the guns. On this bitter day an unheralded squall flings hailstones stinging across our faces. A leafless sapling gives scant protection, and so Sandy moves a few paces to the lea of the church, where he squats uncomfortably on the stump of a fallen tree, his hands between his knees, begging me to speak to him. I remain standing, leaning back against the church. I won't speak to him. I feel resentful that he has taken so many weeks to ask after my welfare, after all I've been through on his account. We cannot have been here more than a couple of minutes, not looking at each other, when Gigha sets up a ferocious barking. I step away from the corner of the church to regard her, hackles raised, fending off a yeti of a gamekeeper. It is the one folk say beats up his girlfriend. He is none too friendly with us either, though he can see at once that we are not vandalizing his hut. Perhaps he hoped to disturb some lovers' tryst, and is disappointed to find us wrapped up in winter overcoats, scarves and gloves – and not each other – for warmth. Or perhaps his anger is the more inflamed because he's been shown to be afraid of the doggy.

The gamey leaves and the brief spiteful hailstorm is over. Gigha stays close to my side walking the short distance back to the car. She has not had much larking around today. I keep my silence, but Sandy is still holding the door open as I reach for my seat-belt.

'I want you to do something for me,' he says. I want you to take a clump of early-flowering snowdrops and plant them somewhere, to remember Heather. I'll dig up a few bulbs and leave them at your gate one day. Tell me where you decide to put them.'

I start up the engine. After Sandy's gone I lean over to Gigha and shed tears into the thick fur of her neck. She waves her tail slowly, unsure if she's done wrong by defending me against the gamekeeper.

Sandy once told me he has scars on his limbs from cutting himself deliberately when he was younger. Self-harm is common among survivors of abuse, and the question is in my mind whether this was the reason for him mutilating himself. He has never confided as much to me, but the suspicion that he may have suffered in the same way that I have makes it easier to forgive him. It also explains why, until that random act on 1st December, he was always so solicitous of me.

A small plastic bag containing mud and a handful of bulbs is left on top of a sack of hen-feed at The Faulds.

I inter the snowdrops along a lane a couple of miles off the route Sandy will take to the market when he goes there. I am staggered that the suggestion of a memorial has been his, as he was so unsupportive a month or two ago. Now he needs a focus for his grief, as I do. The shared sense of loss, which at last he is prepared to acknowledge, creates an unexpected emotional bond between us. Who else is there who knows, without even being told, that I feel desolate? I hide my hurt from everyone else. Even so, I find it very difficult to go to Sandy's farm at Easter Craig and do so perhaps only two or three times in the next eighteen months. Once it is to fetch a stew Moyra has made for a group of church visitors and another time I've been asked to feed the cattle when all the Nicolls are away at a family wedding; so I don't see anyone on that occasion.

Most Sundays I see Sandy at church, where communication between us is limited to a pain-filled, wordless look. Occasionally he will draw up at my gate on a Saturday morning, when he is up to set the heating clock for church the next day; but our conversation then is awkward and strained, inevitably. There are happier times when I have friends visiting from Edinburgh or Paisley. He knows then I'll ask him in to join the merriment that is always present in my kitchen when my guests are breaking their teeth on pizza and mocking my cooking. He seems to relax in company, and it is almost possible to pretend that brief incident on the first afternoon of December never took place.

What I don't realise is that Sandy drives past The Faulds frequently, just to see if any visitors' vehicles are sitting under the ash tree. Nor do I know, until my ever-attentive neighbour tells me, that he sometimes parks outside The Faulds when I'm out. . . Does he want his wife to imagine there is something between us, when there isn't? Is he trying to incite her so that she will make the decision for him and end the sham of a marriage he doesn't have the courage to leave unless he's pushed? She is bound to learn of his every movement: this is a small rural community, where no-one's business is private, where everyone's car is known and where so little happens that a stir can be caused over nothing at all.

March 1996

It is in March, during another spell of raw cold and snow, that news comes of the massacre of the infants at Dunblane. A gunman shot them, soon after their school lessons began, then turned the gun on himself. There is no-one in Scotland who is not stunned and sickened. I invite our own Sunday-school children to place snowdrops around a lighted candle.

In the prison, shock and grief are the locked doors and the iron portcullises that are slammed broadside across the corridors. They are forces more palpable than the actual barriers of incarceration. Many of the prisoners feel the separation from their own kids acutely. Some have fathered children they've never even seen, as relationships seldom stand the test of 'doing time'. These men are affected terribly by the dreadful news from Dunblane. I sense the heavy atmosphere as soon as I walk into the cell-block.

Listening to prisoners and seeking to provide a focus for the expression of public mourning, I shelve my own needs, and pay no heed to the effect bereavement is having on me. It is a couple of weeks until, unable to continue fighting off depression, I phone Freya. I tell her about my clump of snowdrops, and my voice becomes choked. I don't have to say to Freya that there is an association in my mind between the mass murder of the five-year-olds in Dunblane, and what I allowed to be done with what was, scientifically, little more than a collection of splitting cells. My sense of guilt towards Heather is intolerable. Freya knows this, and tries to make me see it is hardly the same.

I find it the more difficult to deal with the choice I made about my pregnancy because my own childhood was torn away from me. I remember another incest survivor describing her gestation as *carrying a grotesque parasite in my belly*. If I'd believed my baby was a male I'd have felt the same way as she did. I have convinced myself, however, that the unformed shadow within me would have developed into an infant girl. I mourn the loss of my own childhood, with hers. For years to come I will pass a shop window and, looking at pale rose knitted baby jackets, and lemon frocks with daisies on the bodices, begin to cry inside.

Feeding Pearls to Swine

June 1996

Sandy is submerging his guilt in whisky and plaguing me with phone calls again. Exasperated, I resolve to tell Moyra Nicoll that I need this to stop. Sober, Sandy is sociable but sensitive and people like his company. Inebriated, he is obnoxious and persistent. I don't know what I'm going to say to her but I need Moyra's help to bring her husband's pestering to an end. Dreading her anger, but believing I have no choice, I telephone her. Will she please speak to Sandy and ask him not to phone me again?

She reacts much more calmly than I expect. Unknown to me, Sandy has already confessed to her that he raped me. Rape. That was the word he used to her, as he did to me immediately after it happened. She has known of it for a week or more. She is speaking gently to me. She asks if they can both come to The Faulds to see me.

'I don't want to see Sandy,' I say.

'Sandy needs to see *you*.'

They pull up at the gate. I go out to them, miserable, but Moyra hugs me. 'I don't know why he did it, but I'm sorry he did.' I am dazed and relieved that she is promising to take care of me.

Inside my kitchen, Moyra reverses roles. She is asking *me* for help. But I am part of this situation, far too involved and hurt to manage a professional position here. I beg them to go to marriage guidance counselling, or to talk to my colleague, Robert Ramsay. 'No. Not to Robert. I already told him about Sandy's drinking,' she rues. 'He came to our house to "counsel" us, and he consumed twice as much whisky as Sandy did!'

I am to conduct the June Communion service in Kilry. It has been difficult enough for me to see Sandy Nicoll sitting in his pew in previous months, but at The Lord's Supper, as the senior elder, he'll be sitting at my side behind the Communion Table. How shall I be able to keep from spilling the wine? Waves of anger, grief and shame all surge over me in succession.

Moyra meets me at the Kirk door. 'This will be difficult for you: it's difficult for all of us. But we'll see you through it,' she whispers.

This will be the last time Moyra ever speaks to me, however. The writing is already on the wall. Moyra is thick friends with Robert Ramsay, despite his incompetence in helping with Sandy's drink problem. And Robert Ramsay and I are not working well together. Our collegiate relationship has been deteriorating for over a year.

Robert sees to all the administration; work that I am glad to leave to him. I prefer 'hands on' ministry to sitting behind a desk. People remark that they never see *The* Minister. I defend him because he is at home or in Forfar doing office or organisational tasks. My loyalty is not returned, however. I'm told that, chairing meetings, Robert implies to the congregation that I can't be bothered being present, even if he knows I am on duty in the prison at that time. True, I don't relish meetings and doubling-up at them is poor deployment of the workforce, as it doesn't require both of us to chair. But I never undermine him in the way he constantly undermines me.

I never wear a dog-collar and many people assume I'm not fully qualified. In fact, I'm an 'associate' minister. The definition of 'associateship' is 'equal partnership'. But frequently I am introduced as 'assistant', which suggests a lesser status. It's just what comes of being female, slight of stature and much younger than my colleague – who is in fact less well qualified than I am. If I sit at a dying woman's bedside and hold her when her soul departs, the undertaker still initiates the arrangements for the funeral with Robert Ramsay, because he is 'The' Minister.

Associate ministry would only really work satisfactorily if we had begun with a clear agreement on spheres of labour. For all Robert's talk, it is too apparent that he thinks of me as only 'assistant'. He has no notion of the Presbyterian principle of parity of clergy! And maybe I'm not good at working in a team: I'm inclined to be too independent.

Robert has certain assumptions about the role of women. At the A.G.M., to the suggestion that elders' district meetings could be held at the Manse as he doesn't seem to have time to go to people's homes to acquaint himself with them, Robert responds, 'That's a good idea: Helen will help my wife in the kitchen.' And no-one protests!

During the 'mad cow disease' beef ban I attend a farmers' rally in Forfar. I wouldn't know how to roast a joint of meat, but many of our parishioners are affected by the B.S.E. crisis and as their minister it behoves me to show solidarity with them. A cattle breeder speaks up at a subsequent church meeting, expressing appreciation of my support. The Clerk relays to me, 'Robert Ramsay sneered. If I could have minuted a "sneer" from the Chair, I would have done!'

I don't understand why I upset him, but clearly I do. Perhaps it is because I am young and vivacious, with new ideas that overthrow the *status quo*.

It is difficult to raise issues with Robert. My directness is counteracted by his preference not to face problems. For example, I asked, six months in advance, if it would be feasible for me to be on holiday a particular week, when he also planned to be away. He agreed readily, but now I hear his gripe from several sources, 'She'd no business being absent at the same time as me. She hadn't permission.' I challenge him about this and he can't look me in the eye. It does not help our working relationship that I have raised the matter. It simply makes him more resentful of me.

I've been working in the six churches of Kilry, Glenisla, Lintrathen, Airlie, Ruthven and Kingoldrum for more than two years and at last the big wooden notice-boards have been replaced. Robert Ramsay has his name and all the letters after his name put up in big print bang in the middle. My name doesn't even appear in the bottom left-hand corner! I am laughing about it. It really doesn't matter to me, although it is indicative of the way he views me. Nonetheless the Congregational Board makes a request that the hefty articles be sent back to have the missing information added. The Clerk sends Robert Ramsay a copy of the ensuing instructions to the sign-writer. The only sensible way to rectify the 'omission' without repainting everything is to insert my name above Robert's. He phones the Clerk immediately, in high dudgeon. 'This will never do! I shall not tolerate it! Helen has a misguided notion of . . . *equality!*' Yes, these are his words, drawing in his breath before the word 'equality' and then emphasising it as if it were some kind of heinous offence!

I am no angel. I am a rebel. Church services are often boring and I can't stand too many of them! Tonight there's a service I'm expected to attend, but in which I'm not actually participating, so I telephone a pensioner who stays along the street from the church in Kingoldrum: 'Jean! It's Helen. Will you put the kettle on about six? I'll be round three minutes after. I'm going to speak to everyone on their way into church, hide behind a tombstone until the latecomers are inside, then race round to your house. Let me in quickly because I don't want anyone to see me. I've bought some iced buns for us! I'll rejoin everyone in the kirk for the social time afterwards and if anyone notices me going back in they'll think I've just nipped out into the graveyard because I was taken short.' I am full of monkey tricks like that.

Robert does suffer from much stress. As an 'associate' minister I suppose I am having an easy ride. I don't have ultimate responsibility for committees, fund-raising or forward-planning. There's no pressure on me to be 'successful' in any sense. It's different for Robert. If an event does not go 'swimmingly' he takes it as a personal insult and becomes worked up about falling attendances. By contrast, on the occasions when Robert goes off sick with stress and is forced to leave me in charge of meetings, the participants lack any of the aggressive behaviour with which he has to contend. I suppose this is because I do not play on my authority and so I do not court resistance. I don't enjoy chairing meetings, but when I do they run smoothly enough. I know I can be a bit 'woolly' on procedure but there is never any antagonism or rancour. I may confuse my 'amendments' with my 'counter-motions', but I admit it if I'm struggling and discussions always end amicably. Robert is far more competent and efficient than I am, but somehow he brings out the worst in his office-bearers and the meetings he chairs can be stormy.

On one occasion the elders berate Robert for not putting in an appearance at some social function. He has taken three services that day and this unwarranted criticism is the last straw. He packs his bags and leaves for his holiday house, leaving me the material for the *Parish Newsletter.* He has written his editorial in haste and in a fit of rage. In it he harangues church members for failing to see how hard he works. It is a lengthy screed and the kind of letter that should be slept upon, re-read in a more rational moment, and not sent. I consult the Clerk to the Board before delivering it to the typist. 'If people read that they'll say these are the ravings of a lunatic!' is her verdict. We take a joint decision not to submit it and

I write a bland few paragraphs on a different subject. On his return I explain our reasoning, adding that he can easily publish it in the next issue if he still wishes. He never re-submits his article, but I suspect our well-intentioned intervention has bruised his self-image.

From now on he seeks to destroy me.

The Trucker

September 1996

Robert Ramsay's tendency to act as though I do not exist is one of the reasons I want to drive a big truck. I need to regain self-confidence. In my imagination, I rev my forty-four tonne lorry up the driveway to Airlie Manse, jump out, toss the keys at Robert and say, 'There! Now you reverse it out!'

There is another reason. Sandy's violation of me has brought back all those childhood feelings of powerlessness and loss of control over my own body. Though I have forgiven, I cannot forget. I want to feel I am in command of something much bigger than I am.

I've been walking the Kilry lanes with my neighbour Christine during her maternity leave. 'James has to take a load of hay to Skye tomorrow. I can't travel with him now and the scenery's so brilliant, up high in the truck. You go with him, Helen!' The Skye Bridge has just opened, and James lets me drive his red lorry from Broadford to Kyle. Leaning down from the cab to pay the toll-man, I feel in charge. Yes, this is what I need!

It is not nearly as easy as I thought. The red lorry was rigid, with straight gears. James now takes me in his big articulated ERF, with a twin-splitter. Only when I almost deprive Dundee City Council of some railings do I realise the trailer does not follow the

90

same course as the cab! Small boys play with tractors and bogeys as toddlers. Axles, pins and pivots are second nature to them. I spend hour upon hour learning how not to jack-knife the muck-spreader and reversing round bales in the field. James's patience and Christine's encouragement should have them in the running for sainthoods.

James gives me a pair of HGV 'L' plates: bright orange, with red 'L's, and about fourteen inches long and ten inches wide. 'If your enthusiasm for lorry-driving wanes, you can always wear them as earrings!' says James. Kenny the MacGas man spies them sitting in my porch and gives me the name of a good instructor, Alex McAra, in Perth. I arrange a fortnight's intensive training during my annual leave.

I hold my own with the men during those weeks, often making them laugh. I am impish. I tell Winko, the proprietor of the burger van on the industrial trading estate where we stop for our morning break, that UHT skimmed milk makes the coffee taste yukky, and I demand real milk in future. Instructor Alex cannot believe I have the nerve to say this, but he is standing behind me and can't see the twinkle in my eyes. I have my full-cream milk the next day and by the end of the fortnight I have Winko setting up for us a picnic table and chairs, complete with floral arrangement, on the delivery forecourt!

My co-trainee is an older man called Bob Wallace and, as he comes from Kirriemuir, we share transport from The Blackbird Inn each day. Bob has been out on a friend's lorry many times, before taking lessons from Alex, and on our way back to The Blackbird one evening he shows me the gash along a wooden fence on a sharp corner, for which he, with his mate's trailer, was responsible. He forbids me to tell Alex.

Needless to say, I tell Alex exactly where this fence is, when Bob is occupied ordering his burger. We take that route later, Bob driving.

'Watch this corner, Bob,' warns Alex, winking at me. 'See some daft bugger's scraped right along that fence. Shouldn't be allowed on the road, the idiot!' Bob glances at me then, and I grin back, all innocence. Alex, Bob, and Winko are foxed by my mischievousness. They have no inkling of my pea-green secret.

I've learned to trust Alex in this artificially intense short period. He is a gifted instructor, sarcastic, but knowing how far to push us.

I have a particular problem at roundabouts. Alex has me in tears one day, bullying me through every roundabout in the city, but I keep going. I have to overcome this hang-up, but when traffic is bearing down on me from all directions, I become paralysed. 'Brake, Helen! Steer! Don't freeze!' Alex has to shout instructions at me because I can't think for myself what to do. Whenever I can foresee a collision, instead of taking evasive action, I dissociate my brain from what is happening around me. This is the strategy I learned, long ago, for coping with the searing pain I anticipated being forced on me. It was a mechanism for survival then, but it is downright dangerous when I'm in charge of an articulated lorry!

Bob is out on test. Alex has walked me back to his house, not far from the test-centre, to wait for my own appointment. He realises I'll be more relaxed in his kitchen than in the test centre waiting-room.

Alex has a collie dog and I make a fuss of Max while Alex pours coffee. Just as the prisoners sometimes find themselves able to say difficult things through the medium of my dog, Max enables me to confess the real cause of my anxiety, which is not just the impending driving test. 'I'm experiencing flashbacks of being raped by a parishioner,' I blurt out

Now Alex understands about the roundabouts. 'I could see your face change, your eyes glaze, every time. . .'

The examiner, a stand-in, is a taciturn man with a florid complexion and protruding stomach like my father's. I do not pass my test this time.

My retest is on Christmas Eve. The town is heaving. Shoppers are distracted, and in their haste are liable to ignore even a heavy goods vehicle bearing down on them. The regular examiner is less than half the size of the stand-in who failed me on my last test and he puts me at ease immediately. He rattles off a stream of inter-mingled observations and instructions as I am negotiating the streets.

'There's more salt on this yard than I've ever had on my chips so don't worry you won't skid so can you go up to twenty miles-an-hour then brake and stop before the marker that's fine now turn left out of the yard and proceed to the traffic lights I've lost my glasses so it's your lucky day I can't see what you're doing I can hardly see the road at the lights turn right did you see that nutter in the Renault he's got so much food and booze in that car it's practically trailing on the ground it's so over-laden take the second exit oh no groan the mother-in-law's arriving today the old bat will be there right over Christmas so you're a minister of the kirk and you don't like Christmas either hey that could be a disadvantage if you pull into the next lay-by we'll have a caramel bar before you do your hill-start.'

I don't know whether to kiss the examiner or Alex first when I jump out of the cab with a pass certificate in my hand. 'Me first, please,' laughs the examiner.

I write to the examiner after the test to thank him. I explain what I told Alex McAra – that learning to handle an articulated lorry was my way of coming to terms with having been raped and with the subsequent feeling of loss of control over my own body. He writes back, 'It is the best letter I've ever received, and I'll keep it. You are probably the only minister who could persuade an old sinner like me back to the Kirk. If there's anything I can do to help you in the future, just ask. . .'

The Love of Small Things

Autumn 1996

One of my prisoners is in hospital. He has been complaining of severe headaches for three years, and now that he is also suffering loss of balance the Prison Authorities have finally referred him to civilian medics. His brain tumour is untreatable by now.

Abe is a Dutch Jew, his cell-mate Colin an atheist, and I the prison chaplain. The three of us are firm friends and enjoy battle in the prison dining hall. Colin and I are missing our Devil's advocate now that Abe is hospitalised down in Dundee. The Governors permit Colin to visit two evenings a week, the Roman Catholic Priest spirits him away to a pub some afternoons, and I go on the days he has no other visitors.

Abe longs to breathe fresh air. He coughs his way down the corridors. We sit outside the hospital block watching the orange sky behind the cedars and speak of dying, of God, and of rare foretastes of eternity – times when the transcendent and the earthly merge into one another. Attired in hospital pyjamas and prison overcoat, Abe drags his sick body over to the peat bed bordering the concrete. He breaks off some heather for me. I sit quiet with it in my hands.

'I lost a wee one. She was called 'Heather'.'

An unmarried Presbyterian minister confessing a pregnancy? Absolute trust exists between those who have faced up to death. After fecund silence, Abe shakes his head: 'You are a wonderful woman, you know.'

My awareness of the value of life is heightened. Whenever I come across a road-accident rabbit with its rear end stuck to the tar but its ears still waggling, I peel it off and, swinging it by its hind legs, whack its neck against fencepost to put it out of its misery. I hate doing this but I cannot let it suffer.

Heavy rain draws out toads, in hundreds, leaping across the path of headlights, splattered leaf-thin. I cannot drive over this battlefield of amphibian agony and so I trudge six sodden starless late miles home. I remember, as a child, fearing to tread in the hornbeam wood, lest I crush wild hyacinths. I hear my father start the lawnmower and I scurry to pick the daisies. As many as possible before they're beheaded. Salvation from shredding.

Moyra Nicoll and her mother-in-law have stopped going to church. They stick their noses in the air when they see me. What on earth possessed Sandy Nicoll to tell his mother what he has done? She has written me a tart letter accusing me of being a 'whore', and turning her quiet, naive laddie into a 'loud-mouthed sot'. Her 'innocent boy' is twenty years older than me and I did not ask to be violated by him, but she is right in one respect: Sandy has changed since he started drinking so much.

His married daughter announces she is expecting a baby and she flaunts the ultrasound photographs in front of her parents and siblings. Sandy, the guilt of 'infanticide' on his hands, turns away and reaches for the bottle once more.

Moyra wants to move nearer their daughter now there's a grandchild on the way. They'll sell the farm. After years of dissimulation, there is little more point in acting as though a real marriage exists.

I walk out of a shop in Alyth one day, right into Sandy. I suspect he saw my car and has been hovering, hoping to engineer an opportunity to speak to me. He needs to spill out what is worrying him. 'Moyra's at the psychiatric hospital. Another one of her "episodes". She's completely off the rails. Psycho-potic. Psycho-something. . . I forget.' I feel genuinely sorry for Moyra. And Sandy is at a loss. They are leading separate lives in the same house but she is still technically his wife and he feels responsible for her, though it's clear he struggles to understand her diagnosis.

I need Robert Ramsay to be a pastor to this distressed couple because it is impossible for me to do so. I do not trust Robert, however, and decide to broach the Nicolls' marital problems at our six-monthly team support group meeting, when there will be witnesses if he tries to twist what I say.

Support meetings are meant to help team ministries resolve difficulties such as failures in communication, minor conflicts, or balancing of workloads. Ours doesn't work, because Robert sits aloof. He will refer to it as 'Helen's Support Group', as if it has nothing to do with him. He dismisses any issue I raise the minute our three 'advisers' are out of the door. The forum is useful, however, if I need to confront him about some disloyalty or deception. Direct confrontation results in eruptions and if there are going to be eruptions I need other people to record what is said. He will probably change the story afterwards.

'Robert, please will you visit the Nicolls? Moyra is in psychiatric care. I can't go because Sandy made a "pass" at me,' I test the water.

Robert is Vesuvial: 'What! An elder in **MY** parish made a pass at

MY Associate Minister, and I didn't know about it! This is ridiculous! Preposterous!'

How can I, now, relay the seriousness of the 'pass' Sandy made? I played it down to protect the Nicoll family and myself. I can never entrust Robert with the full information. Once we are outside Robert's manse Brian says, 'I thought he was going to burst.'

I still love living at The Faulds, although part of the soul of the place is lost when my little cockerel disappears. The self-important Belgian bantam was fine that last night. Hearing my engine return after dark, he crowed his usual welcome from the rafters of the byre. When I went out at dawn, he'd vanished. I never find a single plume from his thousand-flowered jacket.

Local farmer Grumbling Jock calls: 'Chickens roosting in the trees at the foot of Middleton Brae. Don't know how the buggers got there but they're feasting on my cabbages and I'd be pleased to "see them not there".'

Niv and Mary Malcolm from Boarhills are staying at the caravan site in Kilry with Mary's sister and brother-in-law. They always come to me for their supper when they are at Kilry and agree to become intrepid chicken-catchers. We have to wait for dark, to creep up on the sleeping fowl. Niv has this cunning plan that if his accomplice suddenly shines a torch in the birds' eyes, he can leap up from underneath the branch and grab its legs.

We women try to stifle our laughter as the men steal under the tree, snapping enough twigs to wake the dead. Nevertheless they take up position without, they think, the hens having detected them. Silence. On goes the torch, Niv shoots up his hands to grasp their feet and the chickens dive off the branch with cacophonous shrieks, scattering across the field. The five of us give chase, falling over the unlit furrows.

The nights draw in, and the bracken on the hill is cerise in the afternoon light. The geese begin to circle Lintrathen Loch. There will be no more paddling in the burn before winter.

11 January 1997

It has been one year. Sandy arranges to meet me at the end of the lane where I buried the snowdrop bulbs. He has bought a rose for Heather. I am sobbing.

Moyra knows he has come.

Why, after a year, am I still tied to this man emotionally, when he has been the cause of so much misery? He is himself miserable and I feel pity for him. But also I don't feel strong enough in my soul to bear the pain completely alone. Sandy is the one person who knows what has happened. Who else is there? Where else is there? My home, my work and my animals are in Kilry. I have neither the strength, nor the belief in myself, to cut myself free and be cast adrift.

The snowdrops have not pierced through the mud so early this year. I try to remind myself of what I have told the prisoners about Resurrection: 'Where the shit's the thickest is where the plants grow best.' It is language understood by men who have been two'd up and three'd up in a cell, slopping out once a day, the walls caked with excrement.

The shit is going to be much deeper before any snowdrops flower.

PART II
JUDGEMENT

Cloud Cuckoo Land

Spring 1997

What is the point in reaping barley? His children are adults with their own careers and have no interest in the farm. Moyra hasn't been inside the cow byre in years. If they sell up, she can have the big town house she's always fancied and set up a classy Guest House. She's a good cook.

The estate agents having been contacted and the asking price set, Sandy has no desire to watch his crops ripen for someone else's harvest. Nor does he want to cradle his grandchild, about to be born. He cannot face the reminder of Heather. He determines to go away without his family, for the first time in his life. They are furious.

He is on an aid convoy in Bosnia. I don't hear from him while he is away, but he contacts me on his way home. He has reached Perth. He is more inebriated and more troubled than ever. He has an almost drained bottle of strong drink made from Bosnian plums when I see him at the bus stance and he talks nonsense: 'I'll get divorced. We could live in Sarajevo.'

'Aye, Sandy. Divorce, change your name, run away – and we'll live happily ever after? Pie in the sky!'

I leave him to make his own way to Alyth. My car may be littered with chaff, chicken feed and chocolate wrappers, but I draw the line at a drunkard puking up in it. I am on my way to do some hospital visiting.

There is one occasion when, without the aid of drink, Sandy speaks to me of the possibility of marriage. He's seen my car outside the vet's and has waited for me. I am about to make a sarcastic retort but something about his unusual sobriety and earnestness makes me gentler: 'Sandy, I couldn't marry you even if you divorce . . . Maybe I'd be able to bear you hugging me, but the nightmares would return. Eventually it'd all come flooding back. I couldn't sleep with you – or anyone.'

He sinks against his old Land Rover. 'I could cope with that, Helen, just as long as you didn't leave me.' It is partly a whisper and partly a cry. 'You wouldn't leave me?'

I can't answer, and turn away. It strikes me that Sandy, like me, has lost his spirit over the past year. He doesn't even have his dog any more. He reversed over it with the tractor and broke its back.

Could Sandy really cope with a chaste relationship? Can we go back to the time before his lust spoiled everything? Is that possible, once the ground has shifted and the trust is broken? My feelings are mixed.

Was it my fault? Did I ask too much of him, to return my affection as innocently as it was given? Certainly I was naive. I was so happy to have the 'safe' affection I'd craved since childhood that I didn't foresee the jeopardy. Had I realised how his marriage lacked any love or warmth, I should never have been so unguarded.

The End of the Road

February 1997

As Presbytery Clerk, Robert Ramsay is privy to all manner of information about the private lives and difficulties of ministers in the district. Those who visit the Presbytery office are shocked that he divulges information to all and sundry. There is a move afoot to clip his wings. The Business Committee votes to limit the term of office of Clerk to five years. They agree this when Robert is on holiday. He returns and autocratically overthrows the decision.

I am given an inkling that Robert is busy setting a trap to ensnare me. Brian, the minister at Aberlemno, who is Moderator of the Presbytery this year, draws me aside after the Presbytery meeting: 'Robert is on the warpath. Things are not going well for him and he needs someone to blame. He'll target you. You should look for another post. There's a vacancy in Islay. Apply for it.'

March 1997

Something else happens that makes Robert all the more determined to scapegoat me: I find him out to be deceitful and I confront him.

It is his wife's birthday. I say I'll bring a gift for his wife to the manse and he can tell me about his Holy Land trip. He seems strangely anxious to prevent me visiting, so I say I'll just drop off the gift and not stay. But when I arrive, parishioners' cars are parked right up the drive. The party is in full swing. So *that* was the real reason he hadn't wanted me to visit. . . I go to the door anyway, because I need to tell him that a parishioner is dying. I am not invited over the threshold and Robert never does go to see Johnnie in his final weeks of life.

Over the weekend I begin to feel more and more hurt by my colleague's inability to be truthful with me and by his progressive, intentional, alienation of me in public.

Robert's timing when he does deign to contact me could not be worse. My neighbour has dropped in for coffee, leaving her dog in the garden. When we go outside the dog is standing in the rabbit pen, grinning. My two grey rabbits are lying slain on the ground.

These rabbits were given to me by the inmates at Noranside Prison. They had the softest velvet coats, running from cream on their bellies, through every shade of grey, to black-tipped ears. They would lie on their backs in the crook of my arm like babies.

Robert Ramsay chooses his moment to telephone minutes after the bloody-chopped dog and the corpses are discovered. He wants to make arrangements for our weekly meeting. I give him short shrift: 'There's not much point us meeting if you can't be honest with me, Robert!' I burst into tears and put down the telephone.

Robert cannot deal with expressions of emotion any more than he can with having his honesty questioned. I return at night to a message on my answer-machine:

'*I can't work with you any more, Helen. It's the end of the road. I'll be contacting National Mission in the morning.*'

I draw in a deep breath. 'National Mission' is the Edinburgh-based committee that employs me, technically, but if Robert refuses to work with me I'll be redundant. The Faulds is a 'tied' house, and so Robert will put me out of my home as well as my job. I need to talk to someone. Douglas Glen, the schoolmaster, is the only one of my Session Clerks I know will still be up at this late hour. Douglas promises to speak to Robert first thing in the morning.

I receive two calls the following morning. The first is from Douglas, reporting back on his conversation with Robert. Douglas tries not to laugh when he tells me, but apparently Robert delivered an impassioned spiel, listed all my supposed misdemeanours, and made me out to be demon-possessed! 'Somehow I didn't recognise the person he was describing. . . Unless perhaps he was talking about himself?' suggests Douglas. 'What do the letters LLB after his name stand for anyway?'

'It's a law degree, isn't it?' I muse.

'No: it means "Lying Little Bugger"!'

The second call is from Rev Brian Ramsay of Aberlemno, Moderator of the Presbytery. (Brian was also convening the 'support group' that facilitated teamwork between Robert and me, until Brian became so exasperated with Robert that he saw no use continuing.)

My colleague has set matters in motion with alacrity, it seems. Brian tells me Robert has already arranged to meet National Mission staff next Monday. I am to see them immediately afterwards. They will have to find me alternative employment for the remainder of my contract. In the meantime I should consider myself on leave from duty.

I am anxious. The Faulds is my home. If they send me far away I shall also have to abandon my prison chaplaincy.

Brian's recent prediction about Robert using me as a foil has already come to pass.

In the short-term, I have a few unexpected days off. I've wanted to visit a friend near Inverness since she had her new baby. Now I can go.

First I contact the Session Clerks to tell them I'll be absent on Sunday. (I am not fool enough to trust my conniving colleague to relay this message without maligning me.) Then I visit Major Houston and Mr Ogilvie, who have responsibility for the church buildings, including The Faulds. Major Houston believes that the congregation will not favour Robert if he tries to put me out of the cottage. 'Try not to worry,' reassures Mr Ogilvie, giving me an unaccustomed kiss on my cheek. I leave him my friend Emily's telephone number and head north.

Emily and I push babies in buggies and feed ducks in the park. The next day Gavin Ogilvie phones with unexpected news: the four Session Clerks formed a united stand against Robert, who has backed down. I still have a job!

I return to Angus on the Saturday, having been invited to a toddler's birthday party. I have a soft spot for this little one, whom I baptised. Her mother, knowing how difficult my colleague has become, advises me that Robert's daughter Susan, who nannies for her, will be there. 'That's okay,' I say. 'I don't hold Robert's behaviour against his family. I shall speak to Susan as I always do. I'm sure Susan's mature enough to think for herself. She's a grown woman in her twenties.'

Unfortunately when Susan sees my car bumping up the pot-holed track to the house where the child's tea-party is being held, she becomes hysterical, crying and shouting, 'Helen's evil! She's evil!' She speeds out of the front door as I enter the back door. Obviously Robert holds such sway over his household that his tendency to imagine demons has become a *folie á famille*.

So Robert is telling his family, as well as our Session Clerks, that I am 'demon-possessed'. This is not common terminology in this day and age, even within the Church. It's not the first time I've heard Robert use it, however. Discussing a contentious parishioner with a group of elders, he swore, 'If ever the Devil was at work it's in that woman!' Then there was the time he spoke publicly of his most senior elder: 'He's in league with the Devil.' We did not know how to respond to his startling outbursts of slander. Now he's gunning for me. Is there a form of personality disorder, where the sufferer perceives others – never himself – as being 'ill' or 'possessed'?

Brian of Aberlemno relays Robert's wish (since Robert will not speak to me) that I should 'decide when to return to work and make arrangements for our continuation as she sees fit'. Clearly Robert is licking his wounds after the stance the Session Clerks took against him. I do not perceive myself as having won any victory, and am at pains to be conciliatory. I write him a letter:

> The Faulds,
> Kilry
> Tuesday, Holy Week 1997
> Dear Robert,
> I realise Good Friday is going to be a busy day with the
> schools but as you prepared the children last week it
> would make sense for you to continue. Would you take
> both the Holy Week services? I am anxious that the
> congregations should not be affected by tension, and I
> guess you will find it easier if I am not present. I shall
> take the Easter Day services. I suggest we meet next
> week, on neutral ground, to discuss where we go from
> here. If you feel you would be uncomfortable, then with
> your agreement I shall ask a third party to facilitate this.
> Please let me know if you would find this unacceptable.
> I want you to know I am very concerned for you and that
> I shall remain loyal to you.
> Yours, Helen

My intention is to make peace, and it is genuine. Some people, however, become dangerous when their authority is threatened.

Easter Monday, April 1997

I have given up my bedroom to visitors and am sleeping at the front of the cottage. I am woken at dawn by the blood-curdling cry of what I think must be a vixen. That sound is surely not human. Gigha barks. The hair on her birse stands on end.

Making breakfast, I glance out to see a police car and a funeral undertaker's hearse outside the village hall. So the cry *was* human! My ashen-faced neighbour opens my gate. As I run to her she falls into my arms and blurts out that she has found her daughter's body. She has taken her own life.

The village is soon reeling from shock. News of this nature travels rapidly. That meeting with Robert and our 'mediator' is tomorrow morning. I need not be one of the number of folk who will surely phone to inform him of this tragedy today.

The father of the girl whose body has been found hanging has been brought back from his work and I go down to their cottage. They pull me inside: 'Will you help us? We want you to do the service.' I have come as a neighbour, not as a minister, but of course I shall take the funeral if that is what they wish. The man doesn't come to the church and I've seldom conversed with him, but I wave to him when I see him in his garden, which is almost every day. I'm better known to them than any other minister.

On Tuesday I dress in skirt and jacket for the dreaded meeting with Robert – our first since he tried to be rid of me. This occasion calls for 'power-dressing'!

I drive to Malcolm Rooney's manse. I chose to ask Rooney for a neutral venue, specifically because I hardly know him. I do not want Robert to feel threatened by any ally of mine.

Robert is already seated, sullen and oozing hatred, in the corner. He has, as I thought he would, brought a briefcase full of his documentation about me. Papers – whatever nonsense is written on them – are his LLB's version of 'power-dressing'. I am unimpressed. He does not use this opportunity to reveal what it is he has been noting down and filing for the past two years, but it is suggestive of a degree of paranoia that he has dragged such a tome of archives along with him. Clearly I have become synonymous with the Devil in his mind. He has come here with an arsenal. Until this moment I have only ever felt exasperation with him. For the first time, I begin to despise him.

I look at Robert when I speak to him, but when he speaks his comments are communicated indirectly via Rooney. He refers to me in the third person. He cannot bring himself to look at me.

I tell Robert that I have been asked to take my neighbours' daughter's funeral. His eyes flash in my direction for the first time, but fleetingly. Apparently he hasn't heard about the awful death in Kilry. 'SHE arranged this. . . **She** is not the Parish Minister. . . How can **She** be asked to take the funeral!' Normally florid in complexion, his throat becomes deep purple, like that of a sexually-aroused turkey. I am reminded, not for the first time, of Gilmartin in James Hogg's *Confessions of a Justified Sinner.*

'But, but, but. . . this is PREPOSTEROUS!' he squeals. 'That. . . that. . . that. . . an undertaker should contact an **Associate** Minister, and not consult **ME**! Not consult the **Parish** Minister first! **She's** just an Associate! **Just** an Associate! It's ridiculous! That's what it is! It cannot go on! What am I supposed to do now?'

He runs down like a clockwork toy. Rooney and I carry on looking at him, expecting the last nerve-induced shakes of the pullet which has had its neck wrung.

'Well,' I venture quietly, 'you should go and see the family, I would think.'

'So would I,' helps Rooney.

'Well! Of course, that's just what I **intend** to do. . .'

He does not go. He attends neither the funeral, nor the home of the grieving parents. He finally goes six weeks later – and only then because Major Houston's formidable daughter-in-law gives him short shrift, and tells him if he has not been to visit that family by tea-time that very day she will be hammering at his door demanding an explanation.

When he does go he speaks not a word of the deceased girl and tries to blame my actions for his tardiness.

The funeral is today. It is bitterly cold. Even the few flakes of snow that flutter down shiver and think better of it. Nonetheless, I ask the Session Clerk to open the doors at the back of the church so that those who are packed into the vestry or spilled out into the kirkyard can hear the service. So seldom have I buried anyone younger than myself, as was this lassie, I am affected by it.

There is a constant stream of neighbours parking themselves in my kitchen needing to talk about the tragedy. Such waste of life touches the entire community. We see in our minds the contorted face, the epitome of despair, the abolition of hope.

The Net Tightens

1 May – 14 June 1997

It must seem remarkable to the urban dweller that in a place of such idyllic beauty as Kilry there exists so much anguish. As in other farming communities, there are more than a fair share of accidents and suicides.

Farmhouses nestle into the side of the hill and quaint cottages with gardens full of evening primroses are dotted along the lanes. Wild honeysuckle adorns the hedgerows and the sweet scent of newly mown hay is in the air. Yet behind the dykes festooned with blossoms lurk the same anxieties and addictions, debts and illnesses as in any fume-polluted terrace or block of flats. The latest tragedy of a young girl's suicide, however, seems to draw those of us in the tiny cluster of houses around the church particularly close to one another, in a way that we would not otherwise have been. Thus it is that I am torn between my attachment to this community in which I have already spent more time than in any other since my childhood, and the realisation that my relationship with Robert has become unworkable to the point that he is seeking to destroy me. I shall have to uproot myself and my four-legged family all over again.

Rooney agrees to preside at a monthly staff meeting for us. He also suggests a bland statement that the two ministers have had '*a difficulty in communication which has now been resolved*.' I believe it behoves us to offer this much of an explanation to the Session for my sudden removal before Palm Sunday and Robert appears to be in agreement. Typically, however, he subsequently proceeds to act unilaterally and withholds the document. Two elders he respects rebuke him and I am eventually permitted to take it to the church secretary, for copying. I also ask her to type my *c.v.* so I can apply for other posts. I am irritated by Caroline's lack of confidentiality: when I ask about the *c.v.* several weeks later she says she left it with Robert in a see-through plastic sleeve! She might have had more gumption!

Another principle to which Robert assents at our first supervised staff meeting is that weddings, baptisms and funerals will be conducted by whichever of us is working in the relevant parish in the month the event occurs. Needless to say he breaches the agreement within the very first month of its operation and arranges a funeral over my head. It is my month in Airlie and I was with the deceased on the day she died. When challenged at the next meeting Robert is unreasoned and aggressive. He narrowly misses running over Rooney's neighbour's kitten as he over-revs his engine and speeds away in first gear. Rooney says he cannot continue to supervise our meetings if Robert does not co-operate with the decisions reached. I am not, however, happy to speak with Robert without a witness.

I have to find another job. I apply for the charge on Islay as I was advised to do. A couple of hundred miles and a few million gallons of sea water between Sandy Nicoll, Robert Ramsay and me should give me the chance I need to begin a new life. I have an interview arranged for the end of June. Then, at the General Assembly in May, I am standing outside the cloakrooms talking to a friend who, pointing at the poster behind us advertising a vacancy in South Uist, announces, 'Apply for that, Helen. You'd love it.'

'Don't be silly. They'd never entertain a woman minister in the Outer Hebrides.'

'Oh yes, they would! I grew up on that island. It's ninety per cent Roman Catholic and the few Protestants that do exist are liberal. Calvinism never really reached that far down. You'd be in your element.'

We look up the list of commissioners at the Assembly and find one Murdo McKenzie, Session Clerk of South Uist. I leave a note in his box among the long wall of numbered pigeon-holes, asking him to look out for me in the coffee-room. The note tells him, *'I have a pony-tail and tartan legs, and I'm young.'* This last factor alone makes me stick out a mile among church commissioners, quite apart from the trousers with each leg a different tartan.

A gentleman with a mass of ginger hair, a beard down to his waist and a twinkle in his eye accosts me in a strong Hebridean accent. 'You'll be the lady with the varicose veins?' I look must look uncomprehending, so he explains, 'The tartan legs?'

We make for a pub just across from the Assembly Hall but my brief interview is already over by the time we've crossed the cobbles: 'I've only three questions to ask you: do you believe in God, can you preach a half decent sermon, and do you have a sense of humour?'

South Uist sounds like the parish of my dreams. Murdo tells me the previous minister was an Iona Community member and so the congregation is unlikely to be shocked by radical theology or new approaches to worship. There is harmony between Catholics and Protestants, and Session meetings are as laid back affairs as they were in my early parishes. My interest in farming and in nature will be a bonus there. The Presbytery, Murdo regrets, will not make a female very welcome, but nine times out of ten the wind and waves will forbid the crossing to Leverburgh for the meeting in any case.

A week later my *c.v.* is posted. I am baffled by a telephone call from a man pretending he is an S.S.P.C.A. officer: 'I understand you intend to make a pig sea-sick.' It is Murdo, wondering about the dimensions for a sty for Grace and a crate for her on the ferry.

I am within a hair's breadth of escaping to Islay or to South Uist – both of them charges for which few would consider applying, but which I should rejoice to serve.

My enemy, however, is busy casting a net into the water between me and the Isles. . .

There are newspaper reporters sniffing around our parishes. The *Sun* arrives at the door of a family who made a complaint to Robert Ramsay about a presbytery elder touching up young boys. The reporters wonder why, as Clerk to the Presbytery, and indeed the culprit's own parish minister, Ramsay has taken no action. Ramsay knew there were previous allegations against this best friend of his but he still swept the matter under the carpet. Ramsay has legal acquaintances in high places. The story is never printed.

Ramsay must know they are onto him. As his own net tightens about him he is seeking desperately to ensure that I am the first to be entangled. I do not know what he will do but I have prescience of danger. Rats sense when a ship's about to sink, or a cave about to fall in on them, and they run. When they've eaten poison they shovel dirt down their throats to push it through their guts. I can smell there is evil afoot but I don't know how to shovel dirt.

Tilda comes into the kitchen one afternoon, as a number of my neighbours are in the habit of doing in the aftermath of the tragic deaths in Kilry. Tilda isn't a churchgoer and she doesn't know Robert. I also know she keeps confidences. 'Does he have anything on you?' she queries when I express disquiet about his paranoid behaviour.

'Oh, he keeps a file on me, Tilda! I don't know what he'll use against me exactly, but he'll twist it, whatever it is. . . . He knows about something that happened to me. I told him, more or less. But there were three witnesses from Presbytery. And I couldn't really be held to blame. . .'

Tilda has worked with Women's Aid. She expresses no surprise when I explain what took place with Sandy Nicoll. It is similar to accounts she's heard from so many women.

Other than to Tilda, I speak of my anxiety about my colleague's malicious intent only to Helen Ross at Airlie. I've been visiting Helen over a period of illness and know her to be a mild woman not given to gossip. I am circumspect in what I say and taken aback at her vehement response: 'There are plenty of people round here who know things about *him* to his shame. He's got a cheek if he tries to put something on you!'

Little do I know that he is moving in for the kill. In less than a week he will pounce.

The next day I receive instructions in the post:

Airlie Manse,
12 June, 1997
Helen, (no 'Dear')
As of today's date anyone wishing you to conduct a
baptism, wedding or funeral within any of the six
parishes should, in the first instance, contact me at Airlie
Manse.
You may not make arrangements to baptise, marry or
bury (except when I am on holiday and have instructed
the undertaker accordingly), without first having
discussed the matter with me.
Robert J Ramsay

This is now beyond a joke. If I cannot exercise the functions of a minister, how can I remain? My position in the parishes, attached as I have become to the people, has become untenable. So certain am I of the rightness and strength of the pull towards the Western Isles, however, that hope tempers sadness.

Saturday 14 June

Alyth Show Day. Bob Wallace, who was on the lorry-driving course with me, appears at my cottage for a coffee and a blether. I'm pleased but surprised to see him. The talk is of lorries at first, but then Bob drops into the conversation, 'Robert Ramsay came over to speak to me at The Rotary Club this week. I don't know what's afoot but he spoke so menacingly about you! I thought I should warn you.'

'Why, Bob, whatever did he say?'

'He said, "There's more than you think going on up that glen, Bob. Just you wait and see!" I don't know what it was supposed to mean, but it sounded ominous, and nasty.'

'Its nothing, Bob. He just doesn't like sharing the glory of being the minister here, that's all. Look, this morning I had this letter from him. He wants me to scivvy for him, but not to do anything for which I can be given any *kudos*. No baptisms. No weddings. No funerals. He doesn't want me making myself popular by shining in public. He's irritated because the elder for this district – my own elder – booked a date for his son's Christening when I'd be taking the service in that building, rather than Robert. That's all it's about. Petty jealousy.'

In the light of the curt letter I've just received, it does not occur to me that Robert could be plotting any further destruction. I think he has clipped my wings sufficiently for his purpose.

Similarly I dismiss a second warning. Frank Norrie from Dryloch telephones. I know the Norrie children through the village school, better than I know their parents. I am particularly fond of flaxen-haired wee Janice, who has taken to planting herself in my lap while I sit telling stories to the infants in the church. Her father has never previously telephoned me.

'Helen? Are you all right?' he asks. 'Good. Well, it's just to say that if you're going to run away with that young lad, you should just get on and do it!'

'I'm sorry?'

'MacPuff of the Milton's been at our door with the church newsletter and he says you're sacked because you're running off with a loon from Kilry and it's the talk of Alyth Show.'

'Oh? It's the first I've heard of it!'

'We wanted to make sure you're all right.' Frank means this. He's not hungry for me to confirm the truth of the rumour. He is just concerned for my welfare.

'Frank, I've been instructed not to conduct weddings, funerals or baptisms without Robert's express permission. I haven't been sacked. But perhaps you could tell MacPuff I'll be standing at the gate at eight in the morning with my bag packed if he wants to run off with me!' *MacPuff of the Milton* as he's nicknamed is one of the elders at Ruthven and a big bear of a man. Perhaps in his youth a lass would have eloped with him but it takes some imagining!

I've always got along well enough with MacPuff but I know very well that if anything is the 'talk' of Alyth Show, MacPuff will have started it. He hasn't earned his nickname for nothing. I am irritated that an elder should be spreading gossip like this around his district. I ask the Session Clerk to upbraid MacPuff. MacPuff's response is typically boorish: 'Well Douglas, it's a bloody disgrace, and I don't know how you haven't heard about it. Everyone else has!' Everyone else, that is, except me. Still I do not tumble to the fact that I am sitting within the very jaws of the trap, by now only hours away from springing.

I've a wedding to take in the afternoon; a cheerful family ceremony in the upper room of the pub. I leave early in the evening, having a sermon to finish for the morning. That homily is never to be delivered. Several messages on my answer-machine instruct me to contact the Reverend Brian Ramsay of Aberlemno, 'a matter of great urgency' having arisen. I cannot imagine what can be so desperately awry that he will have me drive all the way over to Aberlemno immediately. Can I make it in half an hour?

'Brian, I've only just walked in. It's a fifty minute journey. . .'

As I hurtle down the Balloch Brae I meet Sandy Nicoll's brother Richard's big four-wheel drive hurtling up it. Richard is driving like a Jehu and for some reason Robert Ramsay is perched up on the passenger seat, his face purple and thunderous. They are pursued hotly by another Nicoll family car. We pass at some speed but Robert Ramsay's face as it appears in that second is etched on my memory. It crosses my mind that he and the Nicolls are embroiled in something I do not like and which gives me a sinister sensation, but even at this late hour I do not unravel the knot to see what he is doing.

The Snare

'BUT it was tantamount to rape!' I cry out, aghast. So that is it: the Nicolls are accusing me of fornication!

I stare at them in disbelief. How can they possibly accuse me of something I did not invite and that brought me so much pain?

I'll own up to many sins but never to having lustful desires. Sex is abhorrent to me.

'They say you had an abortion. . . You are telling us he raped you and you fell pregnant?'

'It was tantamount to rape,' I repeat my first words. 'I didn't want him to do it.'

Brian of Aberlemno has already made a phone call to my boss in the Department of National Mission. 'He's your employer: I had to let him know,' he excuses. And a Reverend John Chalmers from the Board of Ministry is anxious to talk to me and to offer 'pastoral support'. I am issued with his telephone number and instructed to contact him. I do not want to talk to a stranger! All these people are discussing the intimate details of my life, without my sanction.

Brian has also arranged for someone to take my church services tomorrow. I don't understand why I am being removed from my work so hastily. It is as if my home has been raided and I have been taken into custody without even being allowed to leave a note for the children coming home from school. The 'sin' took place eighteen months ago: do they really think I shall lead my congregation astray in one more sermon? Or lure other innocent men with my wiles this very night? Banning me from occupying the pulpit is a precipitate action, bound to fire speculation before I can be given a fair hearing.

'Perhaps Sandy Nicoll will admit the truth and confirm what you told us,' simper Brian and his sidekick Helen McLeod. 'Perhaps you could contact him in Bosnia through the charity for which he is working?'

It is no accident that Robert Ramsay and the Nicolls have chosen this time, when my only alibi is travelling in a truck in a foreign country, to spring the trap. They will have me neatly bundled out of the district by the time he returns. I shall be frightened by the threat of an ecclesiastical trial. I'll be under pressure to make a rapid decision because the Superintendence Committee meets in a few days and will require my resignation on the table.

Helen McLeod and Brian of Aberlemno urge me over and over again to *demit*. I think they mean that I should resign from the ministry – *demit status*. This is too drastic a shift for me to absorb. I have felt a spiritual calling since I was a child. I cannot imagine being stripped of my identity overnight. I am in a trance; a state of shock. They are getting nowhere with me. It is only when Brian reveals, 'You'll still be able to apply for another parish. We are only asking that you demit your *charge*, not your *status*,' that I come to my senses. To leave the district, to go to another Presbytery, is reasonable. I already have one interview lined up in Islay and I'm waiting for a date for one in South Uist, on which my heart is really set. I can find another parish. I feel relieved, suddenly, and they have won the end to which they were pushing me.

It is almost eleven o'clock when I leave Brian's manse. In my memory it is dark, although it is midsummer and there must have been light in the sky still.

I'll put off telephoning this Reverend John Chalmers. I don't want to bare my soul, and my woman's shame, to an unknown male. I feel vulnerable and threatened. Imposing an unfamiliar pastor on me is insensitive and cruel. Brian has, however, also contacted the Reverend John Birrell, who left Angus Presbytery recently. He is acquainted with all the characters involved, but will not be on the jury as he is no longer in the district. And I know him.

John is now in hospital chaplaincy and does not have a Sunday service. He is prepared to drive up from Perth to see me at The Faulds in the morning, if I want him to. *If I want him to.* John does not just assume I am ready to speak to him. He also realises I'd feel safer in my own home. Basic tenets of pastoral care that others ignore.

Sunday 15th June

I feel so lost. So aimless. The sermon lies on top of the desk, pen laid beside it. The hymn book sits waiting to be lifted, just as every Sunday for as long as I can remember. The house has become frozen in time. Next door, the church bell is ringing. I stand at the window and watch people parking their cars and walking across the churchyard. Humanity is going about its usual Sunday business outside, but my life has just been cut short. I am locked away in a separate existence.

When John Birrell arrives, he brings a modicum of normality. I pour him coffee, and heat pizza. Ordinary people do this on Sundays. The whole world is not in church.

He has already leafed through his books on Church Law. What

will they do to me if I refuse to resign from my post? I could go against Brian of Aberlemno and Mrs McLeod and face a Church Trial. 'Is there anyone who knew you were raped? I mean, before allegations were made against you?'

'Yes. . . Yes! There were doctors, at the time. Rape Crisis counsellors, too. There'll be medical records. I told my lorry-driving instructor. And the examiner. A long time ago. Yes, long before there was any hint of this ludicrous accusation!'

'Good! So you have corroborative evidence! And what about Sandy Nicoll?'

'He's not depraved, John. He's not some villain. Millions of men do this – to their wives, even. But he knew I hadn't wanted it. He was the one who said it was "just a bit of rape." That's just it: most men don't notice the woman doesn't want to be there.'

'You are fond of the guy.'

'Yes.'

'See if you can contact him and ask him to tell the Committee of Inquiry how it happened. Listen, if you do choose to go to Trial, I'll come as a witness: I know very well that Robert is responsible for this plot. I was Depute Presbytery Clerk in Angus and every week Robert slated and undermined you in front of his colleagues in the Presbytery Office. I reminded him once that you worked in one of Edinburgh's poorest housing schemes and ran a parish of your own in the drug districts of Paisley, before you came here. You were probably a great deal more experienced as a minister than Robert himself. He was still drifting along in his first charge, a rural backwater. It didn't go down too well when I pointed that out to him, but it put his gas at a peep for a short while.

'Your alternative is to cut your losses, resign, and make a fresh start in a new parish. You don't have to go through the rigours of a Church Trial. You would clear your name but what concerns me most is the press. There's no way they'll be kept out if the case goes to Trial. Female clergy? Sex? Rape? They'd lap it up! It will take months for Presbytery to arrange a Trial, but, come the Spring, your front garden will be full of them. There they'll be, cameras pressed against the window panes.'

John points to the patch of grass in front of the kitchen window where the hens are busy scratching and Grace Pig has just stretched out her lumbering frame to sunbathe, oblivious of the hell that could soon descend around her black ears in a few months' time. I cannot face that. I cannot stay and fight. I'll ship my animals to South Uist, very soon.

Before he leaves John gives me a big, kind hug. By this he shows that not quite every man need treat me as if I am a blemished and untouchable slut. And not all ministers think they must avoid showing human compassion, for fear of loosing a safe 'professional distance'. Safe for whom?

A neighbour stops on her way back from Church with flowers from herself and the woman who shares her pew. They are worried by my unexplained absence. Apparently Rev Robert Ramsay is so 'stressed' by the events he engineered that he asked the newly elected Moderator of Presbytery to come to his churches and preach the sermons for him. Mr Maplesden informed the congregations that he brought 'the support of the Presbytery for your Minister, *Robert* and his family'. He made a point of praying 'for strength for *Robert* at this difficult time.' My name was not even mentioned.

I am permitted to tell my neighbour nothing. I take the flowers inside and cry.

Monday 16th June

The phone rings early. Sandy. 'The Aid agency faxed ahead to Sarajevo, with an urgent message for me to contact Angus Presbytery. What's going on?'

'They're taking away my job because of what you did to me. Will you tell them the truth?'

'Yes,' he answers gravely. 'Yes, I'll tell them the truth about what I did.' Then, his voice wavering, he squawks, 'I could be up in the Courts of the Land!'

'Look, you won't. I'm still not going to the Police. You. . .' His coin runs out. We are cut off.

'I am sure when they hear that they'll let it rest,' Brian of Aberlemno assures me on the telephone. 'When they hear Sandy's admitting what he did and that you've agreed to demit your charge and leave the district, they will back down and leave it at that.'

The National Mission Boss is coming at seven o'clock to collect my letter of resignation and Brian half an hour later to collect a similar missive written to the Presbytery. I am surprised, therefore, when Brian's car pulls up outside when I am still receiving the National Mission Boss into the cottage. It is only minutes after seven, and I can see from Brian's face that he has bad news. He explains as soon as he is inside the door.

'Hello, Douglas.' He addresses only the National Mission man. He does not look at me. 'I had to come at once. I've seen the Nicolls and they won't accept Helen's resignation; not unless she's out of the ministry altogether. She must demit her status, not just her charge. No parish away on the island of Islay. No parish on the island of South Uist. No parish five hours on a boat across the sea where she could be forgotten. She's going nowhere. I'm sorry.'

Shock. A towering wave smacks against me, knocking me off my legs and tumbling me round and round. I struggle to fathom which way up I am, whether I shall breathe in air or water. How could they? How? Surely it is enough to have me banished from their Kingdom, without demanding my decapitation? It isn't reasonable! What I've done doesn't warrant this! I am reeling on my feet. Brian says he told them I'd contacted Sandy and that he was backing up my plea; but they were resolute. 'I'll get her out of the ministry for good,' Moyra had sworn.

Robert Ramsay must be at the root of this. He must have egged them on to bay for blood. Only someone versed in Church Law would know the difference between 'demission of *charge*' and 'demission of *status*.' The Nicolls would not have asked for the ultimate sacrifice of my ministry, without Robert's calling the tune. Brian knows it, too. 'This is Robert's doing,' I say darkly.

Brian nods slowly. 'Yes. He is wicked. Truly wicked.'

Brian did his utmost to resolve matters to preserve the peace of the Church, not to compound my hurt, and let the Nicolls feel they'd got their pound of flesh. He couldn't achieve it. The Nicolls were determined that that pound of flesh should be carved from close to the heart and Rev Robert Ramsay was telling them how to cut it. All Brian's good intent was not sufficient to contend with such evil.

Brian tries to tell me what will happen if I do not now demit status. He has brought with him fat hardback tomes. 'There'd be a *Trial by Libel*. I've read up the relevant section on the 1935 Act *Anent* Trials by Libel. It's difficult to follow, but I understand there would be a *Committee of Inquiry* that would hold *Hearings*. Then the *libel* would be served, it would be *revised by the Church Procurator*, then it would *proceed to proof*, and the Trial would be heard . . .'

He goes on. If Brian himself found it hard to follow, how could *I* begin? The very phrase, Trial by Libel, is terrifying. My brain is fuddled. I am not taking in any of it.

'You could fight this, Helen,' Brian looks up at me. 'I've seen people stand up to things like this, but it's destroyed them. You must think what it'll do to you.'

I stare in bewilderment. The National Mission Boss and Brian both think it best that I re-write my letters of resignation and say that I shall demit my status from the ministry altogether. Brian tells me exactly what wording to use:

'Put, "I wish to demit my status because I am no longer able to work with my colleague, Robert Ramsay." I'll take it to the Superintendence Committee tomorrow. They know enough already to read between the lines, don't you worry! You could hardly continue, anyway, after Robert's Papal bull about baptisms, weddings and funerals.'

I do as I am told and hand over the two letters with a heavier heart than I have ever felt. The National Mission Boss says he will put my resignation before his Committee 'in due course', but he wants to see me again with another man in Edinburgh, to finalise the details, tomorrow.

Edinburgh? Drive to Edinburgh, tomorrow? Already two nights without sleep and I am on the verge of collapse from exhaustion. I cannot, safely, drive to Edinburgh. If I sound pathetic, I feel it.

'Please, is there any way you could come here?'

'Yes, I think we could do that.' The National Mission Boss can see that I really am not fit to drive. 'Meantime, you should arrange with the Session Clerks to unlock the church and supervise you while you remove your prayer books.' This comment kicks me in the gut. What do they think I am going to do? Set light to the holy building?

The telephone rings as the two men are getting up to go. Murdo, in South Uist. The vacancy committee has met and they want to interview me for the post.

Murdo, I groan inwardly. Your sense of timing! I have just signed my life away and I am watching all my dreams walk out of the door with these two men. Don't talk to me about your beautiful island, when I shall never see it now! My throat is dry. I muster just more than a whisper to interrupt him, 'I shan't be coming. I'm sorry. I have to go now. I've visitors.'

Murdo rings back, very late. He has waited up to do so. 'Your voice sounded strangled earlier: Do you want to tell me what is wrong? You don't have to if you don't want to. . .' Do angels have gnomish red beards and speak with a West Highland lilt?

I pour out my soul to this man, whose sense of timing is perhaps not so misplaced after all, because he persuades me to think again about resigning. He gives me the courage I need at the point when I had given up the fight: 'Muck sticks, but most of it falls off eventually,' he philosophises.

Murdo was in the Police and he believes what I tell him about my early experience of sexual abuse, and more recent events. It fits. On the one occasion he met me, this percipient man saw the vulnerable and frightened girl beneath the brightly coloured trousers, each leg a different tartan, who was outwardly so spirited and vivacious. 'You were like a bitch that's been ill-treated. My sheepdogs are my passion. The collie I rescued is just like you; so eager to please, but slinking towards me with her belly almost on the ground, cowering when I raise my voice. You must come here to South Uist! You must not give in to the Presbytery of Angus! The island folk will return the love you will give them, with the love and acceptance you need. I know my people. I also know you cannot have invented such a story as you have just told me. But even if it was otherwise, and you had brought it all on your own head, you'd still deserve compassion. Get yourself a lawyer, first thing in the morning.'

So it is thanks to Murdo that I resolve to lift up my head and contest the case.

I lie awake all night again, turning my body and my mind this way and that. My head hurts. My jaws will not unclench. Eileen the cat throws me accusing glares from the foot of the quilt because I am disturbing her. My heart is racing with adrenalin, but there is nowhere to run, and so I writhe here. A knot of sharp pain seizes one of the vertebrae between my shoulder blades. I watch the clock, willing the hands to move quicker towards a half-civilised hour when I can telephone Barbara Lovegrove. Barbara is the only lawyer I know, apart from several illustrious elders of the Edinburgh congregation where I finished my training. This is too trivial a matter for them. I don't know if Barbara will be able to help. She usually deals with property law.

Tuesday 17th June

Half past seven. I can wait no longer to telephone Barbara. I explain the reason for my early call. She tries to encourage me. 'Of course you should fight this! Of course it isn't reasonable to make you give up your status as a minister! You'd have no chance of re-employment anywhere! Come to my office at noon.'

Even if I fight to clear my name and keep my status as a minister, the National Mission Boss has my letter of resignation from this parish. He indicated that I have twelve weeks to quit my tenancy of The Faulds. Then my salary will stop. Twelve weeks! Where am I supposed to go then? Where can I find a place of safety for my cat, Eileen? Eileen is a one-person cat. She sinks her teeth into anyone else who attempts to touch her because she was kicked and abused as a kitten and then locked in a flat with no food. She can do without further trauma in her life. Where shall I put three large sows and a litter of piglets? What if a duck is sitting on eggs when I have to leave home and I can't disturb her?

I drift through the rooms of the cottage, caressing the wallpaper with my fingertips, mourning every inch of the walls. I stand in the doorways and gaze at corners and fireplaces and my body screams with grief. I cry the kind of tears that do not flow but dam up in the chest and hurt there.

I walk the dog to Christine's, half a mile along the lane, and Eileen the Fierce tries to follow me. My little cat can sense there is something very wrong.

The knot of tension in my back has become a gnawing pain and I beg Christine to knead it. She kneels astride my back and I want to groan with pain, the pain of an animal for whom the burden of living has become intolerable, not just because of physical suffering, but emotional anguish.

I expected Christine to have heard about my original decision to resign as a result of Robert's decree. It is her nephew's baptism that precipitated Robert's irrational jealousy. She is amazed when I tell her about the developments since the 'no baptisms' letter. She is less surprised about Heather. She and James have long since realised that my mercurial swings of attitude towards Sandy Nicoll must stem from something that happened between us. They are also aware that the Nicoll marriage has been less than happy for many years. 'You obviously have some feelings for him. . .Wouldn't you go to stay with him now?' she asks gently. I shake my head. I am in so much turmoil that I don't know what I feel or want. 'You'll never be able to fight this in your condition. You've been trembling like a leaf ever since you got here. Your whole body's quaking.'

'It doesn't make sense,' says her James.

Nothing makes sense.

Drusilla, a young mum I've been supporting through psychiatric difficulties, said she would be at The Faulds about ten o'clock. I run back home from Christine's, but not really expecting Drusilla will keep her word. Most times she says she'll come, she doesn't. I've often waited in all day for Drusilla and she's never appeared. This time, however, is one of the rare occasions she does show up. She is looking at the hens with her little girl when I return.

Drusilla may be unreliable, but in a crisis she is nothing short of a wonder. She takes the situation in hand. 'The bastard!' she says, referring to Robert, and then she gets on with the business of organising my affairs. She bundles me into her jeep. 'You must tell my elder, Dr Buchanan, absolutely everything. I'm taking you there first and then to Barbara Lovegrove. You're not f***ing well fit to drive. Come on!' Drusilla minds her private-school-horsey-woman's language in the presence of her elder, but not in front of me.

The Buchanans are both doctors. They do not need to be appraised of Robert Ramsay's twisted behaviour. Nor of the Nicolls'. They are familiar with their goings-on over the years. Heather is the only matter of which they had no previous knowledge. Jim Buchanan is hard of hearing and he keeps disappearing to answer the phone. I have to shout and repeat, the most painful details.

The Buchanan doctors' 'pro-life' views are known to me. I appreciate their position and am all the more grateful that they are supportive of me in my predicament, despite what I was forced to do concerning Heather.

Elizabeth Buchanan does what she knows her Lord would require of her. Though not in the best of health, she drives to Mary Nicoll's house. Mary is just putting on her coat to go across to her daughter-in-law, Moyra, with whom after years of enmity she has found a common cause.

If anyone has the quiet tact to remind Mary of Christ's command to forgive, it is Elizabeth Buchanan. She tells Mary what her current course of action will do to her son, to her family, to the Church. Mary is adamant, bitter, and hell-bent on reprisals. Her son has let her down. She does not care how public this becomes.

Elizabeth Buchanan returns wearied, as if she has battled against evil. I don't deserve her going through so much pain on my account.

She gives me some of her own sleeping tablets. I cannot go to the local surgery: I'd meet half the district in the waiting room. She can see I am dropping with tiredness. It is now so long since I slept that I need to be knocked out artificially to break the pattern. I sway on my feet when I stand, but sleep eludes me when I lie down.

Barbara Lovegrove leads Drusilla and me to the café opposite the Steeple Chippy. She orders three bowls of soup, but I cannot swallow one spoonful. I have not eaten for several days. I feel nauseous constantly.

Back in her office, Barbara makes two telephone calls. The first is to her court partner in Dundee. He agrees to see me, but I must telephone his secretary in the morning to make an appointment. The second call is to Finlay Macdonald, Principal Clerk of the General Assembly of the Church of Scotland. He is being a little testy with her because I hear her say, 'There is another side to this story, you know!' Clearly he has already heard that I have stated a sexual act took place without my consent.

I do not think Finlay Macdonald really knows what to do. Church Law does not have a clause to cover such a situation. The 1935 Act of the Church of Scotland *Anent* Trials by Libel has remained little changed since its eighteenth century original version. It presumes that all ministers are male, and all libidinous behaviour is therefore entered into willingly, and actively, by the accused.

Drusilla takes me home to feed my animals and be ready for my employers' visit. She offers for me to sleep at her house later, and packs an overnight bag for me. Her husband is away. Drusilla is enjoying managing my crisis. I stand in the middle of it all, blinking and staring like a dozy owl. Drusilla will collect me in a couple of hours. I protest. I don't want to inconvenience her any more. I'll drive.

'You can't! For f***'s sake, look at you, darling, you can hardly stand! You need a few gins, a hot bath, and sleeping pills. I'm coming down to get you. And you'll have something to eat.' I give in about being driven, but not about the food.

The deputation from National Mission arrives. The second visit of the National Mission Boss in twenty-four hours. He has brought with him a Reverend Alan Taylor, yet another male I don't know. As they munch my chocolate biscuits, I inform them that I am thinking of standing trial after all and not demitting my status. They exchange glances and make non-committal noises. It is obvious that my change of plan does not suit them. They say they cannot advise me. They are only there to give me twelve weeks' pay and the same time to get out of the house. My resignation, which the National Mission Boss was in such a hurry to pick up last night, has already been accepted. He neglected to tell me that the relevant committee was scheduled to meet today. That will be why he was in such a hurry to collect my letter of resignation last night.

If the case goes to Trial it will take far longer than twelve weeks. Where shall I live? How shall I pay the lawyer £80 an hour, without a salary of my own? Gin, a hot bath, two temazepam. I still hardly sleep, but am comforted by the wind soughing in the trees at Dalnashally, and a change of walls at which to blink and stare.

Playing by the Rules

19 – 25 June 1997

Night after night, terror runs up my arms like rats and perches menacingly round my neck. Ribbed tails of fear cling to my back. Grief gnaws at my thorax with yellowed incisors.

Wednesday, Thursday, Friday, Saturday. The sleepless nights and days are merging into one.

Not just today, but for a fortnight or three weeks, I lean on Drusilla as if she is my sister.

Which night is it that strong Drusilla urges me to write a letter to Sandy Nicoll on his return from Bosnia? She will see that it reaches him. In it I must reiterate the necessity of his telling the truth about what has gone on between us. I must instruct him not to contact me, except through Drusilla herself, who is overanxious to act as go-between. Moreover, I must insist that the letter be destroyed and not kept for his wife to find. . .

Sandy has left things lying around before. He has seemed to be inflaming his wife's wrath deliberately – as when he bought me a pie after the cattle auction and left the receipt in his pocket, knowing she'd check before washing his trousers. Sometimes it was as if he wanted to incite her jealousy; parking his car outside my house when I wasn't even there! It was almost as if he hoped she would throw him out and save him making the decision to go.

Look what all this has brought on me now! My anger is apparent in the letter Drusilla has commissioned, as I repeat in it my sarcastic jeer about him changing his name and living with me in Cloud Cuckoo Land.

[*Sandy did leave this letter for his wife to find. Appendix I.2*]

At breakfast, I pass my effort to Drusilla for approval. Her decree? 'But it sounds so final: the poor man will commit suicide when he reads it! You must add that you love him! You have to offer him some hope and consolation, if you don't want his death on your conscience!'

I don't realise how Drusilla is relishing the drama of it all. She is orchestrating my every move.

And I let her. I am relieved to comply with everything. She dictates a revised version and I write whatever she says. I am so out of it, totally beyond autonomous thought. A puppet on strings.

I don't even remember the letter until it reappears five months later, published in the *Scotsman*. The Presbytery will claim to have gained possession of 'damning evidence' in the form of a missive in my handwriting. In actual fact it says little that is new, and the most shocking revelation is the bad language, which is uncharacteristic of me, to this degree. It sounds more like Drusilla, with her private school 'For f***'s sake, darlings'.

All I recollect is that the temazepam is not enough to let me sleep and I feel so tired I could retch with exhaustion. Sleep deprivation is affecting me. Some conversations and events I shall remember as clearly as the day they took place. Others will be lost to my memory. It is the most hectic week in the most stressful six months of my life. Shock-induced exhaustion sweeps over me. I am dazed. So many people give me contradictory commands so that I no longer know my *own* mind. I am a passenger on a locomotive that has gone out of control. We career down the track veering one way as the points change, then lurching to a halt, shunting into reverse and hurtling backwards.

This whole week, and intermittently over many months, my arms are cold and numb and the blood pounds in my head and neck. My brain is fit to burst, as if a haemorrhage or stroke is imminent.

This is the day the Business Committee meets to discuss the agenda for the full meeting of Presbytery next week. Barbara Lovegrove telephones: 'Helen, will you let me write to the Business Committee asking for time to be given for you to be seen by the Church Medical Officer? You're too ill to know what you're doing.'

'Barbara, they have to give me time anyway. I've spoken to Douglas Murray at Glasgow University. He says they have to let my demission lie on the table until the next meeting. They can't accept it at once. They have to appoint a committee to confer with me and report back. It's in the rules. Dr Murray says I'll have until the September meeting to decide if I can face Trial.'

'But will they? We can't risk it.' Barbara must have inside information that there are those on the Business Committee who have no intention of abiding by the rules. 'I want to ask for time on medical grounds, just to be certain.'

Friday. The Reverend John Chalmers finally contacts me. I have reneged on telephoning him myself, despite instruction. I don't know him! Chalmers has received the request to see the Church Medical Officer. He wants to bring Dr Manson to my home. I think it must be late afternoon, but in my memory all these events take place when it is dark. Pathetic fallacy, surely: the light hardly fails in Scotland in June.

I am frazzled by this time. Chalmers and Manson are big in

stature (or perhaps it is like the nights being dark; they just seem so) and I am intimidated. These men from the Church have not come to judge me. Nevertheless, repeatedly I have to allow males I have never met into my living room and be stripped naked, having the most intimate details of my life revealed. Nowhere, nothing, is private. The cottage, which was my refuge, has become a place where I feel invaded and unsafe.

I am forced to explain what happened with Heather, but I become distraught in the telling. The two big men sit watching me and say nothing. Can men comprehend the depth of a woman's grief over such loss?

Chalmers has left the room to make a phone call. Dr Manson takes this opportunity, when there is no-one from the Church present to condemn me if I make a confession: 'And did you have a liaison with this gentleman?' He is very kindly, and very serious – and for a second I want to laugh! I have never heard anyone use such a quaint expression. No, I did not have a 'liaison' with Sandy Nicoll.

Could I benefit from counselling? The hospital offered me counselling after Heather, but Glasgow was too far away to travel. The grief is still raw, and I still feel vulnerable and scared of men. 'Will you go now, if I recommend that time be given for you to do this?' He turns to Chalmers. 'I think she needs time: she is in a state of shock and clearly not fit to be making life-changing decisions. It could be of benefit all round: it sounds to me as if the Nicoll family could do with a while to calm down too.'

At precisely the same time that Dr Manson is trying to restore a little sensibility to a fraught situation, the Presbytery Business Committee is warring over how quickly they can whip up the storm.

The Business Committee meets, and dissolves into a rammy. If I am asking for time to be seen by the Church Medical Officer before *deciding* about demission, well, then, that could be taken as my *withdrawing* my demission! So they can get on with arranging a

Trial right away, can't they? Yes, they must hold the Trial at once! This cannot be left to wait! Never mind that I have already been signed off sick by my own GP.

Some caution deferment, but Rev Robert Ramsay campaigns for summary execution. He does not think the Trial is even necessary: it is obvious I am guilty. He blurts out the damning content of the letters of accusation that, officially, only Brian of Aberlemno has received and that should remain confidential.

Brian is livid. If I decide to face trial, the accusations will be passed to the Convener of the Committee of Inquiry. No-one else should be aware of the contents, so that there will be no prejudice if the case is dismissed. There is now no longer the possibility of that impartiality.

Others also descend on Robert Ramsay for his indiscretion. He's been a lawyer and ought to know better! He protests my guilt all the louder. The meeting becomes out of order.

As Presbytery Clerk, Robert's word prevails. I may see the Medical Officer, but in the meantime the Trial will be incepted. The attempt to buy me time has back-fired.

Should I be named at the full meeting of Presbytery? A second heated argument ensues. The Reverend Peter Youngson is keen that it should be made public, exposing me at once to the mercy of the press. However, the agreed wording is eventually limited to: 'Allegations of a serious nature have been made against a minister within the bounds of the Presbytery.'

Youngson registers his dissent. He wants my name in bold print.

Of course it is academic at the end of the day. It is a small presbytery, and seventeen members of the Business Committee already know the details. It is only a matter of time before the press will be onto this.

It is now over a week since I slept, apart from a fitful few hours. I pace the floors of the cottage counting the days I have left to live here. Twelve weeks already eleven.

I need to see the Acting Governor at the prison to explain what is happening: 'Helen, just you come in whenever you are able. I'm here all week.' He knows from my voice that some crisis has arisen and treats me with consideration and sensitivity.

It's nine days since the blow was dealt and I think I am able to drive. I owe it to him to learn directly from me what is going on. National Mission has in any case whipped off with my resignation from my post, which I'm told must include that of Prison Chaplain. It makes no difference to them that I have decided to fight the allegation against me: they won't have to pay me a salary during what could be a protracted process towards the Trial.

Mr Morgan makes time to see me at once. And he listens. It is not incumbent on him to do so. He is answerable to the Scottish Office for the custody of notorious criminals and he is responsible for an entire staff. The personal difficulties of a part-time chaplain are nothing to him. My little trouble is a trifle, but he gives me his undivided attention, and the benefit of his experience.

'A colleague of mine once turned up for work reeking of drink and with only half his uniform,' he says. 'I was a junior warder then, and was asked to support him at a hearing. I pointed out a minor procedural error in the manner in which the man had been briefed. The Governors were forced to let him off on that technicality. Helen, this whole process could fall flat on its face before it goes as far as the Trial. An accused person must be given the opportunity to defend himself throughout any disciplinary process, and it seems to me that by taking away your livelihood precipitously they are pre-judging you. I am not questioning your innocence – unlike the colleague I defended, who *was* drunk on duty. All the same, the procedures must be implemented properly and appropriate advice and support provided. The Church can be no different from any other organisation in this.'

I fail, at this juncture, to see the irony of such confidence in the integrity of the system. The Church of Scotland does indeed have such procedures, enshrined in an ancient Act. Mr Morgan is echoing the assumption of my elder Major Houston, from his experience of Army courts martial, that the Church will have to follow procedures. None of us foresees that the Kirk will waive its own rules, at whim.

Mr Morgan is not happy to lose me as his Prison Chaplain. He telephones the head of the Joint Prison Chaplaincies Board in the Church of Scotland offices right away. I hear him telling the Reverend John Thomson, 'Whatever the Church intends doing with Helen Percy, Noranside Prison does not have a problem with her, is very happy with her work, and wishes her to continue.'

His words cut no ice. He puts down the phone and announces, 'I am going to lunch. You have the use of the Governor's office, desk, and telephone. Write to National Mission saying that you were over hasty and wish to withdraw your resignation. My secretary will type it for you and fax it. Post the original. Here are stamps. If they're going to hold a Trial it could go on well into next year. Twelve weeks' salary won't go very far! You can't let them abandon you like that. Meanwhile, you keep coming into the prison. Take time off if you need to just now, but come in whenever you want.' With that, he leaves.

Mr Morgan is speaking sense and is taking control for me when I am in no fit state to act in my own interests. He realises that, at a time when my whole life has been turned upside down, I need the prisoners, and some semblance of routine, more than they need me.

Parishioners

FIONA and Davie Robertson request to see me. Davie's parents are both elders at Airlie, but the younger couple are sporadic attenders. I hardly know them. Fiona however, is a very direct person, and I am comfortable with people who say what they're thinking. She puts down a mug of coffee on the table in front of me.

'We don't know what's been going on, but MacPuff of the Milton's been round everyone's door with copies of a letter – allegations written to the Presbytery against you – and father's furious. Not with you. With Robert Ramsay. That Robert Ramsay can't talk. Not with the rumours that have been flying around about him. And not just rumours, either. I was a Scout Leader with him and I know him very well. But father wants to hear from you what's happened. Now get that coffee down and away across to see him.'

What is the use of lawyers advising me to say nothing to anyone about the story? MacPuff told half the parish I'd run away to a foreign land with a man, when I was at home feeding my chickens! Then he was circulating copies of Mary Nicoll's letter to the Presbytery –

even before I knew I was accused! I haven't even seen this letter myself. My parishioners are better informed than I am, about a matter that should have remained confidential to the Moderator of the Presbytery, to whom the letters were addressed.

Bob Robertson is as blunt as his daughter-in-law: 'I want to know exactly what happened between you and Sandy Nicoll. It doesn't matter if you enjoyed every moment of it, you still don't deserve to have it plastered all round the district. *Did* you bring this trouble on yourself? But I already know the answer, don't I? I know fine well who's at the foot of this devilry: MacPuff doesn't have the intelligence to be the Master of this plot, but Ramsay knows how to choose his henchmen!'

I do not need to say anything. Fiona puts their family's theory to the test by visiting Airlie Manse herself at tea-time. 'Robert, you're the Minister here, as well as the Presbytery Clerk: shouldn't you be doing something about these explosive confidential documents being bandied around?' she demands.

'I haven't had many dealings with schizophrenics but Helen does have severe mental problems. She needs help,' is his slander-ous and unfounded retort.

Fiona is none too impressed by the nature of help on offer, nor by Ramsay's readiness to blab. The extent of my supposed sexual favours increases every time Ramsay is given the chance to tell the tale.

Bob Robertson has survived a couple of wars and has both medals and injuries to show for it. He is afraid of no-one. He rallies the troops. Unbeknown to me, the elders in Airlie and Kingoldrum hear the cornet blast and attend an unofficial Session Meeting at Cookston Farm. They've all seen Mary Nicoll's damning letter, dubbing me an adulterous little slut and a baby-murderer. Despite these shocking revelations, their support for me is unswerving. A docile enough crew under the leadership of their previous minister who guided them gently for three decades, it has taken just three years for Rev Robert Ramsay to rattle their cage sufficiently for them to stand up to him. Now he won't know what's hit him.

Granny Vogan is at Hazel's gate. I have been advised not to speak to anyone, but it is so awkward. I shall be isolated for months. I cannot avoid my nextdoor neighbours! I can hardly remark on the weather and the size of Hazel's cabbages and then let them discover what is going on from some lay-preacher who suddenly appears in the pulpit instead of me this Sunday. That's if they haven't already heard the gossip. . .

They have heard, of course. Everyone has, thanks to Robert Ramsay and MacPuff. Granny Vogan is Mary Nicoll's bosom companion, but she does not condone her friend's vindictiveness. She lets me know that I am as welcome in her kitchen as I have ever been. She and Hazel are two generations older than I. I have no family and we have been drawn very close, especially since I took the funerals of Hazel's daughter and of another close neighbour.

Is it Tuesday when Dennis Leadbeatter chances to telephone? Knowing nothing, but detecting the faltering in my voice, he asks, 'Do you want me to come over to Kilry now?' Dennis, the oldest minister in the Presbytery, drops everything to comfort me, the youngest. He sits at my kitchen table hearing me tell him that, still unmarried, I have been pregnant. His reaction? Dennis *laughs*! Not for one moment does he consider that my misfortunes could be the result of my own immorality: '*Have* you? *HAVE* you?' The merriment in his eyes dies away only because he sees the distress in mine. The ache of loss gnaws deep. Grief has impacted hugely on my reactions towards Sandy Nicoll.

Dennis hears how my colleague engineered the allegation against me and how this very night all will be revealed at Presbytery. I am racked with such sobbing as Dennis has not witnessed in all his years of dealing with human grief: 'What would Robert Ramsay

say if he saw you now? What *would* he say if he saw you, Love?'
'Dennis, he'd be *pleased*!'

The Presbytery meets in full and in public tonight, and I haven't even seen the Big Lawyer to hear his assessment of my chances of acquittal. The press representatives are pricking up their ears, especially when there is a further attempt on the part of Reverends Robert Ramsay and Peter Youngson to name and shame me. Farcically, delegates are sent from Presbytery to inform all my elders (and I shall be named) at an Emergency Meeting of the Kirk Session that Robert Ramsay will convene tomorrow night in Kilry Village Hall.

I can see the village hall from my front window. It is odd, watching the cars draw up outside, knowing I shall be the sole subject of discussion and feeling so much an outsider.

Drusilla and her husband screech to a halt at my gate shortly before the meeting is to begin. Sidney has returned from his trip abroad. He doesn't think Drusilla has been sensible in encouraging me to fight the case and has persuaded her of the folly of it. They both urge me to put an end to the stress, send a letter of resignation to the impending meeting and leave the ministry before matters go any further.

'I wrote a letter to my congregation at the very outset,' I tell them, 'but Barbara Lovegrove would not let me send it. She doesn't believe these are grounds for me to leave the ministry. Here, you can read it if you like.' I reach up to the shelf behind me and pull out the letter I wrote days after I was accused.

> My Dear People,
> You may know that I resigned my position as Associate
> Minister. The lack of love between the two ministers
> could do nothing but damage these congregations.
> Since then I have had to make some very rapid decisions,
> and I owe it to you who have supported me to tell the truth.
> I have not been having an 'affair', but I have shared a

great depth of pain with a man for whom, as a result, I have grown to care. Now I must leave both him and my status as a minister.

I believe that all I have suffered throughout my life has made me a far better minister than I could ever otherwise have been. I am not convinced that the Church can understand this, and I am forced to ask the Presbytery to accept my demission of status as a minister.

I have loved you, and I thank you for the love you have shown me. It is breaking me to have to leave you.

I don't yet know what my future holds.

Yours in Christ, Helen

'I don't know why you and Drusilla maintain it wasn't an "affair",' declares Sidney. 'You and Sandy should just run off into the sunset. You could be happy.'

'You can't call it an "affair", Sidney: it was one isolated incident and she didn't want it,' protests Drusilla.

'But if she still spoke to him. . . Give me the dictionary. . . Look, it says 'a continuous sexual relationship'.

'Well, it wasn't 'continuous'. Sex happened only once. I wasn't given an option and I didn't like it! You can't call talking to someone having an "affair".'

'You're a typical man, Sidney. You can't imagine a woman *not* enjoying your sexual favours, can you? God, testosterone gives men such delusions!'

Sidney's perception as a male human being is not altered, but the upshot is that I have my mind changed for me for the umpteenth time and I place the letter in an envelope.

Sidney and Drusilla speed to the hall where the elders are arriving and give the letter to Dr Jim Buchanan.

He does not open it. The letter is not read.

If only he had done as he was asked the rest of my life could have been different . . .

Lawyers and Nuns

25 June – 2 July 1997

The meeting of the Kirk Session becomes disorderly as soon as it begins. Rev Robert Ramsay 'constitutes' its inauguration with prayer, but ten minutes later does not wait to pronounce the Benediction. It is left to the lay representative from Presbytery to find appropriate words to conclude proceedings.

Ramsay expects to be hailed a hero when it is announced that my depraved and wanton nature has at last been exposed, that I shall for ever hereafter be forbidden to preach in the parishes, and that I shall be put on trial for my immorality. The last thing Ramsay anticipates is Bob Robertson standing up and proposing a motion, 'If she goes, you should go too!'

Ramsay huffs and puffs, then calls for a vote of confidence, which he does not win. A large number of elders stand up behind Bob – and not just those who attended the impromptu meeting at Cookston Farm. Rev Robert Ramsay is visibly disturbed and enraged and strides out of the hall declaring he will henceforth be on 'sick leave'. (It is a Presbytery Clerk's privilege to be able to grant himself medical leave without consultation with his fellow presbyters and without a doctor's line!)

He resigns as Presbytery Clerk the same week, informing the press this is 'to avoid a conflict of interest'. It is difficult to be sure what he means: perhaps that he cannot maintain the necessary neutrality while he feels so much compassion and concern for a close colleague? Whatever it means, it sounds noble and righteous. Nevertheless, his face is like thunder on the only two occasions that I see him after that. On both occasions he is driving his car. My hand is uplifted in wave of greeting and he puts his foot on the throttle and speeds past. He passes in clouds of dust without returning the acknowledgement.

Sick or not, Ramsay makes arrangements to drive Moyra Nicoll to Edinburgh to confront and bring back her wayward husband upon his return from the long trip to Bosnia. Doubtless they had hoped to be able to inform him that I had quit and already left the district, but as it is, the best they can do is escort him home and keep him under surveillance. I can only guess at the coldness and strain of this reunion.

Rev Dennis Leadbeatter is the only source of information I have regarding what is happening in the Nicoll household at this time. Moyra Nicoll's father is still one of Dennis's staunch church members and Moyra and Sandy were married there in his parish. Thus Dennis has a pastoral interest in and responsibility for the family. He drives to Easter Craig Farm the night that Sandy comes home and attempts to restore a sense of proportion in that fraught place where relationships have gone so far awry. He bids Moyra consider what havoc she will wreak for herself and her family by continuing on the course of action on which she is set. It will inevitably bring the raptorial press to her own front door, as well as to mine. Does she want that?

She remains intransigent in her determination to destroy. 'I'll get her out of the Ministry if it's the last thing I do!' she rounds on him.

Dennis relates that their adult daughter is in the kitchen with them as Sandy screams at his wife over and over, 'I raped her! I told you that at the time! I raped her, I told you!'

Moyra bids Dennis leave. Her face is set.

Sandy follows him out into the darkened yard and weeps. Dennis has seldom seen a man filled with such remorse; so broken by the remembrance of his own actions.

I don't know whether I feel most sorry for Sandy, Moyra, or their daughter when I picture the farm kitchen this night.

Moyra Nicoll and Robert Ramsay make a complaint to Presbytery about Dennis 'poaching' on an adjoining parish.

Each successive minister entrusted with the care of our parishes, in Robert Ramsay's absence, visits Mary and Moyra Nicoll. But they don't come anywhere near me. My jurors' interpretation of 'impartiality' is to interview and support the witnesses for the prosecution; but not the defence.

Ramsay does climb out of his sickbed to make one other call – on Sandy Nicoll. He has an important message to deliver: 'If you don't change your story Sandy, you'll end up with a prison sentence!'

My solicitor writes to the Convener of the Inquiry deploring the lack of jurisprudence in tolerating influence of witnesses. Nothing is done about it. In a real court, Ramsay would be silenced until after the Trial.

At last the Big Lawyer has time to see me. His offices are imposing and take up all the storeys of a large Victorian building in central Dundee. The stairs are all carpeted and the reception area is dominated by huge oak counters, heavy chairs with dark leather upholstery and diplomas in grand frames. A clock in a tall case scolds every second. These are intimidating surroundings. I am instructed by a receptionist to follow a long corridor and take a seat in one of the waiting rooms. There is a humming in my head, as at all of these interviews, so that I cannot take in anything anyone says. I want to ask them to shout because I am standing on the far bank of a wide river and can hear only muffled voices across the water.

The Big Lawyer terrifies me. He is genial, but he is physically large. Overweight males scare me. Being alone with him in a room, albeit with a desk between us, makes me uncomfortable. He asks questions and takes notes. He says that my defence – that I had intercourse without consent – can be supported easily. Expert witnesses in the field of child abuse will verify that my failure to resist the advances of a man who won my trust over a period of time, is consistent with my history and background. The Big Lawyer takes down from the uppermost shelf of the bookcase one of the leather-bound volumes with gold Roman numerals on the spine. He looks up a section on divorce law: 'As I thought: "a woman who is raped is not guilty of adultery." '

The interview ends. If I am afraid of my own defence lawyer, what terrors will overtake me when I face the Prosecution?

I have only two temazepam tablets left now. I break them up into small pieces so that they will last longer. I am desperate for sleep. It is only a matter of time before the press will descend on me. The knowledge of its inevitability tortures me. The involvement of the media is like an impending juggernaut. I await the crunch of my own bones under the tyres.

I am driving away to stay with some nuns, who are friends, in England, leaving a bantam hen with her tiny chicks in a pen in the garden. The chickens are the fragile remnants of the disappearing normality of my life.

I have to stop several times because I am afraid I am going to faint at the wheel. My head feels light, my arms cold and tingly.

Sister Elizabeth knows as soon as she opens the door to me

that something is far wrong. I am not my usual cheerful self. I tell the nuns something of my quandary over a pot of tea and then they leave for Mass. I am to put on the vegetables for their return.

While the pots are boiling I telephone my Kilry neighbours, Mary and Gavin Ogilvy, and ask if Gavin will go along to The Faulds and take the house name off the gate. I had the sign painted because I was so happy and settled and proud of the cottage. I am afraid now that it will make it too easy for the newspaper reporters to find me.

'Gavin will drive along right away and do that for you. But if they come when you're back at home, all you need to do is telephone and we'll take you away under a blanket.' The vision of being bundled out of a building into a waiting vehicle with my head inside a grey prisoner's blanket, like a mass-murderer, is at least better than the thought of facing the camera crews completely alone. Mary must wonder if suicide is in my mind. She is careful to ask for my telephone number.

The tatties and greens are simmering when the telephone rings. It is Tilda, from Kilry. Mary has told her of her concern. Tilda has a gift for making a crisis seem what it is – something that won't last forever, however horrific it seems at the time. She tells me this event has brought the community together in a way that couldn't otherwise have happened. She and Mary, for example, live next door to each other but have very little in common, politically, economically, or socially. They have found a link in the need to respond to an emergency, however, and both recognise the other's strengths.

'Ramsay and his cronies keep speaking of the "division" and "upset" caused in these parishes, but it's in his mind, created by his own actions,' observes Tilda. 'You've asked no-one to take sides. A quite extraordinary closeness has developed among us, though, since you dealt with that tragic death in Kilry – and even more since this dreadful event has happened to you.' It's true. Those of us who live in the middle of the village have come to rely on each other in a way we could not have imagined.

I am more secure with the nuns than in my own home at present, but I have to return to Scotland for the Preliminary Hearing of the Inquiry, having received no reply from the Convener regarding the Medical Officer's statement that I am unfit to attend.

The First Hearing

TWO thousand years after the birth of Christ and the Church of Scotland is putting me on trial to ascertain whether I consented to a single sexual act.

The First Hearing of the Preliminary Inquiry is to take place on 3rd July, just one week after the June meeting of Presbytery. Why the desperate hurry? Presbytery is not due to reconvene until September. It seems they want a quick kill.

The Convener – 'Chief Inquisitor' Reverend Colin Caskie – telephones to inform me of the arrangements: 'Thursday evening. St Margaret's Church, Forfar. 7.30 pm. In the vestry.'

'But I've been signed off sick by my G.P. and the Church's own Medical Officer has seen me. He has told you I'm not in a fit state to be held for questioning. He said I must be given more time.'

'The Business Committee has instructed this to be done as quickly as possible. Goodbye.'

He phones back an hour later. 'I am phoning to tell you not to bring anyone with you. I don't want you to bring a legal agent.'

3 July 1997

So the meeting begins.

I ask the Chief Inquisitor if he has received the written advice that I am not well enough to be the subject of this precipitate Inquiry: 'Oh yes, I received the letter – so the medical line has expired now?'

'No.'

'Well, we'll just get on with it anyway. I shall read the letters of complaint and see what you have to say for yourself. They are from Mrs Mary Nicoll, and Mrs Moyra Nicoll, dated . . .'

So he reads the dreadful accusations and then looks up and asks for my response, though it is clear he thinks there can be no explanation for my behaviour.

'I was sexually abused as a child. . .' I falter.

Immediately the token female, Mrs Reid, jumps down my throat: 'Don't start on that one! That's got nothing to do with it!'

Then, where should I begin? That past sexual abuse is the key to everything: to my emotional dependence on this older man in whom I'd confided, my ambivalent feelings towards him, my inability to react when he made advances towards me, either to invite him or to push him away. . . If they cannot understand this then they can understand nothing of what really happened. They've damned me from the start. Useless, my saying that the sexual act terrifies and disgusts me. Useless, my speaking of the secondary victimisation associated with childhood sexual abuse. They will never see that men could misinterpret the childlike openness, the ingenuous lack of barriers, the blithe spirit. . . and be surprised when we then recoil from them physically, shying away from the arm about our shoulders. How can I tell them that the Nicolls treated me as part of their family, the family I never had; how Sandy slowly won my trust; how his marriage had been a sham for years; how in one stupid moment his care for me had been misdirected, but that afterwards he had been filled with remorse and I with confusion. . .?

151

I pass over the letter from my doctor, which states, 'She refused contraception because she was not in a relationship.'

Mrs Reid reacts, 'Didn't you think to use a condom? I'm a teacher. Girls of fifteen carry condoms in their pockets in case of this sort of thing. I think you were extremely irresponsible!' I gape at her. I didn't carry condoms in my pocket when I was fifteen. I wasn't like that; am not like that. Does she think I expected to be raped? Does she think a testosterone-crazed man, intent on discharging himself, would wait while I said, *Just a minute: before you undo your zip, would you mind going into the hall and taking down my red jacket from the peg? I think there's a packet of condoms in the pocket. Check the expiry date first, would you, there's a good chap? They're thirteen years past their use-by-date? I'm so sorry, how silly of me. I don't have much call for these things very often. Perhaps you'd like to pop down to Alyth and buy a new pack from the chemist? I'll still be here when you come back. . .'*

Does Mrs Reid mean what happened would have been acceptable if I'd had a bedside table stocked with contraceptives? It strikes me I can't win: I believed my physician's statement would support the truth of my claim that I had not wanted or invited the man into my bed – but here I am being harangued for *not* using a condom!

'Do you mean to tell us you were a virgin until this?' Mrs Reid demands next.

What is the use? I am trying to tell you what happened, because you demand it of me. You want to open up my compost heap of worms and examine all that is seething there, laying eggs and gorging on the rotting waste of my childhood. You want to overturn it and bang at its sides until every last weevil drops out of it. You are blackbirds, only. You peck over the matter of my life. You want to eye all that is lurid in it, and scratch about in the dirt. You say I must recite chapter and verse of what he did to me. You want me to titillate you by describing abominations of which the Bible does not even speak. Greedy birds with yellow-rimmed eyes, you.

You do not know that it makes no difference how brutal he was: if he 'sodomized' me or if he 'penetrated' me – as you put it with your pursed church lips. So what if it had been 'just a little harmless touching. . . happens to thousands of girls. . . part of their education'? It isn't about degrees of violation, nor about whether it happened a hundred times or only once. What causes the damage is not necessarily proportional to the seriousness of the crime. Perhaps there is no crime, in legal terms.

What I know – and you would know, if your years of university training had taught you anything – is that the boundaries have been fudged. It is difficult for me to know when to trust and when to run.

Forget explicit details. I have forgotten them. The worms have digested them entirely. They are no longer recognisable as animal or vegetable. What my body remembers is a conditioned response: entering a state of paralysis. What my mind holds is the extra-ordinary ability to disappear; to split off; to leap across the wide gap between the stripe of green grass at the bottom of the child's painting, and the blue line of sky at the top. My mind is floating in the air somewhere above the Land of China.

He could have done anything with me; tempted or tortured. I would not have known the difference. He could have enticed me with exquisite delights, or thrown me down among the nettles and the jagged broken glass and bottle-tops. I felt nothing; remembered nothing. In my head, I was in a promised land. I was not there.

I shall not tell you any of this. You know nothing of jumping into horizons to avoid anguish. You have never been to my mountains in the clouds.

I have tried to tell you about the experiences of my childhood and you don't want to hear. I need you to understand about the endless years of fear and shame. I need you to see that I have been wearing a pea-green coat all this time. Then, and only then, could your juridical 'Inquiry' begin to fathom what took place with Sandy Nicoll.

'Miss Percy, were you not vulnerable in your ministry if you were abused as a child?'

Now you are questioning whether I was ever fit to be ordained. I want to ask if you mean was I more susceptible to further abuse by a man I'd grown to trust? A man I pitied because he himself was struggling with the aftermath of abuse?

Would he have shown me the lattice of cuts on his forearms if he had not sensed that I would read their message? A hundred other people have also revealed the raw wounds of their spirits to me, in the few years that I have ministered. Would they have done so if I had worn a suit of clerical armour, as you do?

Why did those hundred others not abuse me too? How is it that I have worked as one of half a dozen women in a prison full of 'bad' men, and I have come to no harm there?

Yes, I was more vulnerable to this particular man.

Some men can pick out of the crowd a woman who has been disarmed already, and they home in on her. . . They smell fear, some men. They may be lawyers, professors, or ministers of the Kirk. Generally, however, such men keep their jobs. . .

I do not say this, either.

'Don't tell me you were a virgin!' Mrs Reid, insisting.

Only once in my life was physical touch sufferable. I cannot tell my jurors about so private a memory:

The man had been tortured as a prisoner of war. He never spoke of it except that one day when he began to recount the unbearable things that had been inflicted on him and allowed me to trace with my fingertips the raised weals of his ancient injury. I had been slit with a tin-opener, to accommodate my abuser. He'd said, 'If you joined our scars together, you could girth a horse with them.'

It was the only time I had seen a naked human torso and not

felt repulsed. The electrical charge was not sexual but came from being so close to another human being who'd returned from Hell alive.

The Hearing goes on for almost two hours and Mrs Reid speaks ninety per cent of the time. Mr Black asks only one question, which he does not manage to finish without interruption from his companions. I fail to mention anything about corroborative evidence – about having told my lorry driving instructor, and the examiner, as well as medical staff, that I was raped. I am not being asked the right questions. I cannot tell them the story, from the very beginning, about the pea-green coat. The style of interrogation is so intimidating that I lose any presence of mind.

Rev Colin Caskie draws matters to a close, demanding my decision about my resignation. I cannot give it and beg time: 'I'm confused ab. . .'

'Don't you dare say you're confused about your feelings,' jumps in Mrs Reid. 'Don't you dare! It's perfectly obvious you're besotted with the man! Why don't you just run away with him?'

I had been going to say I was confused about the procedures, not about my feelings for Sandy Nicoll – but I wither and go back to dysphasia. I thought I could be given time to think. But no. They demand my decision on the spot.

'If you admit you're guilty and demit status you can still go to church,' comforts Chief Inquisitor, so very generously. 'It'll be easier all round, and the Church will deal with you quietly. The press will not become involved and you will not be excommunicated.'

I still do not speak.

'But if you don't confess your guilt we'll just have to advertise in the press for witnesses,' he pursues.

Silence from me. . . He is growing increasingly bad tempered. Still silence.

'Then, by Monday . . . Monday night at the latest. By letter or by telephone. Otherwise the Inquiry moves on and we bring you back here in front of the complainants. Monday night: I must know what you are going to do by then.'

Sanhedrin

4 – 7 July 1997

She is dressed casually, about my own age and I think perhaps she wants to arrange a wedding. She is, however, from the *Daily Mail* and wants to know if I've been suspended by Presbytery. Then she asks if I've had an affair.

What am I supposed to say? If I snap, 'No comment,' or, 'Mind your own business,' the automatic assumption will be that the rumours have foundation. But to deny knowledge of any allegations would be a lie. I've received no advice from the Church on how to handle this situation. I answer truthfully that I haven't been suspended by Presbytery, but that I resigned from my post and subsequently withdrew that resignation. I refuse to be drawn any further.

Now, Mary Ogilvy and Tilda are both in the yard watching my ducklings when a strange car slows down and then stops to disgorge its occupants. I blanch. Mary stands back in the shed doorway with me. Bold as a midday fox, Tilda goes to deal with them. I hear her telling them I am away and she has no idea when I'll be back.

I have to leave The Faulds again. I dread reporters returning. I'll go to friends over in Argyll for safety until Monday, by which time I have to tell Chief Inquisitor if I'll resign; or stay to fight. I telephone Douglas Murray, then Principal Designate of Trinity College, Glasgow University. Douglas is well-versed in Church Law. He is convinced that if I demit status, the Presbytery will be obliged to leave my resignation on the table until a committee has paid me a pastoral visit and reported back to a further meeting. That would effectively give me until autumn to be well enough to face further investigations. This seems a sensible course of action. It will buy me the time Dr Manson advised, but that the Presbytery disallowed. It will take some pressure off me so I can think more objectively, which is the pastoral intention behind the rule to which Douglas is referring.

Chief Inquisitor Caskie has requested that I inform him of my decision, by telephone or by letter, by Monday night, 7th July. He has given me just four days. I write, and post the letter first class on the Saturday morning, after having spoken to Douglas and consulted him on the wording:

> Dear Mr Caskie,
> I offered to demit my status on 17th June 1997. I have at
> no time withdrawn that request to demit status.

It is a statement of fact. I have never withdrawn it. The Church Medical Officer asked for time to be given because I was not in a fit state. The Business Committee chose, perversely, to treat that request as an indication of my readiness to face trial.

He gave me until the Monday night, but I arrive home from my Argyll bolt-hole late on Sunday to find seven messages from him, already, on my answering machine. He has set up the Nicolls to attend the Second Hearing – as early as Tuesday! Each message exhorts me to phone him. Clearly my letter has not yet arrived, and he is anxious to confirm I have received notification of his zealous arrangements.

Why this terrible haste?

Chief Inquisitor Caskie has not given me even the four days he so grudgingly permitted at the First Hearing.

I, too, am irritated. It smacks of the Sanhedrin, so keen to convict and execute the Son of God that it did not wait to achieve a quorum. I feel less than civil. Chief Inquisitor can whistle until my letter arrives through his door at breakfast time tomorrow. That will be quite soon enough, and well before the night-time deadline he gave me.

8th July

Chief Inquisitor Caskie is not a patient fellow. He telephones again, before the morning post. He must see a copy of my original demission. At the double! He is taking his daughter somewhere; he is a busy man. I am an inconvenience. He will meet me in the public car park behind the post office in Forfar.

Another forty mile drive. Argyll was much too far to go, in the state I was in. I am still dead beat.

Chief Inquisitor Caskie's crow's eyes spy me entering the car park. He strides over and takes the documents from me through the open vehicle window, like a military policeman at the border. I half expect him to snap together the spurred heels of his long boots. He peruses my letter gravely, then sets his face.

'This will not do,' he barks. 'This makes no reference to the allegations. You must write that you are resigning because of the allegations made against you.'

'You did not say that before now,' I remind him.

'I'm saying it now. You MUST say your resignation is because you are guilty.'

159

'I'm not admitting guilt.'

'Then I shall not accept it. You must re-write it in terms of the allegations.' When I refuse again, he shakes his head: 'I'm taking you to the Presbytery Office. Get out of the car!'

I am marched up the flights of steps from the car park to the main street and propelled into the building. Caskie throws a meaningful look at the Acting Depute Presbytery Clerk, Helen McLeod, who follows us into the room and closes the door behind her.

We are in that room for two hours but I am not prepared to write a confession. The Second Hearing will therefore go ahead tonight and this time I shall have to face my accusers. I do not relish the idea of sitting there, prevented from uttering a word, while Mary and Moyra Nicoll discredit my character.

Conversing over the arrangements with Helen McLeod, Chief Inquisitor Caskie lets slip that the Nicolls are bringing their legal agent with them. I am infuriated at the unfairness of this: 'You told me not to bring a lawyer with me on Thursday, but now you're letting them bring theirs!'

'For support! Only for support! They asked if they could bring their lawyer and I said they could bring him for support!' he defends, crossly.

'Then it is only fair that I should be allowed to have mine present too. You forbade me to bring anyone with me to my Hearing on Thursday.'

He concedes the point irritably, saying I can bring a legal agent this time, but I can hardly ask the Big Lawyer to drop everything and attend at a few hours' notice. I ask permission to telephone Barbara Lovegrove, mostly because I want to release my anger at this injustice before I thump Caskie, as I am sorely tempted to do. Barbara agrees I cannot summon the Big Lawyer at this hour.

She phones back: 'I really think you should have someone there with you. You know I'm not a court lawyer, but will you let me come?' She says she is quite prepared to drive all the way home to Fife tonight and then back again to Forfar this evening. I don't want her to go to so much trouble, but just having her there will lessen the ordeal, no matter if she has not the experience and relevant qualifications.

I ask for paper to write down the things I wanted to say at the First Hearing, but had no chance because Mrs Reid spent most of the time haranguing me. The Committee needs to know my side of the story and I need to put it in writing and hand-deliver it to them, because Chief Inquisitor Caskie says I shall not be permitted to speak tonight. I can attend so that I can hear what my accusers are saying, but I'll have to remain silent.

The first Committee member's door is relatively easy to find, as the address is in Forfar itself, but locating Mrs Reid involves negotiating the motorway underpass and out onto country roads. Several turnings terminate in dead ends. The house has no name on the gate but Mr Reid is in the woodshed. I give him the envelope for his wife.

'Do you want to speak to her?'

'No. Please just give her this.' Mrs Reid said she was a schoolteacher. I didn't expect to find her at home in the daytime. But he is already walking to the door and calling her, without taking the envelope. Worse than that, Mrs Reid directs me into the kitchen. I can't run away.

Surprisingly, she is far less forbidding on her own territory. She still talks incessantly, but I realise I was mistaken in my first assessment of her. Mrs Reid is no dragon, nor is she condemning me. She has not understood me, but neither have I understood her. 'On Thursday, I was pushing you to admit that you wanted what happened,' she says, 'because I was trying to get you to say he seduced you.'

Seduced? I do not even know the precise meaning of the word. This is language from a Jane Austen novel. It's not used by my generation. The hoary-haired woman is old-fashioned but she is not unkind. Not having a clue about sexual abuse, she has been trying her best to imagine what might have happened between Sandy Nicoll and me. She wanted me to save myself. I don't think she has any perception at all of how frightened I was by her manner of questioning. She had not intended to come across aggressively.

'Ah yes,' muses old Dennis when I tell him about it afterwards. 'Seduction. Of course, it's a word often used in books and stories. Yes, seduction. . .'

'But Dennis, what does it mean? I've seen it in Latin translations at school: you know, when some ancient god or other changes himself into a bull or a billy-goat and *seduces* a beautiful Earth-maiden. Ovid's *Metamorphoses* and all that. But no-one says it these days. What does it mean, exactly?'

'It's a word: *seduction*.' Dennis still does not elaborate. 'Of course Elma Reid has not understood, but I'm glad you found her kinder than the other night. Eat up, Love. Seduction. . . Hmm. . . You will bring Barbara back here after the meeting tonight and tell me how it went, won't you?'

Zealots

BARBARA and I are sitting in her car outside the Bank of Scotland in Forfar. She has acquired a copy of the 1935 Act *Anent* Trials by Libel. It transpires that I do not have to sit in a corner in silence tonight after all. 'The Accused shall be entitled to defend himself at every stage of the Inquiry.' Barbara says that means I can speak. She prays with me. I am so glad of her.

The Nicolls are late. Probably they meant to avoid colliding with me on the way into the building. Richard Nicoll walks in first. He won't meet my eyes. What is he doing here? He's not one of my official accusers. He must have chauffeured his mother and sister-in-law. He will leave now. No, he draws in a chair beside them. He is intending to stay.

Chief Inquisitor Caskie should evict him, but he doesn't.

Chief Inquisitor Caskie opens the meeting with prayer. I suppose there might be a point in this if the Nicolls were any way disposed to Christian reconciliation, or if the Committee's purpose was to attempt mediation. This is blatantly not the case. Mary Nicoll reads out her grievance against me. She declares I've had two abortions. That is a biological impossibility within the dates she gives. I should point that out, but am too humiliated to speak. This terrible taboo is being discussed with reference to me. The word 'abortion' is spoken as if a snotty tissue was discarded in a bin somewhere, along with rotting vegetables and the remains of an Indian carry-out. It is as if sentient life – my life and the minuscule beginnings of Heather's – was not involved; as if there was no anguish, no pangs of grief afterwards. The Chief Inquisitor requires Moyra to add her name at the bottom of the page, after Mary's. It is so cold. They could be immigration officials for all anyone's soul matters.

'And *I* found *this!*' Richard Nicoll pulls something out of his jacket pocket with evident satisfaction. 'It was among my brother's things when I went through them.' He has no compunction about raking through Sandy's private documents. He presents the tiny picture of Heather's simple memorial; the cross made of two small pieces of drift-wood, planted with the snowdrops. He hands the photograph to Chief Inquisitor Caskie with an exaggerated gesture like a Big Top artiste. The Chief Inquisitor holds it between thumb and forefinger, examining it with far greater scrutiny than it warrants. He is enjoying himself. He is playing 'Supercops'.

'Can I keep this?' asks the Chief Inquisitor covetously.

'Yes,' agrees Richard with the generosity of a schoolboy solemnly bequeathing his matchbox of impaled insects to his best buddy.

'I've already told the Committee your brother made me pregnant,' I accost Richard. I can't help feeling satisfaction in watching him deflate. His vital and conclusive piece of evidence is not such a big deal after all. He will not go to the top of the class.

It is Joe Black's turn to ask a question. Black is the quietest member of the Committee and the shrewdest. 'But don't you have any *evidence*? I mean, when my brother-in-law was having an affair we found airline tickets, hotel reservation slips. . . Don't you have anything like that?'

'She sat on his knee!' squeals the elderly mother. 'In front of all his family! In the kitchen!'

'She'd hardly have done that in front of his whole family if there'd been anything covert about their relationship,' objects Barbara. Mary Nicoll, moreover, is the only member of the family who was *not* there. She is the least qualified to place any interpretation on it, and yet she speaks as if she was an eyewitness to some kind of inappropriate flirtatious behaviour. That wasn't the way of it at all. I remember the time it happened. We'd all returned to the farmhouse, very late at night after some church party. I'd left my car there and travelled with the Nicolls to the manse at Airlie, but I still had to drive the mile or so back to The Faulds. I had not accepted any alcohol. Moyra said she'd make cocoa before I went home, to warm us up. We all stood in the kitchen because the rest of the house was cold. I had my coat on, but I was shivering just from walking across the yard. Sandy invited me to share his seat which was beside the hot Aga and Moyra was heating the milk right beside him. I was completely at ease with the Nicolls in those days. Sandy was the kind of father-figure I had never had. His wife heard him ask me for a hug and she wasn't in the least perturbed by it, because it was a candid and innocent action.

Perhaps I can understand why Mrs Nicoll senior thinks she knows what passed. Those who know me best say there are some things about me that are difficult to piece together. In some respects there is still something of a child about me: a lack of sophistication in the way I dress or tie up my hair; my delight in tiny things such as a moth's fur; the fact that I'll drop to my knees to peer at a bumble bee on a cowslip, or a wild orchid in the meadow-grass. I can be impulsive in displaying affection to those I trust, or timid and shy in unfamiliar situations. Mary Nicoll assumes an awareness of the world in me – a street-wisdom or guile perhaps – that most people acquire in the ordinary process of growing up. I don't possess this. I don't know why I haven't developed these layers of adult being. Perhaps, subconsciously, I hang on to aspects of childlikeness to compensate for my premature initiation into human cruelty. I am refusing to let go of vestigial innocence. Far older than my years in some ways, I am far younger in others. This may confuse those who don't know me well.

All the way through the Second Hearing, Moyra Nicoll fixes me with a basilisk stare. I beg her to recall that she agreed that Sandy should to go with me to see Heather's snowdrops. This is when she inflicts her most spiteful barb: 'I don't know how anyone can be so attached to a *foetus!*' Her retort is chilling in its nastiness. The word she uses for my baby slaughters me. It is a clinical word, devoid of any sense of the life I cherished, albeit for so few weeks.

'Anyway,' she spits, 'Sandy said she asked him to experiment with sex.' I am flabbergasted! If that was what he had really told her and not that he raped me, she would never have been so supportive of me, for all those months after he confessed the deed.

Barbara is quick to see through Moyra's lie: 'Helen would hardly have spoken to Moyra, and asked her please to stop her husband from doing it again, if all along she was having an affair with him, would she?' Moyra cannot deny that this was the way of it. Sandy has reiterated my innocence in what took place, in the presence of his adult children, and of Dennis Leadbeatter.

I do understand how Moyra has turned her bitterness towards me recently. She must have recognised that the façade of her marriage could not be maintained. It is human nature to look for someone else to blame and I was the obvious target. My heart goes out to her, even though I am in the dock on her account. Wouldn't I do the same? If someone had betrayed me and my whole life was being thrown into turmoil because of it, wouldn't I try to find some explanation, some rationale, for their behaviour? Wouldn't I try to convince myself, and other people, that something different has taken place to what, inside, I know to be the case? That way, I could begin to re-construct the familiar house of my former days, albeit on the foundations of a falsehood. I see why Moyra is doing this, and I can sympathise, even though I am her scapegoat.

Of course, I know that Robert Ramsay is implicated in this change in Moyra's attitude towards me. He has set out to inflame, rather than to place balm on her woundedness. He is the organ-grinder behind this.

But Mary Nicoll? What possesses a mother to tell the world that her own son has committed adultery? 'It is easier for her to say that, than that her son raped someone,' observes Barbara. Barbara is so astute throughout the Inquiry; so quick to see to the heart of what is going on.

The Nicolls leave and Barbara indicates to me to go out of the room. She requests to speak to the Committee in private. I sit hunched on the stone steps leading to the basement, waiting.

Barbara doesn't tell me much of what was said. She believes proceeding to Trial will prove immensely destructive for the whole Church and not only for the individuals involved on both sides. An adversarial match, which will inevitably be fought very publicly, is no way for Christians to be seen to behave and is particularly nonsensical given the mitigating circumstances.

'It's Caskie,' Barbara tells Dennis later. 'He can't see anything beyond regulations. The other two could see what I was saying, but Caskie's so blinkered. He's the problem. All we can do is wait until the Presbytery decides whether to put her on trial after September.'

It transpires that not only can Chief Inquisitor Caskie not see past rules, but he is also incapable of following them.

Paparazzi

'A lie gets halfway around the world before the truth has
a chance to get its pants on.'

Winston Churchill

30 July – 12 August 1997

I am stuffing clothes into a bag for my stay in Ardgay, Sutherland,
where I am to take Sunday services for a friend and look after his
spaniel while he is holidaying. I did warn Alan Watt of the
accusations and of the Presbytery's actions. I would have understood if he'd wanted to make alternative arrangements for his
holiday cover. Typically, he didn't prejudge me. 'Presbyteries can
be so very clumsy in these matters,' he said.

A couple of weeks have passed since the Hearings and MacPuff
has been busying himself taking copies of Mary Nicoll's libellous
and damning letter round the doors. Robert Ramsay has been
opening his mouth far wider than it behoves him, and Presbytery

elder Evelyn Hood is putting it about that I am 'in need of psychiatric treatment.'

Despite their efforts, all remains quiet in the press. I am lulled into a false sense of semi-security and taken off guard completely when a man from the local paper phones tonight, while I am packing, to ask if it is true that I have been suspended from the ecclesiatical ministry. Once again, refusal to comment will fire speculation, and so I answer honestly that, while I am not preaching in my own parishes, I am at liberty to do so elsewhere. I believe, naively, that I've killed his quest for a good story. I think no more about the phone call.

I am away by six o'clock in the morning and reach Ardgay before the Watts have breakfasted. I promised to appear early so they could head off, but Alan seems flummoxed by my arrival. 'Helen, Angus Presbytery's been on the phone saying there's an article in The *Courier*. Haven't you seen it?' But I left Angus long before newspapers were delivered.

The Presbytery is adamant that I cannot preach in Ardgay. 'How can they say that?' I protest. 'The Moderator of Presbytery said I can. He put it in writing! His letter states, clearly, that I'm still free to preach, baptize, and marry, anywhere except in Robert Ramsay's six churches.'

'Apparently the *Scotsman* and the *Courier* say Presbytery has suspended you.'

'The Presbytery hasn't notified *me* I'm suspended. You can't suspend someone without telling them!'

They've never given me a copy of the rules. I had to borrow an old volume of Cox's *Practice and Procedure in the Church of Scotland* from a retired minister and one of my former university lecturers photocopied pages from Herron's *Guide to Church Law* in the Edinburgh library for me. I checked them both: no suspension can be imposed until the Trial proper has commenced. That will be months down the line. They haven't decided whether there's even a case to answer yet. They can't do this!

How the Presbytery acts does not tally with the procedures that are laid down. Rules are invented and applied retrospectively, as it suits.

Several phone calls later we are in no better position. No-one seems to know who has authority to do what. It is amazing how people backtrack, refusing to take responsibility for anything they said or wrote previously.

'Ah, well,' says Brian, the Moderator of Presbytery. 'I didn't know National Mission was going to suspend you.'

'National Mission's letter, like yours, specifies that my suspension applies only to my duties "as Associate Minister in the six parishes, and as Prison Chaplain". That is where I am employed by them. Not from ministry as a whole,' say I.

'Ah, well,' says the National Mission Boss. 'I wrote that you were suspended from the six parishes, but I *meant* that you were suspended everywhere else, too.'

'National Mission doesn't have the power to suspend me "everywhere else"! Only the Presbytery can do that!' say I.

'Ah, well, I suspended you because I thought Presbytery would like me to.' A lame excuse indeed.

Every one of them precedes his statement with an uncertain, 'Ah, well.'

'Ah, well,' says the Principal Clerk in Edinburgh when I telephone to ask for his definitive decision on the matter. 'It would be my understanding that you could be suspended.'

This is vague and evasive. He's not going to say that one of his fellows has been mistaken. He will put nothing in writing, the spineless creature. It is subsequently to prove difficult to elicit any answers at all from him, on any matter.

'That's very helpful, thank you,' say I.

Alan contacts his Reader, Mary Stobo, who agrees to prepare a sermon at short notice. I feel dreadful about Alan having to deal

with all of this when he is trying to get away on his holidays. I came
to save him trouble, not create it. He assures me he doesn't resent
it. He cannot fathom why Brian of Aberlemno was so reluctant to
speak to me on the phone, when it was clear that I was highly
distressed.

In the midst of it all, Alan takes several phone calls from
newspapers asking if I am in his manse. 'Pardon?. . . What's any of
that got to do with you?. . . I'll thank you to mind your own business!'
I can hear Alan growing angry. Of course they know I'm there.

I'm not even dressed the following morning when the manse
doorbell rings. I'm alone, as Alan and his wife have left for their
holiday. Pulling on a jumper I go to the open sitting room door
and glance diagonally across to the window. There are two men
looking right back at me through the glass. They must be standing
in the flowerbed to do that. I can't pretend I'm not here now. Better
to answer the door, tell them I don't wish to speak, and have done
with it.

I open the door slowly, wishing the Watts' dog was a rottweiler.
Instead she is a dear wee thing – as defenceless as I. My surroundings
grow bigger in my fear and I shrink in my mind's eye. The door
seems of House of Horror proportions and the men loom ten feet
high; larger on top than at the bottom, as if they are falling in on
me. They push copies of the *Scotsman* and the *Press and Journal*
at me, demanding comment. I shake my head and the rest of my
body is quaking too when I close the door.

I don't read the articles, only the headline on the front page of
the *Press and Journal*: 'Minister Flees North.' How can you 'flee'
somewhere in July when the trip was organised in February and
everyone knows the arrangements? It's the same a few months later
when the *Scotsman,* not finding me at home, claims I've 'gone
into hiding'. I am among hundreds of others at a choir festival at
the time – but printing, 'Percy is going out and about in public as
normal,' would not lend the same sense of mystery and implied

guilt. Again the *Paisley Daily Express* will be proud to have 'tracked her down to her home in Kilry,' as though I am an injured animal creeping back to a secret lair.

Next, the phone rings. A man's voice. 'May I speak to Helen Percy?'

'No.'

'Oh. . . . It's all right. I understand. I'm not from the press. My name's Melvyn Griffiths. I'm the Minister of Helmsdale; Moderator of Sutherland Presbytery. Could my wife and I come and see you this morning, to pray with you?'

Mr and Mrs Griffiths drive an hour and a half from Helmsdale, and show much kindness. So I receive pastoral care from the Moderator of a strange presbytery. I am only passing through his patch, am no responsibility of his, and he could easily have dismissed me as a sinful woman who deserves everything coming to her. Most of my colleagues in my own presbytery did just that, after all. Is any one of them praying for me there?

A Mr James Blair, a local churchman, telephones about taking me along to Croick, a local church where families took shelter during the notorious Highland Clearances.

I am expecting Mr Blair when the doorbell next rings and so I answer. But it is another deputation of smartly dressed men commanding the step, one with a huge camera slung over his shoulder. Do they really think I'm going to smile and pose? 'No, I don't want you to take my photograph nor comment. The matter is *sub-judice*.'

'Ah, but it's only a *Church* court,' they argue. 'It doesn't count. We can print whatever we like. So you'd be better to talk, then we won't just make it up.' When I won't respond to threats they try switching on the charm.

An elderly man appears at the gate, just at this moment, who must be James Blair, my tour-guide to Croick. I warm to James Blair before I've even met him: his arrival has delivered me. 'Look, I'm expecting this gentleman. . . Please would you mind leaving?'

'Okay. . . Just one request: would you stand by the wall here for one photograph?'

As if! Their audacity is astounding. 'No, please, I told you, I don't want you to take my photograph.'

'Of course not. We wouldn't take your photograph without your permission.' They are his last words and I, like a fool, believe him.

James Blair comes into the house and appraises the situation. He thinks it would be unwise to go to Croick in case we are followed.

Less than an hour later, I am walking down to the village to buy bread and milk. I notice the two men with the camera on the other side of the street and, in my pitiful innocence, I think they must have decided to have a cup of coffee before heading back to Inverness. I do not see them when I come out of the shop. It never occurs to me that a promise can be broken. I've absolutely no idea that there is a price on my head – that at this point a photograph of me is probably worth tens, if not hundreds, of pounds. And here I am, wandering around buying a pint of milk, wearing a frock I bought at a jumble sale, with my hair tied in a childish pony-tail.

The next morning several national newspapers picture me on their front page, walking out of Ardgay Village Store with my milk. It is as if I have been raped again by the photographer, who broke my trust and as if I am being violated by a whole nation looking at my image in print. It's not as if I'm shown scantily clad: it is the fact that I've been shot unawares. It feels filthy; humiliating.

Months later I discover that the freelance photographer, Peter Jolly, contravened both the Press Complaints Commission's Code of Practice and the Human Rights Convention. The Commission, however, disregards any complaint over four weeks old, no matter how serious the abrogation. Jolly got away with his crime laughing, a rich man at my expense.

That will be the end of the intrusion, surely. I know if the case goes to trial next Spring the press will camp in my front garden and feast on the gory details, but I never suppose the Presbytery will leak documents in advance. Nor that the press will be allowed to print the whole story before it comes to Court. . .

Thus the descent of the rat-pack comes as a shock. I'm not prepared for it to happen, not now. I've lived for weeks with the uncomfortable feeling that the odd press car might be snooping around the lanes, but I wasn't expecting full-scale onslaught; not yet.

Under Siege

COMING to the door in pairs is only the beginning. At half past seven the second morning, out of the bedroom window, I observe a car crawling along the kerb. It stops almost out of view behind the hedge. There is something furtive about it and my flesh crawls. It is a while before the bell rings, however. I ignore it. How am I going to let the wee spaniel out to the garden without being seen?

By half past eight there've already been over thirty attempts to contact me on the house telephone and cars line the road outside. More are on the way. Reporters surround the house and keep me prisoner. If they are not at the front door they are at the back. I creep around the house on my hands and knees, keeping below windowsill level to avoid the camera lenses. I cannot go into the kitchen. There is no corner in which to hide there, as there's a large window and the back door is glass. I cannot make myself a cup of tea or go in there to find a piece of bread to eat. Not that I feel like eating, but I am thirsty. The floor of the hallway is the safest place to crouch down and I stay like that in a foetal huddle for most of the morning. I am clutching onto the spaniel for comfort, but she is desperate to pee now, poor wee thing. The press reporters' slaver seems to drool down the windows. I am so scared.

Between the doorbell and the telephone, the ringing is incessant. My head buzzes with it until I think I'll go mad. I could crawl through to the study and unplug the phone but they'd see me. I've never felt so afraid and isolated in my life and I begin to pick up the phone when it rings, but not speaking, hoping just one call could be from someone who has realised my plight. I don't know any of the neighbours, as I've never been here before, so there's no-one I can call for help. Mr Blair said he would be away today.

There is one friendly call.

My friend Lyndsey has read in today's paper that I am at Ardgay Manse, and she has managed to obtain the number from a somewhat dottled neighbouring minister. She's been alarmed by the newspaper reports. I cling onto the telephone receiver, as if to a piece of a wreck that can still save me from drowning. She doesn't know anyone in Sutherland and there is no-one she can summon to my aid, but at least I know her voice.

Across the road from Ardgay Manse is a small sheltered housing complex for elderly people. The inhabitants, if they are able to come to their windows, must be wondering why the street outside is so busy today. All these cars! Ardgay is not normally such a busy place.

It is one of these pensioners who comes to my rescue. She is a bold wee woman. She puts on her raincoat and she takes her stick and she strikes the road with that stick purposefully as she stalks her way across to the Manse. Up the drive she comes, ignoring all those vile predators, and she bends down and shouts through the letter-box that her name is Vera and she has come to see me and I am to let her in, and if I open the door she vows she will see off any number of them with her stick.

Vera, you are wonderful! You brave going into the kitchen and you make us both tea. You pull shut the heavy curtains in the sitting room, brazenly, right across in front of their prying noses and with the camera lenses pointed at your chest. Then you telephone Mary Stobo and leave a message. When Mary comes home, she runs the gauntlet of the reporters, too, and she takes the dog for a walk, and then she returns with food for me in the evening and her nightdress and announces that she will stay with me in the Manse that night. The Ardgay villagers are strangers but they give me the help I need. They protect the vixen from the baying hounds.

Sandy Nicoll phones once during the siege. There is nothing like the same scale of activity at his end. One set of reporters has been at his door but his son saw them off. A single strange car has been hanging about the farm road end but Sandy dodged its occupants by driving out in a spare van. He had enjoyed the game. There've been just a couple of telephone calls. He is accusatory, however: 'Why are you blabbing to them? They're telling me you're singing like a linty up there!'

The reporters are playing us off against each other, trying to get both sides to talk. They are terrorising me. They've shoved notes through the letter-box saying, 'We just want to print your side of the story! We'll pay you! People in Kilry are calling you a Jezebel! You should defend yourself!' I've said nothing. I cannot convince Sandy that their telling him I am 'singing' is a ruse. He is extremely uptight, which I can understand, but never once does he ask how *I* am coping. He doesn't care that I am having to contend with thirty times the number of phone calls and cars outside, nor that it is *my* photograph appearing in the papers, *my* good name, *my* career, *my* life being destroyed, not his. There is no character assassination of him, no pictures. He is only ever described as 'elder and farmer Sandy Nicoll', whereas I am the 'Randy Rev', whose photograph is blazoned across every bill-board in Scotland, computer-enhanced to make me look like a prostitute.

How I wish someone had prepared me. The Church Press Office might have told me how to handle these twisted characters; what tactics to expect them to employ. It is not much help, when the schiltrons are over the ramparts, to be told, 'Just don't say he raped you. Don't say that.' This is the only advice the Church Press Office gives me. (Why? In retrospect, I can only think it was to prevent the *Church* from looking stupid, rather than advice that was meant to help *me*.) .

I need the Church to issue some kind of restricted reporting order, a decree prohibiting pre-trial coverage. And I need the mob to be dispersed. What I really require is physical protection. I hardly care what they print, if only they would leave me alone. It is all very well the Church Press Office saying, 'It will blow over if you keep quiet,' but other people are feeding the press with stories day after day.

'Don't speak about the matter and whatever you do, don't use the word "rape",' the Church re-iterates. In the ensuing months it is hellishly difficult to follow this injunction and not to tell anyone the facts about what happened. Friends ask me if the allegations are true and I don't know how to reply. I am prohibited from telling the truth to people who have given me their loyalty and their trust.

It makes no difference that I do not speak to the press. When they are bored with watching the house and seeing no movement, they invent tales about there being 'bizarre conversations through the letter-box.' It sounds spicy and helps to build up a character profile of a very strange woman; one indeed perhaps requiring 'psychiatric help' as organ-grinder Ramsay and his monkeys suggest. Mary Stobo is shocked the next morning when she reads these wild lies and invented scripts. She knows there've been no such conversations through the letter-box, nor through any other medium. She was there with me, the whole of the day in question.

The postmistress in Ardgay takes it upon herself to have all the papers delivered to the Manse each morning, just so that we who are under siege know what is happening outside. Mary reads them. I don't. I know what they are saying though, because the reporters keep stuffing material through the letterbox; transcripts of what they are going to print, offers of cash, and enticements to talk. I am aware the Nicolls' letter of complaint to the Presbytery has fallen into their hands. They push faxed copies of it through the door, trying to lure me to speak out in self-defence. Those headlines are the worst, the ones about my having two abortions in less than eight weeks. It is glaringly obvious the allegation is bogus: it's biologically impossible to fall pregnant a second time, test positively, and consult the requisite physicians in such a timescale. But why let accuracy and truth stand in the way of a good story?

When I check the dates that the Nicolls have told the press I was hospitalised, I realise I have cast-iron alibis for both of them. On the mid-June day that they cite, I was invigilating examinations in the prison. My hours are recorded in the prison log-book. Eight weeks later, on 5th August, I was celebrating 'Christmas'. The Paisley 'Gang' – my former Session Clerk and another elder and their families – had not come to Kilry in December because of the snow, and we'd put Christmas on hold until the Paisley Fair. On the 5th August, which was a hot summer's day, we were putting up strings of cards and making a clothes-peg fairy for the Christmas tree. In the afternoon we went carol-singing. We stopped at Easter Derry and called for the young lad there to fetch a tea towel and a pudding string from his mother's kitchen drawer and join us as a shepherd. I was wearing a white sheet and cardboard wings, and Gigha was a Wise Dog, with a crown/collar cut out of stiff gold-coloured paper. We trooped down to West Derry and sang *O Little Town of Bethlehem* until James and Christine plied us with goodies. There was not a body in Kilry who would vouch for my sanity, but I've a host of witnesses when it comes to Mary Nicoll's ridiculous assertion that I was in hospital on that particular day.

I would never want to deny Heather. She was a gift to me, as well as a curse. She was a grain of sand caught within mother-of-pearl, but the friction she caused was never to form a precious jewel. The Nicolls have no need to invent dates to prove that cherished grain existed. I could have told them the hour and the minute that fear stole away my consciousness and she was conceived. Equally, I could name the hour that I woke from anaesthetisation and she was no longer there.

Whenever I think about Heather, I become distressed. Newspapers glibly print the word 'abortion' and each time it causes a searing pain. I steel myself against every other cruel thing they write, but this is an intense hurt, which no-one has a right to make public. Surely this must be against conventions on privacy?

At the height of the media siege, Colin Caskie, Chief Inquisitor of the Inquiry, telephones saying he is sending the charge sheet, or 'Statement of Sinful Conduct', to Ardgay Manse by Recorded Delivery. I am required to sign for its receipt and Caskie wants to be certain I'll be there when it arrives. The man's insensitivity beggars belief as much as does his ignorance of correct procedure. I know the Presbytery is supposed to authorise this official communication before it can be served on me. I tell him I won't be going anywhere for some time: I am trapped, the house surrounded, and the postman will have to fight his way through the barrage of reporters to reach the door. I add that I am very frightened. 'Well, it's your own fault,' he snaps, and puts down the receiver.

Mary Stobo is a godsend. She brings me supplies to see me through the siege and asks the local policeman to warn the cameramen from the door. He has no mandate to shift them from a public thoroughfare, however, and they reinvade private property as soon as he leaves. Mary has her own key and answers the various bells when she is in the house. Two nights she even deserts her family and sleeps at the manse. Vera visits for cups of tea intermittently. I am afraid the reporters will shove her aside and push past her when the door opens but she withers them. Something about this fearless old woman keeps them back.

It continues for days. Ultimately, when there is no let up, Mary reverses her car to the back door and smuggles the little dog and me into the boot. Pretending to put out the dustbin, she spirits me away by a circuitous route to a secret hideout she's arranged. We make a couple of false stops to ensure we're not followed. Mary phones her daughter to tell her where we are going but uses code language. She says something about a 'chocolate Labrador'. Her daughter knows who has a such a dog and works out where her mother will be if she needs to contact her. We are worried lest the phones are bugged. It is that bad. My car is removed from Ardgay Manse to the Police compound at Bonar Bridge to foil the press reporters.

Once the reporters realise they've been duped they imagine I've gone to ground at Mary's own house but no-one will tell them where that is.

Making Hay while the Sun Shines

THE place of safety to which Mary takes me is a close-guarded secret. Rosie Southland, who takes me in, tells not even her mother or her children she is harbouring Scotland's most Wanted Woman. Her daughter telephones from university saying excitedly, 'Mum! There's a photo of our Manse in the papers! This Sex Scandal Minister's in Ardgay!' Rosie is all innocence. Her offspring are dumbfounded when they come home at the weekend to find me there. I bear no resemblance to the man-eating tart the papers portray.

Alexander Southland is just as good at acting dumb: a church member phones asking if Helen Percy will be in the pulpit the next day, given all the stramash in the papers. 'Rosie's playing the organ but I've nae idea wha's preaching,' prevaricates Alexander. He is tempted to say, 'Not likely! She'll be lifting bales in my hayfield all day: it's forecast to rain on Monday!' But my secret is secure.

The Southlands' smallholding is a good hiding-place, being

along a forestry track that goes nowhere. They give me a room upstairs, where I can hide if visitors come to the door. And I am safe enough working in the hayfield, not overlooked by other properties. I have limited freedom: I can take the Manse spaniel, still in my charge, and the chocolate Labrador, into the forest. Being outdoors is an indescribable relief. There was no way of leaving Ardgay Manse without being seen.

The wee dog and I impose on the Southlands for the best part of a week. Rosie feeds me and sometimes walks with me in the forest, where she halts to point out a tiny plant, or teach me to recognise the song of crossbills or of long-tailed tits. I find a soul-mate in her. She is enthralled by wild creatures. Her face lights up with wonder describing an owlet in the shed.

Alexander Southland built his own aeroplane last winter. When we have finished moving the sheep and stacking hay bales he flies his winged creation over the field and Rosie and I run out to wave.

At last the press seem to have given up looking for me and I return to Ardgay Manse. Mr Blair calls again and I meet his wife, who is a gem. Conservatively dressed, she in a neat tweed twin-set and he with a distinguished red cravat, I expect the elderly couple to be shocked by the revelations that have been published; but not one bit of it. We have been prevented from visiting Croick through-out all those tauntingly sunny days of my imprisonment. This last afternoon of my stay in Sutherland, James Blair insists on taking me up there, even though by now I am wearing infamy pea-green.

The little kirk at Croick, with its scratched window panes, tells a tale from Scottish history. There is something very poignant about the names of the fugitive tenants of Glencalvie being etched on the *out*side of the church windows as the scribes peered in and shivered in the blizzard. There is no snowstorm today. The sun is hot and the river sparkles. I have spent the best part of two weeks of summer shut *in*.

Two centuries after the Highland Clearances, there is still a monopoly of land ownership in rural Scotland. Crofting legislation has been introduced but some other kinds of tenancies can be insecure. Ironically, on my way home from Sutherland I think of looking up a couple who were removed in a somewhat arbitrary fashion only last year. Ron Will was a shepherd in my parish but, along with several other families, he was put out of his job and tied house as the result of a land deal. I remember going to see Elizabeth Will where she was working in the potato sheds at Kilry during that anxious time, and riddling tatties alongside her while she explained they had nowhere else to go. Eventually they found a place up at Glenbuchat, in Aberdeenshire.

Ron and Elizabeth are bound to be aware of the appalling scandal about me and I swither over taking the route that passes near Glenbuchat. Ron has a Free Church background. He may well consider me to be consigned to eternal damnation on the strength of what has been printed in the newspapers. I am shamed to the core by it, even though I am not guilty of so much of the licentiousness and wickedness they say I am. Should I really go to visit this Bible-steeped family? What reception will I be given?

I don't know what makes me go there in the end. Perhaps subconsciously I am seeking some kind of absolution, though I've no idea if that is what I will be given. I may just as easily be condemned and spurned.

The light is fading by the time I find them, having asked for directions at two farms. They are shutting up the sheepdogs in the byre. They don't even seem surprised to see me! They invite me across to the house and set about making some supper, as if it's every Saturday night that I appear at their door. Ron has baked a cake. He sits me down with a mug of tea and goes about me in the same quiet way he would lambing a gimmer. Elizabeth tells me what their children are doing. One son is working in the islands. Abigail is still in Glenisla and so, yes, they have heard all the worst of the gossip in the Glen, and they surmised that Robert Ramsay was at the root of it. After we've shared the cake, Ron takes the Bible from the shelf, chooses a passage and begins to read aloud. I am not really taking in the words, but I feel shored up by them. I have found Christ in odd places and in unlikely people – I don't know why I am surprised when I meet him in a Christian household.

I make to go on but as it is already late, they press me to bide with them the night.

Scandalous, Immoral and Improper

13 August – 10 November 1997

The first envelope I open on my return contains a formal document forbidding me to work, anywhere. It is approved by the Deputy Presbytery Clerk, the incoming Moderator of Presbytery, and the Clerk to the Business Committee.

'It is the understanding of the Business Committee that you had been suspended,' it reads, and then they give themselves authorisation: 'Under Powers granted to the Clerks. . .' I am incandescent. No such matter was ever discussed, or minuted, at a meeting of Presbytery. Three people purport to speak for the entire Committee, when clearly others are not of the same 'understanding' – the outgoing Moderator, for example, whose written authorisation to preach in Ardgay contradicts their claim. Moreover, I doubt whether 'Powers granted to the Clerks' for the holiday period really stretch to suspending a minister!

I have promised to marry a young woman in Glasgow –

someone I alone know was abused, as was her mother and her grandmother before her. The pastoral contact I have maintained with this family is special. She has come such a long way to be able to trust a man in marriage. It is important I don't let her down.

I write to the Principal Clerk immediately, for permission to perform this ceremony, which is not in any case to be in a church building.

A month passes. No response. I am forced to phone his office about the wedding, now imminent. He does not deign to speak to me. His secretary relays his message. Yes, my letter was received and no, I may not conduct the wedding.

I also write asking the Principal Clerk *why* I've been suspended, when the Regulations do not allow for suspension at such an early stage in an Inquiry. This action has undoubtedly provoked media speculation. I point to that very first article in the *Scotsman* on 30 July:

> 'The suspension of a minister is an unusual step for the
> Church Authorities to take, particularly when it appears
> that the Committee set up by the Presbytery to
> investigate has not finished its deliberations.'

How can my right to be present throughout proceedings be maintained, now I am no longer entitled to participate in Presbytery meetings?

I never do receive a reply to this letter. I have pointed out fundamental flaws in the Church's judicial procedure and the Principal Clerk finds it easier to ignore me.

My pig-feed merchant brings me to the telephone. 'You're on the radio again. Tay FM News, every hour. There's a meeting tonight in your parishes. Some Very Reverend Doctor or other is going to explain to your elders all about the procedures in a Trial by Libel. Must go: pigs to feed, bloody bank manager to fob off. . .'

It would help if the Very Reverend Dr Weatherhead would

explain to *me* how a Trial by Libel works. They wheel out the experts to advise the Kirk Sessions, the Ladies' Coffee Morning Circle and the Beadle's budgerigar on how they're going to go about putting me on trial – but I'm blowed if I can get anyone to tell *me* what's going on! *I* have to buy a newspaper to find out what they're trying to charge me with and listen to the radio to find out when they're having a meeting!

I am hurt about being kept in the dark so much of the time. From now on, I am cold-shouldered: I cease to be informed of meetings or furnished with Presbytery Minutes. The Board of Social Responsibility, of which I am an elected member, does not go to the trouble of indicating that my services are no longer required: it simply ceases to notify me of dates.

I am more hurt still when the prisoners write and tell me they've been sent an old man as *locum* chaplain. The Presbytery didn't even have the courtesy to inform me what is happening in the institution for which I am responsible. It feels as though I am being ostracised. Information is withheld, deliberately, even when I ask.

Hundreds of letters and phone messages arrive from strangers as well as friends in the aftermath of the phenomenal press coverage. I appreciate them but cannot reply. I can hardly concentrate to write one sentence. I feel swamped.

A sizeable cheque, to assist with the legal costs he knows will not be defrayed, is sent by a prestigious Edinburgh Kirk elder, Peter B. MacDonald. I don't know him and am amazed by his generosity. A former editor, he knows newspapers are seldom to be believed.

'I know nothing of the rights and wrongs of the case,' he writes. He has, however, 'a suspicion you have been found guilty of two serious faults: one, that of being female, and the other, that of being a trifle unorthodox.'

The local police officer drops in. He has been afraid lest I'd take my own life. 'They've no conscience, newspaper reporters. It would just have made an extra day's sensation.'

'I don't know how Princess Diana's survived so long,' I remark several times. Little do I know that in three weeks she will be dead; because of paparazzi.

Just now, I am the household name, not the Princess of Wales. The story has run for day after day, becoming ever more lurid, because it is the 'Silly Season,' when Parliament is in recess and Princess Diana has not yet had her monumental accident. The Helen Percy Saga has all the ingredients of a media mega-feast: clergy, (female to boot), intrigue, and sex. 'I'M NO RANDY REV, SAYS HELEN', proclaims the front page of the *Daily Record*, in letters several inches high – when I have said nothing at all! What the headline means is that I will not confess guilt. Some stupid people think they must have been my very words, however, because the *Daily Record* says so.

'Sex Romps' seems to be the most popular sub-heading in several newspapers. Oh, hardly! Sick with 'flu and with a raging temperature the one time it happened, I wasn't exactly fit to 'romp' anywhere!

It is not going to be easy to face people. My pea-green coat is now phosphorescent.

David Bell invites me to the Glenisla Games Dance. He is willing to be seen out with me, the most notorious tart in Scotland. It's my first social venture since fame – or infamy – struck. I am uncertain, scared. David insists. He is courageous, and sensitive. If it proves too much for me, we'll leave. I have only to say the word, even supposing we have only just paid for our tickets at the door.

Walking into this people-filled place is one of the hardest things I've ever done. Everyone's gaze is on me. But here is not the hostile reception I anticipated: the Kirk elders are shaking my hand and even embracing me and so many of the Glen-folk make a point of coming across to say, 'Well done, you, for coming.' I want to cry with relief. The climax is when one of the farm workers emerges from the bar, clasps my hand with both of his and avers with admiration, 'You've got **balls**!'

Chief Inquisitor Caskie writes to me, desirous of arranging a further hearing between his Committee and me. He wants to 'clarify some matters'. He must have gone back and read his rulebook, because he never did send the charge sheet when I was under siege in Ardgay. He'd skipped the bit about advising the Presbytery he thought there was 'a case to answer' first. Now he's checked what it says and thinks he'd better be sure and get things in the right order. He has himself tied in knots.

It is clear that Caskie has already made up his mind that there is 'a case to answer', though. A further meeting is a pointless exercise. But I am not in a position to refuse to attend. Barbara offers to accompany me again.

One of the members of the Committee of Three is at work and doesn't attend, which arguably renders the hearing invalid. Chief Inquisitor Caskie opens with a prayer for 'understanding and wisdom'. I wish he was genuine and I think it unlikely his prayer will be answered. His mind is closed.

He reads out a letter from Sandy Nicoll's daughter, claiming she saw her dad's car outside my house, once. And Caskie has received phone calls – anonymous phone calls – claiming 'sightings' of me with Sandy Nicoll. The quality and means of gathering evidence is dubious in the extreme. Chief Inquisitor Caskie concludes however that I must have had an 'affair' with Nicoll, on the strength of the malicious calls.

Barbara objects. 'The definition of an "affair" is "a continuous sexual relationship", but this was a single encounter – and one without consent!'

Caskie backtracks, somewhat churlishly. 'Umm. . . an "affair of the heart". That is what I meant.'

'You can't condemn her on the theory of an "affair of the heart"!' splutters Barbara. 'And what about documents confidential to your committee being leaked to the press?'

'Well, they didn't get them from me!' retorts Caskie.

'No? We cannot be certain who was responsible but the resultant coverage has been extremely prejudicial.'

'Why didn't you go to another paper?' asks Mrs Reid. 'You should have gone to another newspaper.'

Barbara is appalled: 'I cannot believe I am hearing a member of a judicial inquiry suggest the accused should put her side of the story to the press!'

'Caskie is so bad-tempered! And obstinate,' despairs Barbara once we return to her office. 'It's impossible to make him see anything . . . It's not your fault,' she comforts, seeing the tears begin to fall.

'Oh, but it is! Some of it is! I was so stupid and I did care for Sandy Nicoll, but not in that way!' I cry.

She hugs me. 'I know.'

The Committee of Three (or sometimes Two) does indeed decide there is 'a case to answer', as I knew they would. Dennis describes the three of them emerging from the Presbytery Office a few nights prior to the September Presbytery Meeting, like righteous executioners.

Chief Inquisitor Caskie informs the Business Committee of his findings. Asked what evidence he has to support his verdict, he becomes ruffled and uncomfortable. 'You didn't tell me you wanted me to find *evidence*. I'm just telling you I think there's a case to answer!'

Rev Malcolm Rooney (Acting Presbytery Clerk since Ramsay's tantrum with the Business Committee at the inception of proceedings) pays me the rare courtesy of a phone call to inform me of what is happening. 'Tomorrow the Committee of Preliminary Inquiry will advise the Presbytery there is a case to answer. You will be issued with "a full and precise Statement of the Sinful Conduct attributed to you." You will have fourteen days to submit in writing any "Objections" to the terms of the "Statement". The Presbytery may amend the "Statement" and will then move on to the Trial itself. But don't worry,' he says, as if I've merely missed a bus, 'you'll probably only get six months' suspension and counselling and you've already been suspended for several months anyway, so. . .'

'I had counselling already. I went to the Rape Crisis Centre.'

'Pardon? Have you told your lawyer this?'

'No.'

'Why didn't you say this to the Inquiry?'

'Because Mrs Reid said at the first hearing that having told someone I was raped didn't count unless I'd told them the day it happened. I hadn't contacted Rape Crisis immediately and so I didn't mention it. There were other people I'd told too, but no-one right at the beginning. Mrs Reid said I should have gone to the Police at once and the three of them didn't seem to understand why I hadn't – why most women don't – so I just didn't say any more.'

'You get in touch with your lawyer first thing in the morning, or I'll phone her myself.'

Rooney does phone Barbara. Neither of them can understand why I said nothing earlier. The reason is that I went through the weeks of the Inquiry in a daze of shock and confusion – stupor, almost. I was drugged some of the time and had difficulty focusing on anything that was said to me. Certain events and conversations are indented on my memory, but others have a dream-like quality. I am a child catching snowflakes, dismayed by the pool of water in the palm of my tiny hand.

The Rape Crisis Centre hadn't taken my surname and I surmise that they probably keep no identifiable written records. Certainly we didn't when I worked for the Samaritans. I have, however, kept intermittent contact with one young woman from the self-help group: Rhona had been the quietest of the eight of us, so badly affected by her experiences that she never uttered a single word in any of the meetings. She had once passed me a note on a tiny piece of paper, shyly. It said that she, too, felt something that I had just described. She accepted my telephone number when I offered it to her at the end of the session. We've spoken a few times since then and I visited her flat once. It was dismal and smelled of rotten carpets because she'd had burst pipes.

I telephone Rhona.

'Helen!' she exclaims. 'I've been awful worried about you. Those crazy articles in the *Scotsman!* I wrote to the Church of Scotland . . . I hope that's ok? I kept a copy. Wait, I'll read it to you:

> I met Helen at Rape Crisis. Only one member of the
> group we were in had made a police complaint. . .
> myself. It was clear to me that all of these women had
> suffered in silence, fearing that no-one would believe
> them even if they did speak out. Helen was no exception
> . . . I cannot comprehend how these allegations that have
> been made against her could be taken at all seriously,
> and I hope that my letter will help you to understand
> why.

'They've never replied, though,' she observes.

Obviously no-one in the Church Head Office in Edinburgh deemed it relevant or important to forward Rhona's letter to my Presbytery. It could have saved my bacon.

I start thinking of other people I told, long before the allegations were twisted against me.

There was Alex McAra, my lorry-driving instructor: I told him. Then there was the H.G.V. examiner, Mr White: I remember that I wrote to him and told him why being in control of a big lorry was so important to me. He wrote back. . . Didn't he say I should contact him if there was ever anything he could do for me?

Little did I think I'd ever need the help of this man I had met for less than an hour. I fish out Mr White's reply to my letter and find his telephone number at the top of the page. It is a woman who answers my call. 'Mrs White, you don't know me. . . I once wrote a letter to your husband about why I had wanted to drive a lorry. He said he'd keep that letter. If he did, it could be a help to me now.'

'I *do* know who you are,' the woman interrupts, 'And he *does* still have your letter. I know why it will help you. You don't have to explain. We've been appalled by the newspaper reports. He'll send you back your letter at once.'

Later in the evening I have a phone call from the driving instructor, Alex McAra. The examiner has spoken to him. Alex wants to know why on earth I didn't ask sooner. He'll write, outlining the conversation I had with him before sitting the test. He'll stand up in the Church Court and testify for me, if necessary.

The Presbytery Clerk *pro tem* decrees it is too late to submit any of these documents.

So Chief Inquisitor Caskie will have his 'case to answer'.

A serious matter comes to my notice from several sources: Mary and Moyra Nicoll are informing folk proudly that the Convener of the Committee of Inquiry visited them, privately, and spent a great deal of time with them hearing 'the many things we had to tell him about that Helen Percy.' What Chief Inquisitor Caskie does not realise (though he jolly well ought to) is that he is denying me my right, under the 1935 Act, *'to be present throughout the whole course of the Preliminary Inquiry and given full opportunity of defending [my]self against the allegations.'* I can hardly defend myself at a meeting that is held in secret!

Dennis is at the Presbytery tonight and telephones as soon as he returns home: 'Do you know what Caskie said? Do you know? I've written it down for you, word for word. Listen: "Miss Percy was present, with her legal advisers, throughout the Inquiry, in accordance with the 1935 Act." And there he was, having forbidden you to have a legal adviser with you and having had that meeting with the Nicolls! Caskie perjured himself tonight, Love: he was lying through his teeth! He perjured himself in front of the entire Presbytery of Angus.'

I was prevented from attending the Presbytery Meeting, having been suspended without warrant. I should never have learned of Chief Inquisitor Caskie's falsehood (because all present presumed his statement to be the truth) had not Rev Dennis Leadbeatter happened to know otherwise.

'Dennis, what about the Support Group that met with Robert and me? It was a year ago that I told them Sandy Nicoll was pestering me. Didn't even one of them have the courage to say so? Brian of Aberlemno? Helen McLeod? The two of them were also there when they first told me of the allegations: they heard me say it was "tantamount to rape". Instantly. They know I didn't have time to make it up! They even encouraged me to contact Sandy to ask him to tell the truth for me. Didn't they stand up for me?'

'Not one of them, Love. They were all prepared to withhold their evidence, and let you hang.'

3rd September 1997

After the Presbytery Meeting, the *Daily Mail* carries the headline, 'Minister in affair row told to clear name or face trial!. . . Two weeks to explain yourself, Percy!' That's not what the fourteen days are for. I have a fortnight to 'present "Objections" to the terms of the Statement', whatever that means. The newspapers exacerbate the sense of pre-judgement.

A certain presbyter is quoted: 'There was no-one in the meeting who believed that there was not a case to answer. We all feel very sad.' This presbyter – and all were defied to comment to the press – was well aware that only three people had considered the *prima facie* case. No information was released to the rest of the Presbytery (except through television, radio, newspapers and the internet!) and presbyters were asked simply to accept the opinion of the three individuals whom they had appointed. They had not been asked to decide if there was a 'case to answer' themselves. Officially, they didn't even know the nature of the allegation against me.

I have a strong suspicion that the author of this comment is not 'very sad' at all.

More likely she is gleeful. She is an elder in our parishes and I know Robert Ramsay supports one of her musical projects, so she is in his pocket. She and a few others will be sorely disappointed if I am acquitted, after all their slanderous efforts.

I suspect the same elder is responsible for a few other twisted versions of events that keep on being regurgitated in the press. I'd once chosen as a text for a children's lesson, 'Man looks at the outward appearance, but the Lord looks at the heart.' *(1 Samuel 16 v 7)* I had wanted to put across to the young ones that it doesn't matter to God how respectable you pretend to be – as long as you're not mean and hateful on the inside. So I wore a calf-length Snoopy T-shirt and bed socks and carried a teddy bear and a hot water-bottle. Snoopy was saying, 'Don't speak to me. I'm grumpy and irritable.' I told the children it's the 'grumpy' bit God minds; not what I'm wearing.

The Snoopy T-shirt – or so-called 'nightie' – has become skimpier and more provocative with every reprint of the story in the press, until today the *Daily Mail* has it: 'Members of her congregation in Kilry were shocked when she stripped to her undergarments while giving a sermon one day.' The Rev Stewart Lamont, a columnist in the *Herald*, actually thinks my 'striptease' is part of the Libel brought against me by the Presbytery.

The morning after Presbytery, I am summoned to Rooney's office to be issued with the Statement of Sinful Conduct, as the Law book calls it. I find it faintly amusing that Chief Inquisitor Caskie has written to me in advance, requesting that I 'be at home or at least available for personal contact next Wednesday, 3 September, the day after the meeting of Presbytery. It is possible that the Presbytery Clerk will wish to give you a letter that day.' He knew fine well there would be a letter to give me: he was its signatory! It is the same Statement of Sinful Conduct he almost sent me weeks ago, when I was holed up by the reporters in Ardgay, until he checked up and discovered he had to tell the Presbytery what he was doing first. He is certainly in a hurry to thrust it in front of me now:

STATEMENT BY THE COMMITTEE OF ENQUIRY
RE: THE REVEREND HELEN PERCY
Having carried out the Preliminary Enquiry, the
Committee appointed by the Presbytery hereby set out
the allegations of **scandalous, immoral** and **improper
conduct** by Helen Percy as follows:
Between 19 June, 1994 and 2 September, 1997 inclusive,
within the parishes of Glenisla, Kilry, Lintrathen, Airlie,
Ruthven and Kingoldrum and/or elsewhere, you formed
and continued a relationship of an intimate and immoral
nature with Sandy Nicoll, Easter Craig, Alyth,
Blairgowrie, the lawful husband of Moyra Nicoll, Easter
Craig, Alyth, Blairgowrie.
J. Colin Caskie
Convener, Committee of Preliminary Enquiry

Scandalous? Immoral? Improper?

'It means adultery,' explains Rooney.

Between 19th June 1994 and 2nd September 1997, inclusive? Do they think I was busy committing 'adultery' from the day I moved in and right up until last night, when the Presbytery was actually holding its meeting? Or do they not really know when or where or what I did or didn't do. . .

Not What You Know but Whom You Know

4 – 30 September

I have fourteen days to state in writing whether I admit or deny the allegations and to lodge any 'Objections to the terms, or to the sufficiency of the Statement.' I don't really know what constitutes 'terms' or 'sufficiency' and the Big Lawyer cannot find time to see me for over a week. So I try to compose a reply on my own.

I think 'terms' must mean the description of my offence, so I write simply that I deny the 'sinful conduct' attributed to me on the grounds that I did not consent to sex. I add that, since the 1935 Act *Anent* Trials by Libel was drawn up decades before women were ordained, it does not allow for the possibility of rape when adultery is alleged.

As for 'sufficiency,' I point out that the so-called 'full and precise Statement' is vague and unspecific – and unsupported by any evidence whatsoever. There isn't much 'full and precise' about 'between June 1994 and September 1997', nor about 'and/or elsewhere'.

I then proceed to make further 'Objections' on the grounds of procedural incompetence. These are lengthy!

I send a copy to the Principal Clerk in Edinburgh, requesting the advice he is paid a small fortune to provide. Needless to say, I never receive a reply to that letter either. The Principal Clerk is very good at ignoring letters that he finds a little awkward.

Fortunately, I've known the Depute Principal Clerk since we were probationer ministers together and am not as much in awe of her as I am of her superior. Her parish is away up in Orkney, although she flies down to Edinburgh for meetings on a frequent basis. I telephone Marjory and ask for her opinion. 'What you've put's fine,' says Marjory. 'But I suggest you leave out the first bit: they'd need to be out of their tree to say rape was adultery. And try not to worry: the evidence against you doesn't amount to a row of beans.'

We are yet to learn just how many of them are 'out of their tree' as Marjory puts it.

I take the completed document to the Big Lawyer. He says it will 'do'. He gives the impression he's not particularly interested in the matter until it goes to Court. I don't doubt that that's where he will excel, but I am not sure I can withstand the strain much longer. I cling to the hope that a trial will be forestalled . . . that I can put this behind me and pick up the remnants of normal life.

The Big Lawyer believes our strongest defence is the one the Committee of Three rejected, through ignorance of the issue. Without understanding the long-term effects of sexual abuse, that primary betrayal of the child's trust, no-one could picture what in reality took place – nor fathom why, afterwards, my reactions betrayed a continuing emotional attachment to Sandy Nicoll. Dr Freya Smith, knowing my background, wrote that it was consistent with what she would have expected. The Big Lawyer wants to call an expert witness to back up this assessment. He also acquires copies of my medical records as evidence of previous abuse, together with confirmation that I sought help to overcome my terror of sexual intimacy at the time of my engagement. There is a note in my medical files to the effect that I believed my female anatomical parts were so badly damaged, through being sliced with a tin-opener, that a physical relationship would be impossible.

Paul, my ex-fiancé, was incensed when he read the scurrilous articles in the *Daily Mail* in England about my supposed 'philand-ering'. He'd known nothing of the alleged 'affair', for we commun-icated infrequently, but he supposed correctly that sexual desire was not a factor. Apparently he wrote to the newspaper and to the Church, explaining that throughout our two-year betrothal we never slept together because, 'like many girls who have been abused she was too scared.' Moreover, he knows for a fact that I 'prefer chocolate'! Needless to say his testimony is not heeded, either by the *Daily Mail* or by the Church.

An expert witness is found – a well-known psychiatrist and psychotherapist who advises the Catholic Church on the care of victims of sexual abuse. She agrees to see me and is happy to assist at the Trial. She has been recommended by Alan Draper, a senior social worker who's been consulted in several disciplinary cases involving Catholic priests. Alan Draper had offered his assistance to the Presbytery early on in the proceedings. For example, he warned that use of the term 'suspension' was likely to imply predetermined guilt and fuel imprudent speculation. His offer was rejected. The Presbytery of Angus acknowledged his advice but they knew what they were doing, thank you very much.

I complain to the Superintendence Committee about the way Rev Robert Ramsay set about making it impossible for me to be given a fair trial. Even before the Presbytery was informed of any allegations, Ramsay was seeing to it that all and sundry heard. My original resignation, if it had been accepted, should have ensured that no scandal would be raised. But Ramsay, as Presbytery Clerk, was determined I should be left without a name. He was intent on destroying me, even if I fled without putting up any resistance. On 19th June, before the Presbytery was aware of the allegations, he marched into Airlie School to tell our Session Clerk, at his place of work, that my resignation was lodged and that things were going to become 'very messy'. The Session Clerk raised an eyebrow as Ramsay further divulged, 'She spent a weekend in Edinburgh with Sandy Nicoll on his return from Bosnia.' Of course, this was untrue.

The same day, a parishioner arriving at Airlie Manse was told that 'a serious complaint' had been made about me to the Presbytery. No-one needed to know this: at that point I'd already offered to demit status.

He told another parishioner I'd committed similar 'misdemeanours' in Paisley and another that I'd had no less than four abortions! Could I be in the Guiness Book of Records?

Most serious of all, Sandy Nicoll told Dennis, and he also told his closest friends and neighbours at Purgavie Farm, that Robert Ramsay has visited him. Ramsay's mission had been to persuade him to withdraw his letter to the Presbytery: Sandy had put in writing that I did not consent to intercourse. Ramsay warned him that if he didn't change his story he would land himself in prison. Sandy refused to change his story, so his letter was secreted under lock and key by Presbytery Officials. *That* one was *not* going to be leaked to the Press. Nor were any of the other statements that corroborated my defence. Nobody was told of their existence.

Robert Ramsay. Surely something must be done about this miscreant's slanderous tongue, and his attempt to frighten a witness? The Convener of Superintendence in Angus Presbytery is young; in his first charge. He writes me a very nice letter confessing his inexperience, but the Principal Clerk at Church Headquarters has advised him that no action whatsoever should be taken. . .

Not long after this, I receive a phone call from Rev Brian of Aberlemno. Hearing my friend's voice is so welcome, after months of ostracisation. My colleagues seem reluctant to have anything to do with me, as if I have leprosy. Brian is the one friend I'd trusted in the Presbytery and I've been longing for him to contact me.

Brian's reason for calling astounds me: 'Have you heard the news? Robert Ramsay's leaving. He's accepted a call to a church in Invergowrie, in the Presbytery of Dundee.'

'You mean they're letting him go? They're sending him to another charge, after all this? Nothing will be done?' I am aghast. This is blatantly unfair.

'Yes, they're letting him go. He's not going far enough, though: Invergowrie's only in the neighbouring patch and these things will follow him. . . Oh, and I wouldn't worry about the charges against you: they'd have more chance of convicting you for heresy! Besides, an unbiased jury can't be found in this whole country: it's become like the Trial of O. J. Simpson!'

Ramsay has been on 'sick' leave ever since the meeting when he informed our Kirk Sessions of my downfall, and elder Bob Robertson turned the tables and led a vote of no confidence in *him*. It so happens that our Bob Robertson, veteran of war, strong defender, big of stature as of heart, is called to meet his Maker this September. I go to him in hospital (suspended or not, I am still his minister) and find him with eyes closed, pyjama top open and chest wired to monitors. He appears unconscious but, perchance he can hear me, I touch his hand. 'Bob? It's Helen. I'm going to win this. I want to thank you.'

One eye opens. 'Aye,' he says. Then both eyes regard me and a victorious grin spreads over his bluish face. 'Aye: Invergowrie, hey? So the bugger's goin'!'

Peter Douglas, the minister to whom I first tentatively confided my sense of 'calling' ten years ago, is livid. He writes to Finlay Macdonald, Principal Clerk, saying his treatment of me is a disgrace. If I'd cultivated the right alliances within the Church of Scotland, I would not stand condemned. Peter reminds the Principal Clerk of one senior minister who's been in fearful trouble for stealing, but strings were pulled by the Church to prevent the matter going to court, and to forestall his exposure in the media. The reprobate subsequently rose to become a Moderator of the General Assembly, no less! The Principal Clerk doesn't answer Peter's letter either. . .

Tarred and Feathered

1 October – 10 November 1997

I am supposed to give a talk about prison chaplaincy to the Woman's Guild at Kirriemuir Old Parish Church. Rev Malcolm Rooney, however, will not permit it 'in the circumstances'.

What circumstances? I have been found guilty of no charge. Even if Rooney regards me as tainted by the very existence of the Preliminary Inquiry, does that negate all the work I've done in the prison? Does he think I'll corrupt the womenfolk of his congregation merely by opening my mouth? I am hurt.

The President of his Guild did not want her Minister to do this . . . not everyone judges me guilty before I am proven innocent.

I am having doubts about Rooney. As Presbytery Clerk *pro tem*, he is not constant in what he says. He appears to bend over backwards to be helpful and supportive, but then he changes his tune. Ironically, he accuses me of 'always shifting the goal posts' and changing my mind; but as I am rarely given much warning of each new move on the Presbytery's part, I feel I am never given time to decide what to do at each turn.

Rooney telephones, trying to persuade me of my guilt. 'If someone my wife knew came to our house and raped her she would never want to see him again,' he declares.

But what if the man were *you*, Malcolm, I dare not say aloud. Rooney is unable to grasp the concept of 'meaningful consent'. I've deliberately avoided the word 'rape' during the Inquiry, because it is suggestive of violence. But physical force is only one end of the scale. Taking a woman's compliance for granted is at the other end. What woman has not experienced that, at some time?

Press harassment is unabating. It intensifies whenever there is a development in proceedings, but even during lulls one newspaper or other will try to catch me off guard. I replace the receiver the minute the caller begins, 'Miss Percy?' No-one who knows me uses my surname. Occasionally a reporter tries to trick me and calls me 'Helen', assuming a familiarity he has no right to. This infuriates me. Even one telephone call is enough to leave me shaking and miserable for the whole day.

Rev Dennis Leadbeatter comes over often and tries to entice me to eat and sits in a chair just watching over me and shaking his head, for hours. That dear old man carries my grief as if it is his own. Without him, I should sink. 'What are they doing to you, Love? What are they doing? How you have kept your sanity I do not know . . .' He has parishes of his own to run but he never grudges me his time. Hardly a day passes but that he telephones, or negotiates my path with his walking stick, and lifts up the burden of my cross and takes its weight on his back. Younger, fitter men avoid me, afraid of the contagion of my sinfulness, or of breaking a rung on the ecclesio-political ladder.

Dennis is answering the telephone for me one afternoon when I cannot take any more. 'It's none of your damned business who I am!' I overhear him snap at a reporter from the *Scotsman*. The next day the print runs: 'Yesterday an unnamed male was screening Miss Percy's calls for her.'

Unnamed male! Factually correct, the words are chosen to imply impropriety and intrigue where none exists. It is obvious, even from his voice, that Dennis is no young stud.

Steven and Annebeth Mackie are with me another day, when two young men in suits appear. I feel sick. Only Jehovah's Witnesses and reporters come to the door in pairs. And the J.W.s visited last week. They had been two older men, who knew who I was and brought words of consolation and then went away. No *Watchtower* . . . No condemnation. . .

I know these two have to be reporters. I ask Steven if he minds dealing with them and Annebeth pulls shut all the curtains in the cottage. These reporters are press agency ones, the worst kind. Commission only. Steven and Annebeth help me pack and escape. Annebeth, ever practical, hangs my wet washing on the backs of chairs in the kitchen. 'It'll go mouldy left in the machine, but it will be pictured on the front page of the *Sun* if you peg it out in the yard!' I am afraid to go outside to peg it on the clothesline anyway. That is the trouble: most times when the press appear I'm on my own and if the door's not answered they hang around, lying in wait for hours. They go to noise up one or two neighbours, or sit in their cars at the village hall, from which vantage point they keep tabs on my movements. If I go out they'll follow me but if I stay in I'm under surveillance.

I have to leave. I feel continually threatened by the presence of reporters or just by the possibility of their telephoning or appearing at the door. I head for Mull, where friends have offered an open invitation. I'll be safe on an island. Agency reporters won't follow me the distance to the ferry and across the water.

Jane and Meme Errington take their whole 'family' – ponies, bantams, Dandie Dinmonts and tortoises – from Fife to Mull every summer. They read the *Scotsman*, know of my trouble and want to help. Welcoming me into their everyday life as if nothing has happened is the best help anyone can give. For a couple of weeks, I am part of the blessed normality of scones for tea, pulling ticks off the dogs and going to bed with a stone hot water-bottle. I look for lost tortoises in the shrubbery. I clamber up through the tormentil and the heather until I can see the Isle of Coll. I wonder at the fragile intricacy of dewy cobwebs strung across the whins at daybreak.

I have to return home in time for the October meeting of Presbytery, only to discover that my medical records and written evidence have been requested by the Business Committee, but that the Big Lawyer hasn't released them as I instructed him to . . . and that it is now too late for the evidence to be considered. . . that, not having had sight of these significant documents, the Presbytery is appointing a solicitor to re-run the Preliminary Inquiry. . . that she will report back to the *November* meeting. . . that there will be yet another month of the hell of anxiety and uncertainty. . .

I do believe the whole matter could have been resolved at this point. I am irritated with the Big Lawyer for not doing as I asked, but this is one of the difficulties of having an ecclesiastical legal system that claims to be totally independent of the courts of the land and yet expects the accused will hire a legal representative from within the civil sphere (at prohibitive expense).

The Big Lawyer doesn't appreciate how the Church works and the Church doesn't appreciate how ordinary Law works. It's virtually impossible to find a legal agent who knows anything about Ecclesiastical Law. There are one or two, but it's certain that no-one in the Church is going to let on where they are. Nor am I provided with anyone from within the Church itself to lead me through the maze of Acts laid down over the centuries. The Presbytery has been provided with two 'Assessors', or advisers, from the Board of Practice and Procedure and has easy access to all the free help it requires from the higher echelons of the Establishment. I am fortunate in having the support of Professors Bill Shaw and Douglas Murray, but they admit that their knowledge is far from up-to-date. Only the Principal Clerk has gnosis of the latest amendments – and he does his best to avoid telling me anything!

Rev Dr Douglas Murray is 'enthroned' as Principal of Trinity College, Glasgow University early in October and I attend the grand ceremony. A few weeks ago Douglas sat me in an armchair in his office up in the corner of The Square, encircled with theological tomes, old oak bookcases, lamp-stands and writing tables. He looked over my 'Objections' to the 'terms' and 'sufficiency' of the Statement of Sinful Conduct, pulled out some volumes on Church Law, and assured me the Presbytery didn't have a leg to stand on. 'All the academics here say this nonsense would not be going on if you were a male minister.'

Freya, married to Douglas, takes me aside at the function in the big hall after Douglas's service. 'Never mind,' she whispers. 'Just wait until they get a *real* solicitor to look at it!'

I am assured that the 'real' solicitor now appointed by Presbytery is from a Catholic firm, and therefore impartial. (It transpires, however, that she is not herself a Catholic: she is heavily involved with a Church of Scotland congregation in Dundee and the minister there is very friendly with Robert Ramsay.) The 'real' solicitor, too, interviews the two Mrs Nicoll in my absence. This may well be done in civil practice but it is not in accordance with the 1935 Act, and once again I am denied my right to be acquainted with the evidence against me. The Act says the accused has the right 'to be present and to defend himself at all times'.

The 'real' solicitor wants to see me now. My own Big Lawyer says it's 'irregular' for the prosecution to request a 'precognition' from the defendant, but it's my decision whether or not I comply. I do see her. She keeps her hair in a Princess Anne bun and wears an alarming red coat with polished buttons and long boots with heels that make the floor reverberate when she strides into the room. Baffled by legal jargon, out of my depth with the things that should be concerning me, I notice only accessories. Unlike Chief Inquisitor Caskie, she makes no secret of the fact that she has interviewed the Nicolls. She fulfills her objective and later asks me to sign a transcript. It is all about fact-finding, however: with whom have I been seen, where and when. It is an inadequate way of assessing where the boundary lies between apparent acquiescence and rape.

This cannot be helped. The Church has already embarked on an adversarial course of action to deal with a matter that would have been better handled with proper pastoral understanding, rather than by legalistic means. There are those on the Business Committee of Angus Presbytery who might have chosen different methods, had the Presbytery Clerk at that time been someone other than Robert Ramsay. He incited the Nicolls to bay for blood and the Presbytery to demand my head on a plate. I don't say this from my own point of view alone: the Nicoll family has been ravaged by the contention, their marriage wrecked at a point when it might well have been salvaged. This process is one of devastation not only for both parties, but also for the local congregations, and for the whole Church. There has been no opportunity for Christian reconciliation.

Something else very odd happens when I am in the lawyer's office this morning. The Big Lawyer tells me he's taken a telephone call from Sandy Nicoll's solicitor, who supposedly told him, 'Sandy Nicoll had sexual intercourse with your client on many occasions.' I feel myself blanch and I think I will faint. If the only other witness to what *did* take place is now getting cold feet and backtracking on his confession, I am finished. Has Robert Ramsay succeeded in intimidating him, with those threats of a term in jail?

'People don't tell their lawyers the truth for all sorts of reasons,' goes on the Big Lawyer. 'Or it may be that his solicitor's trying to protect him from possible criminal charges. . . But if you're not telling me the truth we had better stop now.'

'I am telling you the truth,' I say quietly. I look at him as I speak but he looks away from me.

'Well, then we'll proceed.'

What is peculiar is that I chance to speak to Sandy Nicoll's solicitor many months later, over a different issue altogether. I ask him about his telephone call to the Big Lawyer. He denies having said any such thing. 'I know nothing about Sandy's relationship with you. He's never discussed it with me. Besides, no lawyer would say something like that.' The Big Lawyer remains adamant that the conversation did take place. I don't know whom to believe.

Disaster strikes a second time at the very end of October, when the Nicolls claim to have found a letter written by me to Sandy. The Big Lawyer won't divulge to me the contents of the letter and I've absolutely no recollection of having written one. He does say that, if it is found to be in my handwriting, my chances of acquittal will be reduced seriously. A Trial is inevitable now, unless I plead guilty and save myself further months of torment. To hire him to defend me, he says, will cost me tens of thousands of pounds. 'I am not saying how many tens, but it would be tens of thousands of pounds.'

I attend Mass at St Anthony's Roman Catholic Church in Kirriemuir that Sunday morning, as I have taken to doing since the trouble began. It is the only place where I can have any contact with the prisoners, four or five of whom are Catholics, and are brought out to Mass in the prison van. I always sit in their pew in the chapel. I need them. These convicted criminals make room for me among them and I am thankful for their acceptance of me. I feel cast off by the majority of my clerical colleagues but the prisoners are my friends.

I was the prisoners' chaplain, their spiritual guide, but they are the ones who show me Christ. Their humility humbles me. Some of them will not go up to take the Communion but sit tight in the pew while I, guilty of life, and not even with the virtue of being a Catholic, receive the Bread. 'I'll take it when my sentence is over,' Jamesey explains. 'We're being punished for things we done – but you ain't done nothin'.' Another lad tells me the same thing. They make me cry. I am always in tears when I take the Bread at the Mass.

This morning the tears are rolling down my cheeks already when I enter the chapel. The priest, also a prison chaplain, and a man with the heart of Christ, takes my arm with both hands. He is used to my blotchy face on Sunday mornings, but not to this degree of distress. 'They've decided they're having a Trial!' I tell him.

'A full Church Trial!' He is shocked, and draws in his breath in horror. He looks at me with pity. 'Rome could hardly have mustered such a mighty cruel machine as this! It's Draconian!'

I go to my seat beside the men from the prison and they do their best to console me.

Afterwards, at coffee, Toe almost manages to make me laugh. Toe is so named because he is said to have chopped off his own big toe for a dare. The tale is apochryphal but it is sufficient to put awe and fear into the hearts of younger cons. Toe is notorious and a recidivist, but this time he was innocent of the crime for which he was sent down. 'You need an Advocate!' he declares. 'We'll find you an Advocate. Mine was brilliant. We'll get you Joe Beltrami!'

'He didn't do you much good this time, Toe,' I jest.

'No, but he got me off plenty of times when I *was* guilty!' At least he makes me laugh.

I don't have great reserves of courage and strength and neither do I have the money to pay an Advocate. I don't know how to face the impending Trial. Where can I run? I go to Sue Hewer at Over Ascreavie Farm.

Sue has been a member of our congregation, but has transferred to the Episcopal Church since her husband's death, and so she is at a sufficient distance for me to confide in her. She offers to help me with money but I cannot accept that kind of help.

Sue calls her friends Ruth Dundas, Honorary Sheriff, and Eileen and Alan Draper. They come up to her house at once. Alan is the man who advises the Roman Catholic Church in matters of discipline and I have enormous respect for Ruth Dundas, too. 'What did you say in the letter they've found?' they ask. I don't know. I haven't seen it. 'Did you say you were going to run away with him or something?'

'I don't think so! But Dennis says the Presbytery Clerk wants me to "throw in the towel". He wants me to admit I am guilty and have done with it. He says that'll avoid trial and another five or six months of press intrusion, and the Presbytery will censure me forthwith. But I have to admit "all or any of the allegations in the Statement of Sinful Conduct".'

To which of the allegations should I admit? That I was 'scandalous' or ' immoral' or 'improper'? Sue, Ruth Dundas and the Drapers do not think I should resign, but they realise the pressure on me is phenomenal. We discuss the three named 'sins', and we plump for 'improper'. This sounds the least heinous of the triplet.

Sue e-mails the Presbytery Office for me, intimating that I will accept the charge of 'improper' conduct. There is no time to correspond by Royal Mail. As always seems to be the case, a sudden major decision is required only days before a crucial meeting.

I still haven't seen the 'letter' that is supposed to have sealed my guilt. I am so sick with anxiety over it that Dennis telephones Rooney, the Presbytery Clerk *pro tem*, and begs him to reveal the contents so that he can relay them to me. This is done. Dennis has me sit down on the end of his bed (to which he is increasingly confined, and the worse for his grief over the Presbytery's treatment of me), and begins to tell me what, supposedly, I wrote.

I listen. Slowly, I recall sitting up in bed in Drusilla's upstairs room, at the beginning of the nightmare, following her instructions to write to Sandy and ask him to tell the truth for me and to confess

212

to the Presbytery everything that happened between us. Yes; I did write that, but Rev Brian of Aberlemno had also urged me to write and ask Sandy to tell the truth for me. I had told Brian of Aberlemno that I had done so, and I had told Dennis, too. The letter went on, however, to say some things I am sure I didn't write, albeit I was suffering from sleep deprivation and was stuffed with temazepam. I do remember Drusilla having me amend the letter in the morning, saying it would drive Sandy to suicide when he read it if I didn't lighten it up a bit. So it is spattered with a few swear words (the kind of language Drusilla uses all the time, in a pukka voice that makes it sound not at all shocking) and with considerable sarcasm. The sarcasm would be lost on anyone who gave it a straight reading, however. It would damn me.

There are parts of this letter I remain convinced I didn't write, though I now know that temazepam sometimes causes people to do and say extraordinary things they would not otherwise do. Could someone have tampered with the letter? Why has it turned up *now*, at the last minute before the case is dismissed forever and when there has been a dearth of any real evidence for all these months? Are they so desperate to find something against me? It is too peculiar. There are many questions surrounding that letter, but the thought of involving forgery experts, and C.I.D., is too much for me. It has all become too messy, too far out of hand.

'It's not in the public domain, this,' Dennis gentles me.

'No, but it will be,' I answer darkly. Every other damning document has been leaked to the press. There is no reason to think whoever is responsible will sit on this one.

Alan Draper helps me to draw up a press statement, highlighting some of my concerns about jurisprudence. It concludes, 'I now hope that, in the course of that action on which it has embarked, the Church will be driven by Gospel values of truth, justice, and compassion for all those involved.'

None of the newspapers print my words. But, oddly, they quote

Rooney, saying, 'The Presbytery has represented the Church of Scotland with truth, justice, compassion and love.' He stole my line.

A friend and deacon in Easterhouse has offered to drive from Glasgow to sit beside me at the meeting on 4th November – but there's no point: I'm precluded from hearing relevant items of business, taken in private, because of the irregular suspension imposed on me. It infuriates me that the *Scotsman* will keep commenting, 'Miss Percy was not present at the meeting last night' as if, cowardly, I have chosen not to face it.

The Presbytery arranges the night of Judgement for the following week, 11th November. I am free to speak to the press now that the case is no longer *sub judice*.

Is it better to speak, or not? If you do they twist it; if you don't they fabricate it entirely. A former prisoner knows one of the editors of the *Daily Record* and persuades me, against my better judgement, to grant an interview. The *Record* offers to 'protect' me (or, more likely, protect their 'exclusive rights') from other newspapers by putting me up in an hotel. This is the last thing I want. I am so desperately lonely and cling to familiar surroundings, such as my hens scratching in the back yard, as if these can preserve my life. Then the *Daily Record* breaks a press embargo by printing a story on the day of the Presbytery Meeting. I should have known they would.

All the papers are excited about my 'sudden confession'. None appreciates that I never did deny what took place – but *still* deny having given consent. The *Scotsman*, a 'respectable' broadsheet, is by far the worst, making wild and damaging suppositions about what exactly I've 'confessed'. Headlines such as 'SEX SHAME REV TO BE DEFROCKED', 'KIRK BOSSES WILL BOOT HELEN OUT' and 'SEX ROW REV FACES EXCOMMUNICATION' abound. What must it be like to have your parents read such things? I am so thankful that I have no-one to whom I really matter.

The *Daily Record* does at least acknowledge that I am denying moral culpability (though it goes completely over the top and describes my 'rape hell'. Robert Ramsay shoots back, with libellous accusations in every newspaper, and even on television: 'She denied it all along . . . just concocted this story now to get herself off the hook . . . doesn't know the truth from a lie, and never has done.' Ramsay, of all people, knows I've told the same story from the beginning. He is the one who tried to make Sandy Nicoll change *his* story and damn me.

Once the scavengers of scandal have had their fill and abandoned my carcass to the bleaching sun, one or two of the prettier birds arrive to eye my bones. These are the forensic experts of journalism. They are in search of the truth. They find the secrets in the sand around me rather than by tearing at my flesh.

Sandy Nicoll shows some courage by speaking out, despite the threats, in *Scotland on Sunday* on 9th November. And he confesses to 'rape', the word that the church press office forbade me to use, and which I have avoided. [*Appendix I.1 and I.3.*]

Ramsay and his witch-prickers are seen in a huddle after the service this Sunday, then going across to Airlie Manse. A copy of Drusilla's 'letter' is, as I predicted, leaked to the *Scotsman*.

It is printed, in full, on Monday: the crucial day before the Judgement. It is a dirty, dastardly trick.

'A Penny for the Guy'

THE first week in November is feverish with activity. I am afraid to be in my own home because of continual harassment. I don't want to stay in one place too long, either, in case my hidey-hole is discovered. Consequently, I stay with different parishioners every night – at Ascreavie, Newton or Dryloch. I borrow a vehicle from Dryloch, concealing my own old banger in the tattie-shed, so that I can sneak home to check on my beloved animals. There is a strange car at my gate and a woman with a notepad in the garden, so I drive on and return to Dryloch by a circuitous route, anxious because I have been unable to see the pigs.

Sitting on the floor in the front room at Dryloch, Valerie and Frank ask me why on earth I am sticking pins into a lump of their children's plasticine, which I've shaped into a human figure and wrapped in a piece of blue cloth. I explain lightly, 'I saw they've built a bonfire at Kilry in the field behind my house: I think they must be intending burning me for a witch! There's a Guy Fawkes competition in the village for the best 'miniature guy', so I'm entering one as a voodoo version of me! I'm dressing up my 'guy' in a pale blue cassock just like the one I wear on Sundays and I'm going to tie a note around its middle saying "A Penny for the Minister".'

'Don't!' They shriek with laughter but they can see the reaction it would bring in Kilry if I did put the 'voodoo minister' in the competition. My ability to laugh at my own direst predicament is my salvation.

It can also be my downfall. People misjudge me by it, thinking me flippant when in fact I am worst wounded.

At this moment there is a loud knock at the back door, dogs bound through the kitchen and cats fly out of chairs. It is the firearms officer, checking Frank's gun licence application. The firearms officer is soon filled in as to who I am, shares the joke about the plasticine Minister/Guy Fawkes, and looks at me with amusement, and kindliness. Mine is the countersignature on Frank's gun licence. Since the Dunblane incident, firearms officers are required to double-check the countersignatories and so my presence at Dryloch has saved him a trip up to Kilry.

11 November 1997

It is through the firearms officer that the Police are able to locate me after Sandy Nicoll's confession was published in *Scotland on Sunday* at the weekend. [*Appendix I.1.*] Our local MP has declared publicly that the Police should become involved because Sandy Nicoll used the word 'rape'. So a sergeant from the 'Child and Female Protection Unit' is obliged to interview me. The sergeant insists on bringing a female officer with him to my home in Kilry. I tell them it isn't safe for me to be there. With the 'Sentencing' tonight, I am under enormous pressure.

I have very little time. I need to be at the Presbytery Office in Forfar by midday. I don't want to see them, but they are adamant that they must speak to me, even if a longer interview is postponed for a few days. So I go home to Kilry to meet them.

No sooner have I let myself and the police officers in through the door of The Faulds than the television crews appear. They set up tripods at the gate and wave big black mops on poles over the garden fence. These are part of the sound equipment. The police officers say they cannot prevent the cameramen filming over the gate. I am shaking all over and pour tea onto the table, missing the cups. The police draw my curtains shut. I don't like that: it makes it seem as though I've given in to the terrorisation.

I am looking after an old terrier for a friend who is on holiday and have to carry the creature out of the house. The police escort me. Their presence does not stop the mob from filming me, with the little dog in my arms. It does deter them from hassling me for a comment quite as much as they usually do. Nevertheless, they push me to the weakness of tears.

The Elect and Elite of the Presbytery have requested an audience at noon to appraise me of the arrangements for the evening's 'Sentencing'. Having evaded the camera crews as best I can, I drive to Forfar to attend.

I am so weary from lack of sleep. I was up all last night trying to compose my 'plea in mitigation' for the 'Sentencing'. Apparently I can refer to the circumstances in which my 'crime' took place, but I'm not allowed to 'enter into the substance of the case'. It makes no sense: how can you say *why* you did something without saying *what* you did?

The Censures of The Church

'I acknowledge myself most heartily to be the chief of
sinners,' said David.
'There must be more than a general confession,' said the
Moderator. '. . .You must confess the heinousness of your
guilt on the precise counts I have expounded, admit
your grievous errors and your abhorrence of them, and
humbly submit yourself to judgement.'

John Buchan: *Witch Wood*

MR Maplesden, the new Moderator of the Presbytery of Angus,
speaks in tones as precise and perjink as the ornate timepiece on
the end of his gold watch-chain, which he fondles regularly as if to
remind himself of the import of his office. 'First of all you will be
asked to read out the Charges to which you have confessed. The
presbyters will be furnished with copies. The Honorary Moderator
will then call upon you to make your plea in mitigation. This, Miss

Percy, is the Statement of Charges. . . You are familiar with them?'

'*Them?*' I am querulous. 'I have admitted only *one* charge.'

He hands me the document disdainfully, like one returning a soiled handkerchief. 'Please look at it, Miss Percy.' He speaks as if I am a tiresome, trying child. I do look and I read the document with dawning horror. I can see that these twisters have taken it upon themselves to extend my short confession. The first sentence contains the word that Sue Hewer, Sheriff Ruth Dundas, and Alan Draper and I had decided best described my 'crime' but they have augmented it:

> 'I, Helen Percy, of The Faulds, Kilry, Alyth, Blairgowrie,
> do admit the charge of improper conduct as follows:
> 'Between 19 June 1994 and 2 September 1997 inclusive,
> within the parishes of Glenisla, Kilry, Lintrathen, Airlie,
> Ruthven and Kingoldrum and/or elsewhere, I formed and
> continued a relationship of an intimate and immoral
> nature with Sandy Nicoll, Easter Craig, Alyth,
> Blairgowrie, the lawful husband of Moyra Nicoll, Easter
> Craig, Alyth, Blairgowrie.'

This is what they've printed out to give to all the presbyters in attendance tonight. They have left out the word, 'scandalous', but otherwise it is identical to Chief Inquisitor Caskie's original 'Statement of Sinful Conduct' served on me in September.

'I've admitted no such thing! I wrote to the Presbytery Clerk saying I would accept the charge of "improper conduct". I have admitted nothing more. I accepted nothing that you have written here in your second paragraph.'

'But that *is* the improper conduct, Miss Percy: the second paragraph *describes* the improper conduct.' He sighs to demonstrate his exasperation at my obtuseness.

'The second paragraph uses the word "immoral", ' I retaliate. 'I specifically denied having been "immoral".'

'Then, what, Miss Percy, may I ask, is your understanding of the word "improper"?' He is infinitely polite, to the point of condescension. He purses his lips through his neat grey beard, and each time he enunciates his pretty 'Miss Percy', I want to kick him.

'I mean that it was inappropriate to form a close friendship with a family residing in my parish.'

'I see.' There is an uncomfortable silence in the room. Maplesden puffs out his narrow chest. The watch-chain swings, settles. Always when bewildered by great complexities I become distracted by irrelevant details like buttons and watches.

'Then will you accept the second paragraph if we omit the word "immoral", so that it reads "a relationship of an intimate nature"?' interjects Rev Brian of Aberlemno, the outgoing Moderator. I look up from Maplesden's hypnotic watch-chain.

'No! It wasn't "between 19 June, 1994 and 2 September 1997 inclusive": the incident took place on 1st December1995. And it wasn't "within the parishes of Glenisla, Kilry, Lintrathen, Airlie, Ruthven and Kingoldrum and/or elsewhere": it was in my house. And you can't say I "continued" something that took place only once.'

'Will you accept that it was an "intimate relationship"? We really don't have time for this.'

'Can't you consult your lawyer?' asks Rooney.

'I don't have a lawyer any more.'

'You sacked him?'

'I can't afford him. He charges £80 an hour. And I shall be unemployed as of tomorrow. I won't have any income with which to pay.'

'The Nicolls' farm fetched £650,000 when they left the district. Can't you ask Sandy to pay?'

I am gob-smacked that the Presbytery Clerk is suggesting I ask Sandy Nicoll for money.

'You should have someone with you,' he says. Clearly he is thinking that it is not going to look good on the Presbytery if I am thrown into the lions' den alone. They think the presence of a lawyer will make what they are doing to me seem 'above board'.

I don't want to bother Barbara Lovegrove again. She's said often enough that she isn't a court lawyer. The only person I know who has experience both of legal matters and of church courts is Professor Shaw, who was Principal of St Mary's College and lectured me in Divinity. Once again I've been given far too short notice of the Presbytery's intentions. I don't even know if Professor Shaw's in the country at the moment. I know he sometime lectures in the United States. I suppose if they give me a telephone book I can phone and, if he answers, he may be willing to give me some advice about the wording of this confession they have prepared for me.

I ask to be allowed to use the telephone that is sitting on the desk in the room where we are holding the meeting. They don't offer me privacy. Professor Shaw's number is answered by a recording machine. All I can do is leave a garbled message. My accusers telephone the Principal Clerk at the Kirk's administrative headquarters at 121 George St, Edinburgh. Finlay Macdonald is away but Marjory MacLean is covering for him. Rooney tells her I am quibbling over the wording they want me to use. She offers to speak to me if they will put me on the line. She advises me to re-write the Statement, conceding as much as I am prepared to admit and hope that the Presbytery chooses a punishment to fit the crime. If the punishment seems inordinately severe, she says, I'll be at liberty to appeal to the Judicial Commission for a reduced sentence. She then asks me to hand the telephone back to Rooney.

Obviously Marjory tells Rooney what she has just told me. She warns him against accepting too narrow a confession from me, because the Presbytery will want to punish me for a greater crime and may be limited in the sentence it can reasonably impose. Rooney is irritated. He puts down the receiver and turns on me.

'You'll be suspended for at least five years,' he growls.

'Five years! But if you sentence me to five years I'll have to leave my home and my prison chaplaincy.' I am aghast. Such a long sentence would seem inordinately harsh, even if I had *enjoyed* many nights of passion! But for two minutes of being used by a man, followed by two years of distress and mourning? 'Then I'd *have* to appeal to the Judicial Commission,' I plead, desperately. 'A few weeks ago you said I'd be given six months, backdated to when I was suspended in the summer.'

'The sentence will run from tonight.' How conveniently he forgets his previous tune, sung so very short a time ago. 'You can't live in Kilry, nor exercise your chaplaincy. The suspension will apply to all other denominations, in this country and abroad.'

The assumed power of his *pro tempore* Clerkship is making Rooney more like his predecessor Robert Ramsay with every passing week.

I really am a stupid little sheep amongst prowling wolves.

Helen McLeod goes out to buy her accomplices some sandwiches while I re-write their Statement. They grumble and tell me I've wasted their precious time. I was only invited to this planning meeting 'as a matter of courtesy'. They hadn't allowed time for 'trouble'. They express their impatience.

I scribble hurriedly, while they tuck into their filled rolls and sip hot coffee. I capitulate and agree to include the word 'intimate', and that meets with their approval and acceptance.

Dennis has made me promise to have tea at his house and he will take me to the Sentencing in his car.

'I'm glad you're here, Love. I've just finished my speech for tonight. I'm going to move that there be no censure whatsoever – for how can they censure one who is innocent of any crime? . . . Have you brought that damned mutt with you? . . . Of course she's a mutt! . . . Not damned? Well, I grant that she's very well behaved, for a mutt. . . Come, sit down and have your tea, Love. You must eat something. . . John Forbes phoned. He wants to sit with us tonight. And your Professor rang to say he's coming. We'll meet him in the Bank of Scotland car park and then I'll drive all three of us right into the churchyard to avoid the cameras.'

'Professor Shaw? He got my message? He's coming? Oh, I'll love that man for ever! You know, when he ran the "Church Law" seminars for the Church of Scotland ministry candidates at St Mary's College I exasperated him: I never really took it seriously then. I didn't see the need for a Christian community to be governed with a byzantine rule-book. I wasn't interested in the heavy tome of Cox's *Practice and Procedure*. Now I see how crucial it is to have that guide and to follow it properly: used wisely, the Law of the Church should be an instrument of pastoral care. It's only in the hands of the ill-intentioned or the ignorant that it damages, confuses, and confounds.'

'You are right there, Love. In the hands of Zealots. Of Pharisees. Yes, that is what they are. I am not afraid to speak my mind when I defend you against them. We must never be afraid to be in a minority of one. Our Lord was in a minority of one. And your Professor is coming. He is appalled at the way this matter has been mishandled so far, and he wants to support you as best he can. Yes, you can iron your dress, Love. Bring the ironing board through to the kitchen. I've spoken to that nice young presbytery elder of yours from Lintrathen – Ian? Yes, Ian Ramsay, that's right. He's going to second my motion. A farmer, isn't he? . . . He sounds a sensible sort. He hasn't been swayed by all the rubbish in the papers . . . You haven't eaten very much, Love! How you have not lost your sanity. . .' All the while, Dennis totters about on his bad knees, humming to himself between phrases.

I relate to Dennis the whole saga about the Presbytery office-bearers changing the wording of my confession. 'They were using three words to say the same thing! They'd said "scandalous" and "immoral" and "improper" but really they just wanted me to say I'd committed "adultery", however many words they dressed it up in. But I'm not married, so I *can't* commit "adultery". Even "fornication" – sex before marriage – wouldn't really describe something I did not do willingly, would it? You know, the Catholics studying theology with me used to argue, "It's not a sin unless you enjoyed it". . . I don't know if that's really part of their Canon Law, but they thought it was logical, and I half see their point. Anyway, the Presbytery officials went round and round the houses this morning and they were becoming really irritable because I wouldn't agree that "improper" amounted to the same thing as "immoral". I finally agreed to them putting "I formed an intimate relationship" and they seemed content with that.'

'*Intimate* relationship? You can't say that! It wasn't!'

'Yes, it was, Dennis. I was friends with him.'

'But that isn't what *intimate* means, Love.'

'Yes it does. It does in Dickens's novels and in Jane Austen. You know, like Miss Bennett was "intimate" with her bosom friend, or her sister. It means they shared confidences with one another. Well, I shared confidences with Sandy Nicoll. I *am* guilty of being intimate.'

'But, Love, that isn't what they mean by it *here.*' Dennis gazes at me with a half-bemused, half-serious expression.

'Well, what *do* they mean, then?'

'They mean well . . . intimacy! Intimacy. . . it means "sexual concourse".'

I am flummoxed. 'I didn't know that,' I say very quietly. 'I crossed out the "immoral" bit because I thought that's what *that* meant, and I wasn't "immoral" because I didn't give consent. . . I didn't know "intimate" meant just the same thing! It's yet a fourth word for adultery? Why didn't they tell me?' To my mind sex and intimacy are two entirely separate things. I was openly affectionate towards Sandy Nicoll, as I am to Dennis himself, to my former landlady, to a few friends, my auntie and my dog. . . but sex is not an element in any of these relationships.

Always, this confusion over quaint language. When church folk announce there'll be a coffee morning, they 'intimate' the event. Do they have sex at the coffee morning? Why can't they use normal language? Why don't they have 'notices' like any other organisation? It was the same with 'seduce'. I don't tell Dennis I've never heard the word 'concourse' either, except to mean a shopping mall or a row of departure gates at an airport. For once I understand the gist.

Dennis says I must omit the word 'intimate'. Brian of Aberlemno said I could change the Statement up until the time I deliver it, so that's fine.

Professor Shaw will arrive in Forfar for a quarter past seven. He told Dennis to warn me that, whilst he has his LLB, he has not practiced law for half a century. By chance, tomorrow morning he will be defending Rev Dr Robin McKenzie, the Minister of Brechin Cathedral – also against Angus Presbytery, and also as a result of Chief Inquisitor Caskie's work. Unlike me, Dr McKenzie has not been accused of any immorality or wrongdoing. It's just that a faction in his congregation has tried to oust him. The troublemakers bent the ear of the Presbytery. They claimed that the Cathedral was in an 'unsatisfactory state' and asked that the 'pastoral tie be dissolved'. The Presbytery tangled itself in legal knots and suspended Dr McKenzie. Not only that, but they wrote to him – quite erroneously – that he was barred from preaching or from celebrating the Sacraments, anywhere, and not only within that particular parish. They weren't letting him apply for another job. They were removing his ministerial status altogether. They were acting outwith the bounds of their power. But for two dissenters, the presbyters voted with their leaders, like lemmings incapable of independent thought. Professor Shaw fears they will do the same tonight. He is in no doubt that the Brechin Cathedral matter will be thrown out by the Judicial Commission, however, because the Presbytery of Angus has demonstrated its utter incompetence.

Dr McKenzie and I have been under suspension at the same time, and so each has been prevented from being of any practical assistance to the other. I doubt if I could have done very much for him anyway. He is far superior to me both in intelligence and in experience of ecclesiastical matters. If I was the dunce in Church Law seminars, Dr McKenzie must have been the star pupil. I did write to him, however, expressing dismay at the way he has been ostracised by the Presbytery and vilified in the local newspapers.

I have met Robin McKenzie's wife and three daughters – a whole clan of kindly, quick-witted and humorous people. How difficult this past year must have been for those girls at school. So thankful am I that I have no children who would be affected by adverse publicity and pending loss of home and income.

What it means to have one's sacramental office wrested away! If a sense of priestly destiny is genuine, then the wrench is experienced as a piercing of the soul and as a loss of meaning to life. If, tonight, the Presbytery confirms the suspension it has already imposed on me and removes my ministerial status permanently, they may as well tear my limbs from my body. Yet, from the arbitrary fashion in which they have amputated Dr McKenzie, I suspect that they will be oblivious of the devastating effect of their action.

We meet at the Bank of Scotland. Professor Shaw folds himself into the smaller vehicle and Dennis drives us the short distance into the dark forecourt of St Margaret's Church, which is to be the scene of Sentencing. As I step out of the car a figure runs towards me bearing an exceedingly bright spotlight, completely blinding us. He thrusts it so close to me that I feel the heat of the bulb. Two or three others are behind him. I hear Professor Shaw scold, 'For goodness' sake!' I cannot see the path, nor understand what is happening. It is the first time I've been shot after dark.

If the experience of those first few yards' walk is alarming, it is nothing to the battery that confronts me on turning the corner of the building. A barrage of reporters, camera-folk and T.V. crews pile across the route, ten or twelve rows deep. Dennis and Professor Shaw flank me; two veterans, a lame leg and walking stick apiece, protecting a frightened young woman. The mob bars our path, bombarding me with questions and shining their lights into my face.

My two aides urge me to keep walking, and the rowdy throng begins to move backwards as one body, keeping no more than two or three feet in front of me. 'I can't see where I'm going!' I cry out, turning my head away from the effulgence. At the same moment there is a stifled shriek and a commotion at the rear of the throng, as one of their number tumbles backwards down some unseen steps.

Someone comes forward from the wings, stepping into the short gap between my horde of tormentors and me and puts something into my hands. It is a large bar of chocolate. I look up, and see that the hand that proffers it belongs to Colin, the Salvation Army Captain. He was my colleague at the prison, together with the priest. Overwhelmed by a situation beyond my control, once again my mind fixes on one small detail: it is milk chocolate. I like milk chocolate best. Of all the inappropriate emotions, in this instant I feel a surge of delight and joy. Here in the crowd is one, unexpected, friendly face. The rest are a blur. Impulsively, I throw my arms about Colin's neck, kiss his cheek and grin as though I'm on my way to my coronation, not my execution.

Colin has braved a daunting and hostile crowd to offer what comfort he could. The rabble is desperate to learn the identity of the young man who stepped out of the crowd to wipe sweat from the brow of a condemned woman. He's not in Salvation Army uniform and he will not tell them who he is. His friends in London spot him on *ITN News*, however, and when word reaches the ears of his superiors, he has his knuckles rapped. To my mind he should rather have been lauded for coming to the aid of someone in great trouble, without judging her.

Achieving the doorway, forcing the scrum to fall back to allow us passage, we come across another supporter. A lone parishioner is asking for the Presbytery Clerk to come out and accept a petition – signed by some two hundred other parishioners. The names were gathered on one Sunday alone, Remembrance Sunday, and in only three of the six tiny parishes.

The petitioners are asking for me to be allowed to remain a minister. I have been pilloried in the media for four months and left without a name. I am amazed at the strength of their support. They have judged me by what they know of me and not by what my enemies have spread abroad.

Robert Ramsay will comment to the press regarding my popularity, that it is a pity that many of the signatories are 'only' people who 'live in the parishes', and 'not all of them regular church-goers'. He implies, disparagingly, that such support is of no account. To me, the sheep on the hill are every bit as important as those within the fold.

I am directed, not into the courtroom as I expect, but into the vestry. There I am faced by Moderator Brian of Aberlemno (dapper little waiscoated Maplesden has a prior engagement tonight), by Clerk *pro tem* Rooney, and by his Deputy Helen MacLeod. These are the same figureheads with whom I met just a few hours ago. Now they inform me that they have reconsidered my Statement of Confession and are not prepared to accept it. I *must* admit to the charge of immorality as set out in their version of the second paragraph. 'I cannot,' I defy them. 'I told you I'll admit "improper", but not "immoral". I didn't give consent.'

'But "immoral" is what *we* mean by "improper".'

'In that case,' retorts Professor Shaw, 'you have worded the charge very poorly indeed. You gave three words – "scandalous, immoral and improper" – and now you say they all mean the same thing. She cannot confess to something she has not done.'

'Then I shall go out and tell all the reporters and the TV crew she has changed her mind!' snaps Rooney.

'You shall do no such thing,' Professor Shaw puts Rooney in his place. 'She has not changed her mind: you have.'

Rooney rocks back on his heels slightly. He had thought he was Lord of this outfit and had not expected to be countered. Recovering, he rounds on Professor Shaw: 'You shouldn't have come here without having studied the charges beforehand.' This is totally unreasonable since Professor Shaw has had but a couple of hours' notice, as Rooney knows full well. It was Rooney who gave permission, early this afternoon, for someone to come with me tonight. He knows Professor Shaw was not in his house when I telephoned him, and that he has had to travel some distance to attend. Goodness, only at eleven o'clock this morning was I myself given the Presbytery's version of the charge!

The meeting should have begun at half past seven. Dennis is knocking on the door asking if he may enter the vestry. He has been hovering in the corridor, anxious about the cause of the delay. The senior presbyter's presence soothes me. I have become very precious in his big heart and he makes no secret of his disgust at his Presbytery's behaviour. 'There can be no censure tonight, Dennis,' Rooney explains. 'There must be a Trial. She will not admit to immoral conduct.'

'Of course she won't admit to it!' fumes Dennis. 'She hasn't done it! This girl has done nothing immoral – and she doesn't know the meaning of the word 'intimate' either. I have spent many hours talking with her, which you have not. What she means by 'intimate' is not what you and I mean by it. You cannot make her say she is guilty of something she has not done.'

Rooney is growing more than impatient. 'We spent quite enough time discussing this at lunchtime today. Presbytery is waiting! We have already delayed the start of the meeting more than forty minutes. We must proceed.' With this, he swans out of the vestry to 'proceed', although I know not quite what he is 'proceeding' to do. Brian of Aberlemno, robed in the majesty of Moderatorial vestments, follows in his wake.

Shortly, the Presbytery Officer appears. She leads me through to the great hall. I only know her name as 'Liz'. Her role is that of a Steward. Apart from her monthly six seconds of glory as the 'Black Rod' at the start of each meeting, when she bellows 'Moderator!' so that all will stand for the monarch's grand entrance, her tasks are lowly. Liz always treats me with a kindness and consideration that is lacking in those of higher station.

I follow Liz through the avenues of power. The Judgement is to be taken 'in private' but the faces of the scandal-hungry mob are at the windows as I pass through the corridor.

Liz shows me to a seat in the front, with Professor Shaw, Dennis, and John Forbes. The platform is taken up by a long trestle table, draped in cloth and presided over by the Clerks, the Church Press Office Representative, and the Assessors. The Moderator is already enthroned and, having invoked the Almighty in prayer, commands me to stand at the rostrum. I am surprised that he asks me to make my plea in mitigation, without first reading the Statement of Confession. This seems illogical, but I begin:

> 'In as far as to have established a special friendship with
> a family in one's parish, and to have entrusted that family
> with confidences about one's past which were betrayed,
> might be construed as improper conduct, I accept that
> charge. I accept nothing more.
> 'You are being asked to decide a suitable punishment,
> knowing nothing of the facts of the case except what you
> have learned from the media. It is not permitted for me
> to present my side of the story here.
> 'This morning, the Police assured me they would protect

me from the press, or from anyone else, interfering in their investigations. It is already too late here.

'I never once commented in the media until I knew that the matter was no longer *sub judice*. It goes without saying that I accepted no remuneration for what did appear in the press.

'Contrary to what most newspapers have stated, my story has been consistent from the outset. The only thing that has changed is that I have exhausted both my financial and my emotional resources to continue to Trial.

'Had I committed the most heinous crime on this Earth, my pillorying in the media has already been punishment enough.

'Procedures were not always followed. . .'

[Here I highlight the denial of legal representation, intimidation of the witness, and the secret convocations with my accusers about which Caskie lied in the Presbytery.]

How am I supposed to make a plea in mitigation when I am forbidden to 'enter into the substance of the case'? I try to hint at what has been my experience:

'Some years ago, as a student minister, I remember sitting at the fireside opposite an elderly man who had been a Prisoner of War. He recounted to me many horrific tales. Then he said, "I can talk to you, my dear, because you've suffered too."

'I believe that all I have gone through will make me a better minister, if only I am allowed to remain.

'From the time I was first ordained, whenever I have celebrated the Lord's Supper I have taken the Bread and the Wine before offering it to anyone else in my congregation, because I am the chief of sinners.'

I go back to my seat. John Forbes whispers encouragement; that I have spoken well. Immediately, I am recalled to the rostrum.

'Miss Percy, would you read the Statement of Confession for us?' requests the Moderator from on high. To do so now, after the plea of mitigation, still seems odd. Nevertheless I do as I am told:

' "On 1st December 1995, at The Faulds, Kilry. . ."'

'No: I want the Statement we prepared earlier,' he interrupts.

'Oh . . .I'm sorry ...You did say I was still at liberty to reword it . . . It's here. . .' I fumble to find the original document:

' " Between 19th June 1994 and 2nd September, 1997 inclusive . . ." '

I am forced to include the words 'of an intimate nature' even although I now know they will be understood differently from my intended meaning.

'Why do you deny the charge "immoral"?' persists the Moderator.

'Because I did not give consent.'

I am being escorted out so that the Presbytery can talk about me out of my hearing. Another single woman has joined the Presbytery in this last year and is a minister in one of the fishing towns. I like her and had hoped we should be friends. She rises from her seat as I pass her. 'Helen, you know me, but it's very difficult.'

'Yes, I know.' I gaze at her for a second or two before being led away.

It *is* difficult. How can they be my friends and also my judges and jurors?

I am relegated to the vestry for some length of time. Professor Shaw is sitting with me. He is not permitted to remain in the hall during the Presbytery's deliberations. Liz, the Presbytery Officer, brings us tea, and waits with us while we partake. She has an aura of calm, even in fraught circumstances.

Eventually two female delegates are sent from the big hall. 'This is Catherine Coull, one of the Assessors, a solicitor,' Helen McLeod introduces the younger woman. 'We've to come to persuade you to admit more than you have yet admitted. Presbytery cannot censure you if you will not confess to more. You must confess to immorality. Otherwise there'll have to be a Trial by Libel. It'll take months.'

'I cannot confess to something I haven't done,' I answer.

'Then there must be a Trial. Why don't you see sense?'

'You can have your Trial by Libel and I shall have no lawyer. I've already made my plea.'

'So you won't confess?'

'No, I shall not.'

Brian of Aberlemno comes into the vestry to remove his Moderatorial stole and gown after the meeting has fallen flat. 'Does this mean you still won't be able to speak to me, Brian?' I ask of him, who was my closest and most trusted friend among the local ministers.

He looks sheepish. 'It's very difficult.' Those same words of excuse again.

The last words he ever says to me.

Muirskeith

LIZ lets us out of a side door while the reporters are having an audience with the Presbytery Clerk. They will not expect me to stay in Dennis's spare room at Muirskeith tonight: so that's where I am to be concealed. What ever would I do without Dennis?

Sandy Nicoll has been at Dennis's door during the time he knew we were at the Sentencing. He left a bunch of flowers on the step and a note saying, 'I'm sorry.'

I am ungracious. I think he isn't as sorry as he should be. Dennis scolds me for my lack of charity. 'The lad's suicidal, Love. He phoned me this morning from the harbour. I really thought he'd throw himself in. The lad knows what he's done, Love. He really does want to make it up to you.'

'With a bunch of flowers? And he's not a "lad", Dennis: he's old enough to be my father! He should've known better.' Dennis thinks me unnecessarily hard. Dennis has such a vast capacity for compassion. There is no doubt he abhors the act Sandy has committed, but that does not prevent him from offering pastoral care to the man, who's been to see him a number of times since the night he broke down in tears in front of him. Dennis reminds me of that night again now.

'You know, Love, when I went down to the farm to see that family, he was shouting at his wife, "I told you I raped the lassie! I told you from the beginning!" He said it in front of me, Love, and when he followed me out into the yard he wept. The police sergeant wanted to see me, too, this morning. I told him all this and that Sandy was at the harbour. . . They're going to take his guns away from him. They're afraid he'll kill himself.'

'I know, Dennis,' I sob. 'He's not a wicked man, whatever he has done to me. I did feel sorry for him and I did care about him. Drusilla told me he'd commit suicide if I didn't write and tell him I cared in that letter. It's just that I'm going to lose my job and my home, everything I've trained for and worked for and loved doing . . . and the Presbytery's not putting *him* on trial, is it? No-one's asking *him* questions about where he spreads his favours. *He* was ordained an elder and an elder he'll remain. *He* won't have to pay for this.'

'No, Love, and I've heard you weren't the first.'

'No. I don't suppose I was.'

I feel safe at Muirskeith. I can hear Dennis humming to himself in the kitchen. But I cannot sleep.

I hoped it would all be over. Instead I still have months to face: trial, judgement, more cameras and more press intrusion. . . It is unrelenting. I don't know how much more I can take of the public scrutiny of my private life.

Most of all there will be no end to the loneliness and isolation from my colleagues. I long for my colleagues to speak to me again, but now that there is to be a Trial they cannot, or will not. I think of Valerie and Brian, both saying 'It's difficult' and then looking away.

There are other reasons why I did not want to stand trial. One is Rhona, from Rape Crisis: how can I call her as a witness when she'll have to say that she, too, has been raped and abused? Can I let her experience that rape again, in front of a court of male strangers, on my account? I see her face in my mind's eye, frightened and too timid to utter a sound even among eight women who *know* what she's suffered, because they've also been victims. I couldn't live with myself if I let a Church court strip her naked, as well as me.

Rhona most of all; but there are other friends and witnesses whom I am loathe to burden. Were my liberty at stake, I could justify it; but just for my job. . . ?

The next day there is a hard frost and even though the sun shines, no thaw. There is a knock at the door soon after breakfast. I hear Dennis telling the reporters, in his most enchanting manner, that their services are not required. Someone from the Presbytery has guessed my whereabouts and betrayed me.

Several hours later I am desperate to go home to my animals, but Dennis's neighbours telephone warning that press are still lurking at Muirskeith road end. There is another way out, by a steep, rough track, but informants say paparazzi are also parked up at Kilry. Will it never end?

The Trial is unlikely to be completed before next May, if then. There is much procedural rigmarole. The jargon means nothing to me: the 'Libel' will be prepared after Presbytery meets in February, passed to the Church Procurator to be 'revised', 'certified' by the Clerks, 'adjusted', and 'subscribed'. Lists of witnesses and productions must be prepared before the Libel is 'transmitted' to the 'accused', who then has twenty-one days to lodge notice of a 'Special Defence'. Further notice must be given of the date of the 'First Sitting', at which the 'relevance' of the Libel must be established. The 'Cause' will go to 'Proof'. Another minimum of twenty-one days' notice will be given before the 'Diet of Proof' and the hearing of evidence on oath. It could be some time before the findings are reported to the whole Presbytery, and longer still before the Presbytery either concurs, or hears the evidence anew, 'delivers judgement', and 'determines censure'.

The 1935 Act *Anent* Trials by Libel is little changed from the 1707 Act. Making sense of the ancient legislation is daunting at the best of times. Stressed as I am by the continued presence of the press, and suffering from depression and exhaustion, it is totally incomprehensible.

Intervention and Interference

AS soon as it is safe for me to leave Muirskeith, I am obliged to attend the Police Station in Forfar to give a full statement. I don't wish to do this but Sandy Nicoll's own confession in a national paper necessitates it.

I am taken into a room, where the two officers who previously came to my house have spread out on a coffee table both the article from *Scotland on Sunday*, and that from the *Scotsman* including 'Drusilla's' letter to Sandy. They ask me what is meant by it. 'I was asking him to tell the truth,' I say, candidly. My answer is accepted, and no further reference is made to it. In this and in every other way, the police enquiry is entirely different to that of the Church.

When I am asked to give the details of the sexual encounters of my childhood, and of the more recent one on 1st December 1995, I am interviewed by the young female officer, alone. The questions she asks are distressing and intensely personal, but she is sensitive in her approach and does her best to put me at ease. She brings us each a mug of coffee before she begins and tucks up her legs z-wise on the soft chair as she writes. She is not in uniform. She listens to everything I say. Forfar Police Station is next door to the Presbytery Office but they may as well be separated by the Berlin Wall.

She reassures me that my reactions were not uncommon: I'd always thought there was something wrong with me because I'd learned to hold my breath until I blacked out and remembered nothing. I would 'wake up' aware of a great weight on top of me, of my lungs being compressed, and gasping for air when it was all over. The paralysis I describe to her is a recognised phenomenon amongst adult survivors of childhood abuse. I did not know that, nor that entering into a deep hypnotic trance is a classic protective reaction to subsequent sexual approach.

'Do you think you were raped?' I don't know how to answer. I had not resisted because I had been *incapable* of resistance. Clandestine injury was certainly comitted, but rape implies violence and it would be unfair to charge Sandy with that. On the other hand, he knew that I was not willing. I tell the constable that I don't want to put myself through any more of the trauma of the past five months and that I can't see what good it will do anyone if the man goes to prison. He is rough when he drinks but he isn't dangerous. Enough misery has already been created, without adding to it years of wretchedness, or the possibility of a man's suicide.

The constable does not think the Fiscal will prosecute if I don't want to press charges, even though there has been a public confession. Clandestine injury – taking advantage of a woman while she is asleep or in a hypnotic state – is a crime in Scotalnd but convictions are rare.

There would be one enormous gain from the case going through the Criminal Courts: the Church places no restricted reporting order during its proceedings, but with a real Court I'd at long last be afforded protection from the media.

Or so I thought. A woman from the *Daily Record* telephones me about a week afterwards, excitedly informing me that she has been 'tipped off' by someone in the Police: Sandy Nicoll has been interviewed at Perth Police Station and has 'admitted what he did, on tape'. She wants to produce a reaction. I give none but I know her information is correct. Sergeant West has confirmed that Sandy gave 'no trouble', and confessed.

I am disillusioned. I express concern at the continued leaking of information to the press, even by the Police. I am interviewed again, this time on tape, and by two police officers, both male. One is extremely tall, a giant, and I am frightened by his stature. This time it is more like a Church interview. They push me into saying that the time Sandy brought the soup was not the only time he had intercourse with me. 'Did you have sex with him again? Did you? Did you? *Did you?*' until I tell them whatever it is they want to hear, just to make them stop. Bullying tactics make me regress to the powerlessness of the five-year-old victim of abuse.

Without Professor Shaw beside me, I should probably have done the same at the Presbytery; confessed to something I didn't do, just to put an end to it all. I am ashamed of my weakness.

One minister who is supportive of me is a prison chaplain in Edinburgh called Jennifer. She meets me at The Elephant Coffee House that Saturday and we wallow in hot chocolate. She knows how difficult the Church can be as a place of employment for women.

Jennifer is appalled that the *Scotsman*, in particular, has printed all the evidence against me before the case has gone to Court. Nevertheless the Church is intent on proceeding, when an equivalent Court of the Land would be obliged to desist for the want of an unbiased jury. She has discussed the matter with a member of her congregation, Lord Davidson, who has been

Procurator of the Church. He, too, is greatly concerned by what the Trial will do to me and by what it will do to the Church. Jennifer urges me to speak to him, as I am to be attending that church tomorrow. Tonight I am staying with Steven Mackie, who has retired as a lecturer at St Andrews University, and with Annebeth. They are living in Edinburgh now, and they also know Lord Davidson and attend the same church.

I am introduced to former Church Procurator Lord Davidson. Tall, and not much stooped with age, he wears a lengthy coat of mole-grey wool and carries a walking stick over his forearm, more for decoration than as a prop. Pulling on his gloves in the vestibule, he bows his head, weighted with wisdom. He is the kind of man who warrants regard and does not need to command it.

'Had I still been Procurator, I should be doing all in my power to see that this did not go to Trial. . . You will, however, need someone to defend you. . . The legal expenses of the defendant are not met, of course, which is a difficulty. . .' He further inclines his head, thoughtfully. 'We must see what we can do.'

It transpires that I know an Advocate of whom Lord Davidson approves. This Advocate attended Mayfield Church in Edinburgh, where I carried out my assistantship as a minister. His wife had gifted me a pair of elegant grey curtains for my first manse. We are 'intimate' enough to be on Christmas card terms. And he is willing to advise me.

The Advocate bids me come to his house in Edinburgh and tell him everything, from beginning to end. He gives me four hours of his time – for which he could have charged me hundreds of pounds.

It is a relief to talk to him. He understands about sexual abuse and he is far more positive than I hoped, even given the nature of the letter that was published in the *Scotsman*. He does, however, have reservations about the case being heard by Angus Presbytery:

'In a city presbytery, like Edinburgh or Glasgow, I don't doubt you'd walk free. There'd be enough people who'd appreciate the issues. But in a small, rural presbytery you're going to have to 'educate' people first. And when people don't understand they easily become alienated. I can't say which way it will go.' Nonetheless, he promises to find me a Queen's Counsel.

Steven and Annebeth Mackie are delighted by this development. They are both so angry about 'this idiotic preoccupation the Church has with sex,' as Steven calls it.

The Advocate telephones, having talked over the case with a well respected QC, who will defend me gladly.

Friday 28th November 1997

A few days later the Advocate phones again, excited. He has been trying to broker a meeting. He's spoken to his friend John Chalmers in the Ministry Department and also to my Presbytery Clerk. Both are agreeable to 'mediation', as he describes it. Would I be willing to travel back down to Edinburgh? He will act as mediator. He believes this is the Christian approach and that he can achieve a resolution. John Chalmers has already made arrangements to use the offices of Palmerston Place Church on Sunday afternoon.

What can I say? He is so enthusiastic about mediation as an alternative to an adversarial approach. So idealistic. So persuasive. I know nothing about mediation. I imagine he will facilitate an agreement, to the satisfaction of both parties. Perhaps I can keep my cherished prison chaplaincy?

That hope is dashed at once: my job at Noranside Prison has already been advertised! Rev Isobel Birrell, chaplain to three hospitals in Angus, informs me that the advert for the post incorporating both our jobs is in the *Ministers' Forum,* and in the vacancy sections of two national newspapers. A glance at her Presbytery Minutes (which I have not received since my suspension) confirms that Angus Presbytery agreed to my post being advertised several months prior to deciding to put me on Trial. Indeed, even before any allegation against me was made, plans were already being drawn up. It seems that my departure from Angus has been a *fait accompli* for some while.

Isobel has been given three months' notice. She intends going to an Industrial Tribunal claiming constructive dismissal.

Another telephone call is, on the face of it, more positive. National Mission will meet my legal costs. Initially I am relieved, but then realise I'll never be able to repay such a huge loan, especially if I lose my job at the end of the day. If an ordinary court lawyer intends charging 'tens of thousands', how much more is a Queen's Counsel going to cost?

Saturday 29th November 1997
The last straw. The arrival in the post of two obscene items. It has been going on ever since sleaze concerning me was first printed in the newspapers. Sometimes there are pictures of me cut out of the *Sunday Mail* or the *Record*, superimposed onto pornographic material. Or, in different hands, there are anonymous threats of rape, or descriptions of what the author would like to do to me, or is doing to himself while he pores over my photograph. Today, the envelopes contain used condoms, and a photo of a naked woman's torso with my face stuck on top.

It's not that I'm shocked: I could hardly have worked in a men's prison and been prudish. I assume these letters to be from perverts, men sick in the head, who peruse the *News of the World* but don't know me. Nonetheless the volume of them, the cumulative effect, makes me feel degraded and filthy; even more than the newspaper articles themselves are doing.

I cannot take much more.

The Going of The Minister

'The censures of the Church are admonition, rebuke, suspension, deposition from Office, and excommunication, and they are administered **only on confession or proof of sin or of offence**.'

J.T. Cox:
Practice and Procedure in the Church of Scotland

Sunday 30th November 1997
The advocate/mediator explains first of all that his role is neutral. He is not there to support or advise me, but to enable both parties to reach an agreeable solution.

It quickly becomes apparent that the agenda has been set in advance. They have already decided what the outcome will be.

I am given three options, although the last two amount to the same thing:

1. The *status quo:* there will be a Trial by Libel.

2. Presbytery could suspend me *sine die* ('without limit of time').

3. I could demit status, and leave the ministry (with the possibility of reapplying, 'at some future date', to the General Assembly rather than the Presbytery).

What of the first option? Should I continue being afraid to stay in my own home, answer the telephone, or open the mail? Should I run up a huge debt, with no hope of keeping my job, since they've already advertised the post? Should I put Rhona in a witness box to re-live her hell, as I'd have to re-live mine? And let them dress me in a pea-green coat, and drag it from my shoulders to examine every inch of my nakedness?

But I am in floods of tears when they moot leaving my ministry. The second option is impossible: I cannot envisage Angus Presbytery restoring what it has so gleefully removed, for many years to come. I picture Robert Ramsay's presbytery elders revelling in their power and denying me the right to preach, or to pastor to people I love, for all time. Such is my mistrust of the Presbytery, a mistrust not without foundation, that I am loathe to remain in its hands. Moreover, I don't see why I should be tarred with the indictment of 'suspension', when I have never been found guilty of any charge.

On the other hand, the idea of standing up in front of hundreds of people at the General Assembly terrifies me. The mediator tries to convince me there will be a 'dignity' about doing so. 'Dignity' is one thing of which I've been robbed by the Inquiry. My hard-won self-confidence has been smashed to smithereens in these few months. I crave 'dignity'.

They don't tell me that, even if I choose to put my future in the hands of the General Assembly, a national church court that ought to be less partial, the local presbytery will still be consulted and must interview me. This is part of a new Act, with which I am unfamiliar. They also fail to say that I'll first have to pay a substantial fee to go before a Committee and that *this Committee is headed*

by a man who has libelled me in the local and national press. All
this I discover too late.

They are offering me a way out at a time when I am particularly
vulnerable. I'd expected the matter to be disposed of at the
Judgement Night, but now am totally deflated. Had they left it
another week I'd have regained strength and courage to survive
the months until the Trial.

There was no advance warning of the choice presented to me
and so I have had no time to consult advisers. I don't think of the
longer-term future. I should have made a different decision. . .

'We're going to find you guilty anyway,' says Rooney, the
Presbytery Clerk *pro tempore*. 'Adultery was committed even if you
didn't consent.'

'Whoa! Now, I think we should be careful here,' warns the
mediator.

'I didn't say who! I didn't say who committed it!' Rooney is
unabashed.

'And what is the Libel going to say?' I ask him. 'What are the
charges against me?'

'Helen McLeod and I went to see the Presbytery's solicitor,
who's agreed to be our Prosecutor. As far as I understand it you
were pregnant; and you didn't go to the Police.'

'Few women go to the Police! A tiny minority. And prosecutions
hardly ever stick,' I protest. 'What good would it have done? Wasn't
there enough damage? It would have made things a hundred times
worse for his family, for me, for him, for everyone. He knew what
he'd done. The guilt of it turned him to drink. And I never denied
that he impregnated me. That doesn't mean I was a willing party.'

'You were pregnant and you didn't go to the Police. Those will
be the charges.'

I am shaken. There is no hope of being given a fair trial. If the
rest of the presbyters are as blinkered as their Clerk, I don't have a
snowball's chance. 'Please, I need more time to think,' I implore.

I've been crying since the meeting began.

'We've wasted enough Presbytery time on this!' Rooney is irascible. 'This has been going on for months!'

'You'll have to make up your mind by five o'clock,' interjects Chalmers. 'I want to hear my son singing in the choir this evening.'

'And I want to be back home in Kirriemuir for the evening service,' adds Rooney. 'Presbytery meets on Tuesday. You can't have any more time.'

There is a sense of fatalism. I am powerless as in the mornings of my childhood when my abuser made me climb into his bed. I could have resisted, but it was as if my limbs and my will were not mine. I'd no choice but to do someone else's bidding. In the presence of these three men I adopt the same passive role.

'What do you suggest?' the mediator asks Rooney.

'We'll draw up a statement, and release it to the press. I'm sure I can persuade my Presbytery to agree. Something along the lines of:

> "As a result of unresolved issues from her childhood and
> teenage years Helen regrets that she found herself in an
> emotional relationship which moved outwith her control
> and influence. In this relationship there was a single
> sexual encounter which she states was without her
> consent. The Presbytery recognises the difficulties which
> Helen has faced over a number of years. The Church of
> Scotland has offered Helen continuing support and help
> of a spiritual and pastoral nature to enable her to
> address these difficulties. She has accepted the Church's
> offer and has offered to demit status to seek appropriate
> counselling. Presbytery remits the matter to the Board of
> Ministry to provide appropriate support. Presbytery
> reaffirms that she may seek restoration of her status by
> application to the General Assembly." '

He's obviously given it considerable previous thought. It sounds fluent, rehearsed. I am wracked with tears by the time he's finished reeling off his spiel.

Chalmers makes approving noises. He can't speak for National Mission, but he imagines the offer of six months' stipend, or salary, will stand. I'll have to be out of the house in twelve weeks.

I blubber that only three months' stipend had ever been offered.

Everything that gave me any sense of security is slipping away like shingle under the tide. I hate crying in front of them. I try to control my trembling facial muscles but the corners of my mouth turn down like an ugly fish.

The mediator suggests a break. Chalmers and Rooney exit. I struggle to regain my equilibrium.

'Well, what do you say?' coaxes the mediator. 'The Presbytery Clerk's statement is a good one. He's come a long way. He's being very reasonable. . .' He cajoles me for twenty minutes.

I still haven't stopped sobbing when he calls the others back into the room.

The mediator is a good man, I'm told. He's given up his Sunday afternoon to resolving this. I want to please him and I cannot think for myself.

I am distraught.

I nod my head in assent to their will.

Half-past four. It's taken little more than an hour for my spirit to be broken.

They finalise the niceties of Rooney's statement. Rooney wants to include that I'd been pregnant and had an abortion. I protest that that is unnecessarily cruel.

It is after five by the time they've typed it up in the back office. My life is over. Fourteen years of training, hope and service destroyed.

But at least Chalmers makes it in time to hear his son singing in the choir.

The only concession the Church has made is that I don't have to say I am guilty. They've been pressuring me to demit status since June – but they've kept saying I had to do so together with an admission of guilt. I've refused to give them that admission.

Now, all the evidence against me having been leaked to the press, and a fair trial being out of the question, they are releasing me, 'to seek counselling'. They wouldn't allow that at the beginning, when I asked. Rooney's statement makes the Church appear so generous, so compassionate, with its 'continuing support and help of a spiritual and pastoral nature.' But that support and spiritual help never is to materialise. This afternoon, the Church will have washed its hands of me.

The mediator insists that a solicitor be involved in the transmission of Rooney's statement. I no longer have a solicitor. Rooney says Barbara Lovegrove will oblige. He knows her through some business club in Kirriemuir, her office being next door to his church. I don't want to involve Barbara. I've let her down by giving in. But the mediator says he'll contact her. He claims this is to 'protect' me.

Monday 1st December 1997

I have spent the night crying in the shed, with my head against Grace Pig's flank. I am so miserable and cold and exhausted that I don't contact any of my friends to say what has happened. Dennis has asked me to go over for my tea but I don't feel fit to drive.

At about three o'clock I telephone Barbara's office. She will already have heard from the mediator. Hearing her voice on the line I burst into tears and cannot speak. 'Stay where you are. I'll come as soon as I've finished at the office,' she says.

She brings Dennis with her and a copy of Rooney's statement. Dennis doesn't think I've been right to agree to it. Neither does Steven Mackie, nor John Forbes, when they are told of it. But I'm not to be given time to reconsider. The Presbytery Business Committee meets tonight.

Tuesday 2nd December 1997

Barbara is contacted by the Business Committee, just hours before Presbytery is to meet. They are proposing to omit from the press release, 'In this relationship there was a single sexual encounter without her consent.' I am adamant it should remain, to put an end to the silly headlines. Without this crucial sentence the press will latch onto the 'emotional relationship which moved outwith her control and influence' – wording that is unhelpful, untrue, and open to misinterpretation.

What happens? Presbytery meets and Rev Peter Youngson and Rev Allan Webster move that the crucial sentence not be released. They are opposed by Dennis and John Forbes, but the motion is carried by thirty votes to twenty. Rooney telephones me from the Presbytery Office, while the meeting is still in progress. I am dismayed. 'There's nothing you can do, Pet,' he says. 'You can kick the sofa but the vote's been taken. The Presbytery didn't think it'd do you any favours to mention the word "sex". You can't alter it now, Pet.'

I don't know whether to laugh or spit. My name and 'sex' have been linked together on the front page of every newspaper in the entire country. Presbytery had the chance to lend a sense of proportion and has voted not to do so.

Chalmers and the advocate/mediator both agree the Presbytery 'sold me short' and are displeased with Rooney. Chalmers does do his best to rectify the broken treaty, by contacting the Church Press Office with a correction. Most newspapers, however, have already received the abridged version of the agreed statement. It is after eleven at night, and they are going to print.

Wednesday 3rd December 1997

The result is unmitigated disaster. The *Telegraph* and Ceefax describe a relationship having 'spiralled out of control'. BBC and ITN News run away with Rooney's 'outwith her control and influence' and, as it is unqualified by 'a single sexual encounter without her consent', they make out I've been having rampant sex day and night!

'Didn't I tell you this would happen?' Dennis accuses Rooney. Rooney pouts.

Not even in this last act can Angus Presbytery do right by me.

Rooney maintains that the removal of my income, my home and my honour, is 'not a punishment'. Dennis requests that I be given time to consider my rash resignation, but the majority of the presbyters are opposed to extending this 'courtesy' to me. Finlay Macdonald, the Principal Clerk, advises that under new legislation it is unnecessary.

Thus it is that, forty-eight hours from my resignation having been engineered, my name has been deleted from the register.

Rev Peter Douglas rings me in the afternoon. I tell him ruefully, 'I made the wrong decision, giving in.'

'They wouldn't have given you a fair trial: only a public execution.'

PART III
SENTENCE

Expediency

December 1997

Every day I rue the fact that I resigned. The night the Presbytery refused to accept my confession, I had expected the Trial to be over. In stead I faced another six months of male colleagues prying into my life, threatening letters, and the salacious interest of the press: unless I agreed to go. My spirit was at its lowest ebb when they prevailed on me to quit. Nevertheless I shouldn't have allowed them to take away my ministerial status and with it everything that mattered to me. I was given no time to think. I was tricked into it.

I've been powerless to say either 'yes' or 'no' ever since the initial abuse of authority over me as a child. The effect of that original disempowerment is that, whenever confronted by people who enjoy their power, I revert to the five-year-old who wet herself with fright when Santa Claus defied her to blow his cover.

Sandy exploited my vulnerability, but he realised subsequently that I had been psychologically incapable of saying what I did or didn't want, and he regretted his actions. The Church agents had no such compunction. The extensive media coverage was an embarrassment to them. My departure became a matter of expedience. They procured it by stealth.

Within weeks, I am well enough to face trial and I beg to be accorded that dignity, even though I have resigned. I write to the Principal Clerk and I write to the Presbytery Clerk. They will not allow it. They are afraid I'll be found innocent and that will reflect on their handling of the matter.

I learn afterwards that one well-respected Angus minister wrote to the Clerks saying he 'regretted that the Presbytery sought to defend its good name rather than pursue justice.' Another expressed his opinion that the Presbytery had acted 'precipitously, insensitively, and discourteously.' A third that the Presbytery was 'entirely lacking in compassion'. Their voices went unheeded.

Dennis is ever faithful, as is Rev John Forbes (though he is forty miles away and about to retire). Once it is all over I have a telephone call from the Rev Laurence Whitley and an invitation to his manse at Montrose. I accept gratefully. Laurence is enough his own man not to need the approval of the 'boys'. He has certain perspectives on Angus Presbytery and its petty politics.

Nobody else makes contact. I had hoped that after I'd removed myself from the protracted trial process my colleagues would be free to speak to me and there'd be an end to the terrible sense of isolation and loneliness.

Now that it is done and dusted, Angus Presbytery has been invited to look at the legislation and make 'helpful comments' to the Board of Practice and Procedure.

Presbytery's comments, when its critical review is complete, amount to back-patting and self-congratulation. Two suggestions are offered by Angus Presbytery for the edification of less experienced presbyteries, should such a situation arise again: firstly, enquiries from newspapers should be handled by the Church Press

Office in Edinburgh (they say this is to ease the enormous pressure on the poor Presbytery Clerks!). Secondly, they should stick to the 'letter' of the law rather than its 'spirit'. The irony of this would be funny if it did not make me so angry.

It is Dennis who reads me this extraordinary brief report in the Presbytery Minutes. He expresses a mixture of amusement and bitterness. 'And has anyone from the Board of Practice and Procedure asked how *you* experienced the process, Love? Have they? Of course not! These are lily-livered men, Love: lily-livered, I tell you! I've asked Brian of Aberlemno why he won't visit you, I have: I've told him, the girl's desperate. And all he says is "Ah, well, Dennis, it's difficult." Difficult? What's difficult about it? I see her! I'm holding a torch for that girl, I tell them all.'

Dear, dear Dennis. If it was not for him, could I live through this time?

I burned my boats. They say I surrendered all my rights the moment Presbytery accepted my demission. My only option is to stand before the General Assembly and ask for my status to be returned 'at some point in the future'. The further into the future, I am advised, the better my chances. It seems so very unfair, since I have been found guilty of no wrong.

I cannot 'dissent and complain' about any of the actions of the Presbytery of Angus, because 'associate' ministers cease to be members of a presbytery if they are suspended. Neither can I appeal to the Judicial Commission, because I haven't been 'at the bar'. I am stymied. Predictably, the Principal Clerk refuses to advise me.

One of the most senior ministers in the Kirk writes to the *Scotsman* claiming that 'of course' the Church of Scotland has left me a right of appeal and that a young woman in my position would 'certainly not' be expected to endure the rigours of the Assembly. The Judicial Commission, he declares, is made up of churchmen and legal persons of the utmost integrity. But he is entirely misinformed of the facts.

The next day, his comments are refuted, accurately and succinctly, by a Dundee minister, Alan MacKay, and by a lawyer, Maggie Morton. Both are unknown to me. Maggie is about to take up a seat on the Judicial Commission and she knows the true limit of my rights.

Rev Robert Ramsay is also elected onto the Judicial Commission this year. . . a reward for his jurisprudence and fairmindedness, no doubt.

After the Presbytery has accepted my demission of status, the National Mission Boss telephones, informing me that my demission has 'certain implications' for my employment with his department. He means I'll receive my P45. My salary, pension contributions, and other allowances will all come to an end. And I'll have to find somewhere else to live. The National Mission Boss does make an arrangement to meet me at a Perth hotel, to carry out the necessary transactions over a pleasant lunch. When the day arrives I call off sick. I cannot face his cheerfulness. I am perpetually in tears.

The National Mission Boss asks if there is anything his department can do for me.

'Could you find me another job?' I plead. 'Anything. Office-cleaning. I need to feel I have a use.'

'Oh! I didn't expect you to ask that. . . I'll have to think.'

He never comes up with anything.

The humiliation of being unemployed affects me deeply. I'd gladly perform a menial task, just to have a sense of purpose and a role.

I lose contact with a number of friends because I cannot afford gifts, petrol or telephone calls to keep in touch.

Unemployment is a socially isolating experience. After some time I treat myself to the bus fare to Orkney. One of my friends there is the minister of Kirkwall East. He doesn't know how thankful I am that he insists on taking me for a meal and to the flicks, refusing to let me pay my share.

My life-style was always simple. I never did buy new clothes. I don't have a television and keep only one room warm in winter, so my daily living expenses have changed little. Monetary hardship isn't the worst aspect of being on the dole: it is loss of self-worth. Before, I had a part to play in the community. I married the young and buried the dead. I am of no use to society any more. Now I have to attend funeral services for people for whose souls I tended, whom the stand-in minister scarcely knows, frustrated by the impersonal service when I could have given a true last honouring of the dead, with greater sincerity. I would not have used words that were empty of meaning. I would have believed in the hope I offered. Most of these ministers speak of 'Resurrection' and 'the Peace of God which passeth all understanding' as if they are reciting their breakfast menu.

I sink lower into depression as time goes on. Rather than coming to terms with loss, I bend under the enormity of it.

Several more times I write to the National Mission Boss asking if I can be found work elsewhere. National Mission doesn't employ only ministers, but also lay and field staff. There is a desperate shortage of prison chaplains: surely they don't fear I'll corrupt criminals? The answer comes back that only ordained ministers may serve as prison chaplains. I point out that I *am* still ordained, that Noranside is an open establishment where there is no need for me to carry out sacramental functions and that other prisons have unordained chaplains. They say that doesn't count. I've carried out the work for several years, winning the respect of staff and inmates alike, but that means not a jot. Nothing I have done has any value. The whole of my ministry has been negated.

It's surprising whence inspiration comes. The Anstices live in the vast former manse in Lintrathen. Shortly after my demission, they ask me for a meal. Little do I think that a man of such wealth and standing as Michael Anstice will be able to identify with my sense of hopelessness. A few years ago he was a senior figure in a big company with outlets abroad, but I didn't know he had been made redundant. For him, too, change in financial circumstances was not as devastating as loss of sense of purpose. Mr Anstice turned to restoring old bathtubs. If he could pick himself up, so can I.

The Anstices are members of an Episcopal congregation in the local town. All my life I've gone to church on Sundays, but now the sense of shame prevents me. The Anstices are offering to take me with them. I can hardly believe that they are unashamed to walk in the door with me.

I do go with them for some months; until the Sunday we hear a sermon on the Red Dragon of Revelation, waiting to gobble up a baby as soon as it's born from its mother. I cannot return after that.

Their Rector is a help to me, despite his grotesque sermon. He shares with me a similar experience with the press when he left the Catholic priesthood in order to marry.

Some of my friends cease to 'phone or invite me out and it hurts. On the other hand, there are those I expect to be cold and judgmental, who turn out not to be that way at all.

I enrol for Scottish dance classes in Kilry hall. It'll always be hard to walk into a room full of people who will have read those tabloid newspapers. For the rest of my life those scabby headlines will haunt me. I steel myself to enter. Just inside the hall door stands one of the forbidding farm wives – and she puts an arm round me: 'Great to see you, lass!' This is not the accolade I expected and feared.

Local farmer George Pattullo is over-wintering cattle in sheds at Mid Derry. I help him shift his stirks along the road one day. He looks in at The Faulds afterwards, for beans on toast. He's never been inside my house before. It is at a time when all Scotland believes men cross Helen Percy's doorstep for one thing alone, and that is not to eat toast! I don't know if George is very hungry, or if he simply has a kind heart. He sits at my table with his vehicle outside for the world to take note and dares them to gossip.

George's father dies at the lambing time the following Spring, on a foul night when they've twenty-six wet lambs drying in their small kitchen. Even by then, I still assume the older folk in the parishes will be scandalised by what has been in the press about their little minister and they'll spurn me like the Devil. They are not like that though, most of them. I go to see the widowed Mrs Pattullo, who presses me to stop for tea and is the same with me as she's always been.

Many is the time I come home of an evening and cry because someone has spoken a soft word, the fish-van man has given me a herring without charge, or because the milkman collected my empty bottles and left a huge bunch of his home-grown chrysanthemums one day. It is kindness, rather than cruelty, that moves me to tears.

The library-van-man cheers me up. Not that I can concentrate to read. He stops at my gate anyway, to see how I am coping. He has an uncanny knack of arriving just when for some reason I am in despair. More than once I go out to the gate and burst into tears. He'll take a mug of tea until I've calmed down. Here is another courageous man, prepared to risk his reputation in the house of Magdalene. Invariably he'll share his loot – tablet or shortie – gifted by a particular book-borrower further up the hill. She is a church-going lady with a viper's tongue, upright as a telegraph pole in her tweed skirt and decency, and never more venomous than when she speaks of me. What apoplexy the old girl would have if she knew I was being plied with her shortbread!

A woman I don't know telephones from Arbroath. She says she was a presbytery elder at the service when I was first introduced to the six parishes. It struck her then how young and how vulnerable I seemed, and she'd wondered how I'd withstand whatever lay ahead of me. She hadn't predicted quite such a cruel baptism!

Christmas is more difficult than usual. Rev John Forbes sends me a voucher to spend in the supermarket. On another occasion he leaves cheese and some fruit in my porch. More tears.

On Christmas Eve I go to collect pig meal from my feed merchant. The sight of Alan in the shed doorway, broad shoulders, number one hair-cut, wielding a shovel, is sufficient to strike terror into the heart of men. The inside of Alan is fluff. Sometimes we do not speak for months, but he is there when I need him. He is one of those who kept me sane by 'phoning during the press siege in Sutherland. His office is ankle-deep in mouse-dirt. Atop a pile of boars' performance records, bills, and hygiene certificates sits an ancient sandwich, a syringe of wormer and a carton of sour milk. What air is in the room is, incongruously, filled with Mahler's symphonies on his CD player. Reeking of pigs and uttering profanities, Alan confesses he cried when he read the *Scotland on Sunday* newspaper article about the snowdrops I planted for Heather. He asks if I've ever wanted a baby. . . Yes? For how long have I wanted one?

I count up the days of my grief in my head and whisper, 'One year, forty-nine weeks and five days.'

Between Christmas and Hogmanay I receive a recorded delivery missive from the Church. I have ninety days to get out of the cottage.

Salvation of Souls?

'I am not the face the Kirk wishes to show to the modern world. The most plausible way of dealing with me, then, is to find me insane.

'Letters have been flying between the Presbytery, and 121 George St; the phone lines have been buzzing with conversations, faxes, emails, all with the problem of Gideon Mack as their theme. I imagine a file somewhere in the depths of 121. . . the file becoming a drawer in a cabinet, the cabinet being moved to a bigger room. . . the Kirk's officials droning like worker bees as they construct a model of my madness. . .'

James Robertson: *The Testament of Gideon Mack*

January 1998

The Presbytery has 'remitted' to the Board of Ministry my 'continuing care of a pastoral and spiritual nature'. 'Remit' is a good Kirk word, in this case meaning, loosely, 'Pass the buck and forget it'. The Presbytery can now ignore me without a twinge of guilt.

The one and only occasion on which the Board of Ministry

gives me a dose of the promised 'pastoral care' is in the second week of January. The Board is personified by Chalmers. He arranges to meet me, with the mediator, at a busy café off the High Street in Edinburgh at lunch-time. We sit at the cramped table in front of the service counter. People are carrying trays and tripping over the legs of chairs. I am embarrassed because I cannot stem my tears and my distress is witnessed. Could they not have taken me somewhere more private?

A few weeks later I am due for my second dose of 'care' in the same crowded Edinburgh High Street café. I have been travelling on stuffy buses since early morning and decide to walk in to the city centre from the south side. An organisation, *Women Onto Work,* has opened an office in Causewayside. Attracted by its promise, I enter.

The young woman apologises, but the service is only for the benefit of ethnic minorities. Seeing the disappointment in my face, she says I may use the small careers and resource library in the back room. I thank her but start to cry. I blurt out that I was sexually abused and lost my job because my employers tried to make out it was my fault. They've pilloried me in the national media and my confidence is so shattered that it is impossible to find another job. And I've only a few weeks to find somewhere else to live. She gives me tea and a list of addresses connected with tenants' rights and housing and of an organisation for survivors of rape. Mine is not a story new to her, though the media exposure is unusual.

In the event, Chalmers doesn't show up to give me any 'care'. He has a more pressing engagement.

To my mind, a crowded café and a fixed appointment is not a natural context for 'pastoral care' – but Chalmers didn't turn up anyway and neither he nor anyone else from the Board of Ministry is ever to offer another time or venue. On a number of occasions Chalmers comes up from Edinburgh and holds forth at meetings in Kilry. Never once does he tread the few hundred yards to my lighted cottage and enquire after my health.

A succession of locum ministers in the parishes visit the Nicoll family to offer pastoral support, but none comes near me. I have a contagious disease. Christ's Church will not toss a crust to a leper.

I go into the lawyers' office in Blairgowrie – the one with a 'Legal Aid' sign outside – to ask if I have any rights as far as my tenancy is concerned. I've offered to pay rent but the temporary minister from Angus Presbytery who is looking after my parishes withheld this information from the office-bearers. Consequently I've been served notice. Members of my congregations protest: if I need counselling and care, the least the Church can do is afford me the security of a roof over my head. They are ignored. The lawyer says I could buy myself time by squatting until the bailiffs pull my furniture out in the road, but I have no rights. 'You do have grounds for claiming unfair dismissal, though.' he adds. 'You could take the Church to an industrial tribunal.'

Such action hadn't occurred to me, but the lawyer tells me an appeal to the tribunal has to be lodged within twelve weeks of losing my job, so I don't have long to make up my mind.

First Chalmers and then the mediator spend forty minutes apiece on the telephone attempting to dissuade me from taking the Church to a civil tribunal. The mediator says Jesus wouldn't like it. (We should remember that Jesus *never* resisted authority or spoke out against injustice! He didn't? Perhaps I was reading a different version of the Bible.) If I 'make a fuss', Chalmers warns, it will make it much more difficult for the Church to re-instate me in the future. Chalmers is correct in this prediction – and he will turn out to be the instrument of its fulfilment.

There are strong echoes of parental voices telling me that family loyalty is the unequivocal meaning of the Fifth Commandment. I am forbidden to tell anyone outside what horrors happen within our house.

But I am no longer ten years old. I am growing up. This time,

I am not going to be bullied into acquiescence. This time, I am intractable. If I were to keep my mouth shut about the injustice and promise to 'be a good girl in future' I should, implicitly, be admitting past culpability.

They want to palm me off by sending me to a counsellor. They would even pay one to say I am crazy, but the one I have heard is the best psychiatrist and psychotherapist in Scotland sees patients only on the National Health Service, so they don't need to shell out for her fee. Dr Treliving agrees to see me for an extended assessment period, at the end of which she informs the Church that she sees no reason why I should not continue to work as a minister. She's seen a number of male clergy who were far more 'screwed up' than I am (her words, not mine), who remained in office. This is not what the Church wants to hear, so they ask for a second opinion! For six months I am sent to an astute, no-nonsense psychoanalyst, who reaches the same conclusion as Dr Treliving. Her personal advice to me is that I should shake the dust off my feet: 'Why on earth would you want to go back?' she says. 'They will only heap more shit on you from on high!'

I've been forced to repeat the most intimate details of my life in front of team after team of strange churchmen. I cannot heal until this hurt is acknowledged. I need someone representative of the institution that has perpetrated this injustice to watch my tears.

Steven Mackie writes to the Moderator of the General Assembly asking him to give the time to see me. He refuses. It would be 'inappropriate in view of her approach to the Industrial Tribunal,' he excuses. Besides, he understands I am 'already receiving plenty of pastoral care'. I wonder who could have given him that impression?

Likewise, the ensuing two Moderators decline. Then we stop asking.

To rub salt into the wound, Sandy Nicoll's friends tell me that the outgoing Moderator, the Right Reverend James Simpson, has written a pastoral letter to Sandy. The Moderator has offered Sandy a listening ear, any time Sandy feels he needs it. I am *persona non grata*.

The press continually paints Sandy Nicoll as a 'broken man' who's been left with nothing. In fact the attitude towards Sandy from fellow males tends to be, 'The young Lady Minister? Wow, what a conquest!' Sandy Nicoll has not been stripped of his office as an elder of the Church of Scotland. If he turned up on Communion Sunday he'd be given his place at the Lord's Table. Indeed, I'm told that his Long Service Certificate, signed by the Moderator, hangs on his sitting room wall.

Eventually an 'interim' minister comes to the parishes. I've been acquainted with Leslie Barrett at university. He'd just started when I qualified. I write him a note saying I am sure he'll find people kind, as I have done. I want him to know I've no intention of interfering in his task. I've moved to a far-flung corner of the parish and never darken the church door except for occasional funerals, but Leslie would be welcome to drop in if he found himself this far up the glen. Not one of my former colleagues has ever done so. Dennis and John Forbes have both retired out of the district. I'm not surprised that Leslie never responds to my note, but I am desperately hurt when I'm told by a third party that he's actually been instructed by the Church to have nothing to do with me. I had not realised that the ostracism I am experiencing is official policy.

The new minister is being housed in Mary Nicoll's bungalow, and the Kirk is paying rent to the Nicoll family. So much for neutrality and so much for the business of the Church being the salvation of souls.

The Excommunication Party

"Wherefore the Presbytery of Aller, in the name of the
Lord Jesus Christ, the sole King and Head of the Church,
and by the power committed by Him to them, did, and
hereby do, summarily excommunicate David Sempill. . .
delivering him over to Satan. . . and hereby do enjoin all
the faithful to shun all dealings with him as they would
not be found to harden him in his sins, and so to partake
with him in his judgements."

John Buchan: *Witch Wood*

February 1998
I can't shake off Chief Inquisitor Caskie's words, 'If you confess
your guilt the Church will deal with you quietly and you'll still be
able to go to Communion.' I have admitted nothing. I must
therefore be debarred from the Sacrament. I could not have
predicted how painful I should find this exclusion. Deprived of
Grace, I hunger for it.

I don't know whether the veto extends beyond the Church of
Scotland. I am desperate to regain a sense of belonging to a worshipping community. I try attending the Episcopal Church in the town.

In this church, even young children are invited to receive the Bread and Wine. I watch children go forward and kneel at the altar rail, while I remain in my pew. It feels right that they should be welcomed at Communion. By contrast, however, I feel so rejected that I am in floods of tears.

It is hard to walk into any public place, let alone a church. I am aware, acutely, of condemnation, gossip, and shame.

I do go to Mass in the local Roman Catholic Church. The priest knows my whole story, yet he is prepared to offer me the Bread of Life that the Church of Scotland withholds.

Strictly, he should not give it to me as a non-Catholic. In his book, pastoral need takes precedence over ecclesiastical law.

The Roman Catholic Chapel is full of young families and there is a sense of the significance of the Eucharist; of something important happening, however intangible. I always cry when I receive the host, poignantly aware of being disgraced within my own Church.

There is need for a rite of passage. One day I was the minister of six parishes and the next I wasn't. I've been found guilty of no offence and yet I was summarily dismissed.

There was a whip-round and a tea-party for Robert Ramsay when he left. Only awkward silence surrounds my departure. It is as if I never existed.

The parting, the mourning process, demands some recognition of the past.

Had my open letter to my parishioners been read out, back in June when the allegations were made, that would have brought healing. I feel I've let them down in some way and have been denied any opportunity even to say I am sorry. Nothing is tied off. Without a proper burial, grief remains raw.

So I arrange my own wake. I book the village hall at Kilry for an Excommunication Party: the World's first!

The creation of the invitations is my cleansing ritual. I cut the

Statement of Sinful Conduct into strips and run it around the edges of a sheet of paper. Then I butcher various newspaper articles and stick the headlines sideways and upside down all over the page, together with details of the event: I'll provide drink and chocolate cake. Guests are asked to bring savouries, a shovel in case of snowfall and sleeping bags if they want to kip on my floor.

My Pythonesque sense of humour, my ability to mock myself in the face of tragedy, is not an indication of insanity. Rather, it is my preservation from it.

The party is a kind of coat of many colours disguising the pea-green dress I wear beneath it. One friend flies from Germany. We inflate balloons and hang streamers.

About two hundred people turn up at my Excommunication Party. Parishioners bring children and grandchildren who've been in my Sunday schools. Youngsters and adults alike, we play silly games and laugh. Hands tied behind our backs, we try to eat Smarties from bowls of flour. Then we tie strings around our waists from which teaspoons are dangled and, still hands-free, wriggle around trying to deposit the spoons into milk-bottles that are placed on the floor behind us. Sir James Farquharson, the oldest guest at ninety-two, keeps the stopwatch. Later the band arrives with fiddles, drums and whistles. The dancing is wild and merry. A couple of people take the stage and recite poems. Young Linda has brought her bagpipes. Little Mary from Glenisla performs a jig.

I've always said that if I invited all my friends to one party they'd be a strange social mixture; and so it is: the prison Governor and several former inmates, retired Army officers and school cleaners, owners of rich Edinburgh apartments and tenants from run-down housing schemes, Indians and Greeks, Fifers and Borderers. The couple who hid me from the paparazzi in Sutherland are prevented from coming by bad weather, but former parishioners from Paisley carry in a determined supporter, who's recently had his leg amputated.

No-one becomes drunk. Two usually quiet women become a little pink-cheeked and vociferous, to the embarrassment of the local hedge-cutter, whose good looks they are praising. There is plenty of merriment, but no-one is raucous.

About two in the morning we join hands for Auld Lang Syne. Everyone stays to sweep floors and collect rubbish. There is to be a Sunday service and neighbours warn me there'll be one or two church-goers looking to criticise if so much as one sweetie paper is in evidence.

Fifteen people are staying in my cottage tonight and so I give up my bed. I wrap myself in a downie and sleep in the kitchen, and am woken at seven-thirty by the lads from Paisley, who've brought ferrets to go rabbiting. I make up rolls and Lorne sausage for breakfast for them and for those of the sleepy-heads who surface.

There were a few ministers there last night. One of them telephones me and remarks, 'The Church is always bleating about having no young folk. There were hordes of youngsters at your party last night. It's potty. In rejecting you, the Church has turned its back on them.'

The papers report that the 'worshipping community' of Kilry clambered over 'piles of empty beer cans strewing the church steps' on the Sunday morning following Helen Percy's party. My elders snort when they read this. They've no recollection of it having been a drunken orgy or anything like it. Not so much as a ring-pull from a coke-can had been left. Obviously there is still one enemy in the camp, who delights in making a little pocket money selling lies to the ever-hungry press.

Monday is remarkably warm for February. My neighbours and I take mops and scrubbing brushes and wash the floors that have already been swept clean. Hazel is spitting mad about the news-papers: she attended the morning service yesterday and knows there was no trace of any litter, around the church or the hall or anywhere else.

Granny Vogan supplies buns and flasks of coffee and we sit outside the village hall in the unaccustomed sunshine. We don't even need our coats on today. Granny Vogan wasn't at the party. She'd been afraid her friend Mary Nicoll would find out if she went. She had prepared flowers and a basketful of food and sent them over to the hall before the party began though. It deeves her that her friend has been so vindictive towards me and towards her own son. The younger Mrs Nicoll's behaviour doesn't surprise her. She's often enough been cut to the quick by Moyra. But it's Mary she doesn't understand, nor the sudden alliance between the two Nicoll women. Moyra had always been so rude about her mother-in-law. Perhaps Mary was unaware of this, as the snide remarks weren't made to her face.

Granny Vogan once ventured to say to Mary, 'I'd speak to Helen if I saw her.'

'But you can't! You're *my* friend!' was Mary's retort. So we keep our frequent associations a secret. Only Hazel knows that I drove Granny Vogan to her granddaughter's graduation in St Andrews, or that Granny Vogan lent me her big jam pans and helped me make elderberry jelly. There is a special bond between those of us who live about the centre of the village, even though there is half a century's distance in age between Granny Vogan as the oldest, and me as the youngest. The link became stronger after the Easter tragedy with Hazel's daughter and my subsequent removal from the pulpit.

Loss of Innocence

DORA and her husband, Grumbling Jock, tenant a hill-farm above Kilry with over six hundred ewes and a hundred and twenty cows. They're members of the church but are usually too busy to attend on Sundays as they have no employees. Dora says they're 'hill-run' like the Scottish Blackface sheep, which dislike being brought down to the sheds. She is timid, tending towards agoraphobia, and seldom goes as far as the village store in Alyth without Jock. I feel honoured that, every now and then, she ventures as far as The Faulds to share a pot of tea and blether with me. I don't go to their farm often, but when I do Dora says I have an uncanny knack turning up just when everything's gone wrong and she needs to talk to someone. I could say the same about her. She is a generation older than I am, but there is a quiet understanding between us. Perhaps she leads a life I would have liked, up there with the company of sheep and clouds.

Dora is not well enough to come to my Excommunication Party. 'I didn't even bake for you,' she rues. 'The doctors say there's nothing wrong, but I'm being sick all the time. I can't eat.' Eventually Grumbling Jock takes her to a private doctor who admits her for tests. I go into the hospital to see her, but she has been taken away from the ward for an endoscopy. When I come home, the phone is ringing. 'They've told me I'm going to die. Please, will you tell Jock?' Then her voice breaks.

She survives just a few weeks.

I go to the farm each day at the crack of dawn to feed the sheep and, if the truth be known, to make sure Jock is still alive. Up that lonely track, he could easily not speak to another human being for weeks. Jock and I are both thankful to be busy. It's a relief to be on the hill in the mist, emptying bags of feed into the troughs. The soul-stirring cry of the curlew carries from the moor. It's harder to dwell on events up here. I am absorbed in the needs of the flock, listening for the bleat of a lost creature in the unfolding light.

Over all the plates of broth into which we stare without hunger, all the times I know he wants to die and he does not hide it from me, neither of us so much as puts a hand on the other's shoulder. A year later, the night before he flits to a smaller farm, I am leaving him amidst his boxes of belongings, having helped sort out Dora's clothes that he has put off sending to the charity shops all this while. As I turn at the gate I see him silhouetted against the light from the porch. His head suddenly drops into his hands and I go back to him as he breaks down. It is the only time I ever hug him.

Grumbling Jock is the decent, old-fashioned kind. The day of Will Pattullo's funeral we are working together in the fields beforehand, but I won't go along to the church with him. We go separately. I cannot bear for anyone to speak about Jock the way they speak about me. My reputation is tarnished and I don't want his to be by association.

I am furious, but unsurprised, when certain neighbours insinuate to newspaper reporters that I do more than just feeding sheep for Grumbling Jock. Jock says it doesn't matter that folk tittle-tattle:

he has a clear conscience and he's right glad of my help. 'Dora thought much of you and she was never been wrong about anybody's character.'

Jock's pain tears at me. We breathe deeply into our tea mugs and say little to one another. We have our respective griefs.

Two years after the allegations are made the hurt is no less. One afternoon, lifting lambs and clasping their legs so they cannot kick while Jock cuts their tails and puts rubber rings on their scrotums, I feel the breath of each lamb hot on my cheek. Tears are streaming down my face, mingling with the blood spurting from the docked tails. We continue working in silence but eventually Jock cannot ignore the state I'm in. He asks if one of the stronger lambs has belted me. I shake my head. A dozen animals on, I'm still crying into the lambs' necks.

'Are you gaein' tae tell me what's wrang wi' ye', lassie?'

'It's just that I've had enough of always feeling shamed,' I sob.

The whole experience with the Church has been one of loss of innocence: loss of the childlike belief that goodness outweighs wickedness.

1998

My erstwhile parishioners are incensed that their Petition to the Presbytery has not even received the courtesy of an acknowledgement. The Presbytery Clerks binned the official document, which was signed by over two hundred church members and one hundred and thirty-seven prisoners, without so much as listing it in the record of correspondence at the next meeting. It beggars belief that none of the ordinary presbytery members ever has the gumption to question what is being done in their name. They grant 'powers' to their elected leaders and nobody ever asks what the limit of those 'powers' should be. My parishioners tell me I should not have resigned and I know they are right.

'I've heard naebody speak ill of ye. Only the toffs that run the kirk roun' here,' says one farmer. 'They're half-boil't kind o'folk onyway. Ye affronted them because ye showed an interest in what ordinary folk were daein'. It was naethin' t' dae wi' all that rubbish in the papers. And, if y'd a face like the back o' a bus it wud never hae happened at a'.'

I don't think I could live if my neighbours ignored me or treated me any differently. Each time I knock on the door of someone I have not seen since all the publicity, I expect to be slighted. Almost without exception I am welcomed and offered tea. Those who do this for me, in St Andrews, Paisley and Edinburgh, will never know how much I am glad of the embrace of Christ I feel through them.

Kindness breaks me. I cry because the farm wife from Cammock shouts across the street that I must come for supper. I cry because my parishioners make a point of stopping at my cottage when they are carol-singing.

There are men who treat me with honour. There are many loyal friends. I have a collection of former landladies, parents of friends, and my godmother, who treat me like their own offspring.

A local lad who was at the mercy of the press during the folly of his youth comes to me to empathise. His father was a local minister. The day I learned that the Presbytery intended holding a Trial, he took me to the tumbling river at Killiecrankie. It was a magnificent mid-autumn afternoon. The bright burnished beeches tumbled gold coins down the steep banks into the water and the sky was azure. The glory of it contrasted with my despair and I craved rain to match my misery. Needless to say rumour (or a certain female elder in Kilry) is now making out I've been holding hands with the boy and have slept with him, for a fact!

In the village, Hazel and Granny Vogan are my life-line. Our little corner of the village has been marked by tragedy and it has brought us close to one another in a remarkable way. Now I understand the verse in the New Testament about 'the fellowship of Christ's sufferings'. I may be found stirring porridge at Hazel's stove at six in the morning, or she will call over the fence at tea-time, 'The tatties are on!' Likewise, on days when the dank mist creeps down Balduff Hill and seeps into our beings, I find solace in Granny Vogan's kitchen.

It's through Granny Vogan that I hear many of the wicked things that are being said – by the Nicolls, by one or two of the Kilry elders, and by the Reverend Robert Ramsay. Since Ramsay moved to Invergowrie he's been claiming I'm 'hanging around' his new parish, stalking his family, pulling faces at them through windows, and ghoulishly attempting to give them the heebie-jeebies. I've never been to Invergowrie in my life!

I spend less and less time away from the security of the cottage. I've been conceded twelve weeks to find somewhere else to live and the thought of being torn away from it is more than I can bear. Everything that held any meaning has gone. My ministry was not just a job, but a belief I lived out. My prisoners were my friends, and my parishioners' lives were integral to my own. I have no sense of purpose any more. I am holding on to the will to survive by a fragile thread. That thread is The Faulds, and it is about to be cut.

It is not possible to salvage the flotsam and rebuild the wrecked bark of self in twelve weeks. So many bits have floated away on the tide and I cannot nail together the few remaining fragments.

In the middle of March I hear from Church headquarters in Edinburgh that I am not to be thrown out of the cottage just yet. I have been granted a reprieve until the industrial tribunal has taken place. Nevertheless I expect Ramsay's henchmen to arrive to harangue me on 1st April – the date originally proposed for my exit. They don't appear. They are dirtier than that. It is the press they send.

The first I know of the *Daily Express* being on the prowl is through a warning call from the couple at the Old School House. The offending vehicle is making its way up the back road towards

The Faulds, stopping at each dwelling on the way to rake muck. At the first farm, the occupant is asked if I've ever set my cap at her husband. 'Oh, she's welcome to him!' she retorts, knowing full well that John is listening through the open kitchen window. At the next place the vulture is given an equally curt reply to the same impertinent question. My loyal neighbours, one after another, are incensed on my behalf. The subsequent front-page report, headed 'FOR GOD'S SAKE GO!' depicts a 'close-knit' rural community 'rocked' by the scandal involving their minister and campaigning for my eviction. The fact is that not one villager has said they want me out.

Burns, the female reporter to whom I do not answer the door, has won prizes for her journalism, apparently. The judges' criteria had nothing to do with accuracy or quality of research, obviously! Burns stays overnight at the Glenisla Hotel. Failing to extract any juicy gossip from the bar staff and without having set a watch on my house to substantiate her tale, she writes, 'Men queued at her door.'

Some people ask why I stay on in Kilry instead of running away to start a new life where nobody knows me. The answer is that I have nowhere to run; no family to shelter me. Besides, Scotland is a small country and rumour will be my precursor. I am better staying where everyone knows all there is to know and has made up his or her own mind whether or not to believe it.

I am angry that I was never given the opportunity through the Trial process to clear my name. There has been no reconciliation, no healing. I have been abandoned by the Church, hung out to dry like a discarded rag.

Since all the scandal-mongering, it is so hard to go out in public. I'm not 'me' any longer, but someone the press assassinated. People's view of me must always be coloured. They're thinking, 'She's the one who had sex with an elder.' I feel sullied. I'll be remembered all my life for a single incident, which was over in a few seconds, in the blinking of an eye and in the eclipse of my consciousness. Why the hell should anyone have the right to know? I wake up every morning feeling shamed. How do individuals whose lives have been destroyed by the press continue to exist in neigh-bourhoods where the trades-folk and shopkeepers have read all their darkest secrets?

In fact, local folk make it just possible to carry on living. 'Ah keep tellin' folk Ah ken that lassie awfy weel – aye, *awfy* weel – an' she's far bonnier than her photie in the *Courier*,' declares the dust-cart driver. The postman cuts out a rare kind comment from a newspaper. A couple I married bring me a huge lettuce, others leave a few tatties; a man whose wife I buried, a flowering plant.

My neighbours help me survive the shame. The man who rents the field opposite the church has nodded to me once or twice when feeding his ponies, but on the night of Airlie Dance I feel obliged to explain my unaccustomed frock and lipstick when I see him. 'There's jigging tonight,' I make conversation. 'I hate going in on my own but it'll be fine once I'm there.'

'Just you hold your head up high! Take no notice of them.' I didn't expect the horseman to perceive the anxiety behind my remark. 'The ones that speak about you have done far worse things than you've ever done. Aye, and I could name them too . . .You enjoy yourself, lass. Come and crack with me any time you like. Proud to have met you, so I am. . .'

Chic never elucidates about the people he could 'name' and I don't ask. He does, however, speak angrily when I tell him about one elder in the glen who seems intent on knocking me down in her car. 'Her? Run you over before she'll look the road you're on? Do you think she's never done anything bad? Because I could tell you otherwise. My, oh my! Folk have short memories!'

Chic observes one day, 'You back away when a man comes near you, don't you?' In fact I am not afraid of Chic any more than are his beloved ponies. The old man sometimes gives me 'a wee bit cuddle' in front of folk – just to wind them up and 'make them speak about us.' He does it for devilment. I never mind. I sense the difference between his harmless tomfoolery and other men's mixed intent. He's right; I loathe being touched usually. I curl in on myself, a hedgehog ball, fending off assault. My skin is so sensitised that the softest, repetitive, touch on my upper arm feels as if I'm being scoured with a wire brush. I am not sure if it is my mind or my body that hurts so much. I startle easily too, as do many survivors of sexual abuse. If someone comes up behind me suddenly, a strange loud sound emits from my throat. It's like a turkey gobbling. I don't know whence it comes and my own weird cry scares me as much as the person who has made me jump in the first place. I cannot repeat that noise if I try and I have never heard anyone else make it. It is the utterance of sheer terror.

Hazel's grandchildren are forever running up the road to ask me to play skipping, sleep in their tent in the garden, or race dogs in the hayfield. Their light-heartedness is infectious. Their great grandmother, auntie and cousins are over from Canada this summer. They treat me as part of their large family. At New Year we all go to Auntie Connie's at Auchenblae. Whenever I see Connie she hugs me to her bosom and tears well in her eyes as she recalls my troubles. I don't deserve the love of these people.

Hazel knows everything that goes on in the village, no matter what time of day or night and yet she never passes on gossip. She arrives at my door one evening to rebuke me, 'Next time you're away out for the day you must make your bed first!'

'But no-one sees, Hazel! Only sheep! My bedroom's at the back,' I object.

'*I* see! I went round the back and looked in the windows!'

I laugh and laugh. Only Hazel would admit she looks through people's windows to see if the beds are made. I don't mind. When Hazel sees my sheets on the washing line are all holes, she doesn't tittle-tattle in the district but does something practical about it:

she procures some good second-hand sheets that Granny MacKay is putting out.

At six o'clock one morning Hazel telephones. The housebound woman up on the hill, for whom she cares, has gastric 'flu and is too weak to sit up: 'Can you come?'

It is the first of many mornings when I wash and dress the sturdy soul because she is off her legs, or because Hazel herself is ill. It is an honour to do the most basic of tasks for the old woman and we develop a mutual respect. She is quite deaf and says little but she is grateful whether for a few gean twigs in a jar, a bunch of her favourite variety of daffies that she can no longer go out to pick for herself, or just being dried properly after washing so she doesn't develop sores. I admire her gracious acceptance of the help that enables her to carry on living at home with her dogs around her.

I doubt if Hazel would have asked for my assistance when I was a 'proper' minister of the Kirk. My fall from grace has brought me to where I always understood my ministry belonged – with my sleeves rolled up and my arms plunged into the muck of human suffering and sinfulness. People's perceptions of me have changed; for the better. They know I am one of them.

It would hardly have been possible to have suffered so much humiliation without becoming a better minister for Christ because of it. Yet even well-disposed members of the clergy do not understand this when I tell them about washing the old woman. 'Perhaps you should train as a nurse,' they enthuse. 'Maybe care of the elderly is your *real* vocation!' Clearly they think I was out of place in the ministry; that that was not my 'real' vocation. I say no more to them. I wipe bottoms *because I am a minister*, not because I should have been a nurse or a social worker. Ministry was a way of life and being. It was not something I did to earn a living or so that I could feel good about myself by serving others. It was a nagging, a gnawing, a pulling, a destiny. It was what I'd always known, deep down, I *had* to be, no matter what the cost. I am totally bereft now the Church has taken this away from me.

Someone asks me what was the hardest loss of the many – of my home, my baby, my livelihood, my youthfulness, my dignity – I start to weep. The loss of my ministry was the loss of my reason for being. It was the loss of my self.

A few ministers understand – mostly those of an older generation. My former university lecturer Rev Steven Mackie, and Annebeth, are unremitting in their support. Steven writes to tell me that this is 'not just because of the injustice you have suffered, nor even because of the affection we bear you, but also because of your undoubted pastoral gifts and evident calling to the Christian ministry'.

Rev Bill Crombie sends me a cheque for the fee required by the Readmissions Committee. Rev Phil Petty, aged, virtually blind, climbs aboard a train to meet me in Dundee. It's funny, but when I first knew Phil I was afraid of him. He is enormous of stature, but as lacking in ferocity as a fieldmouse.

Gastric 'flu strikes me in September, not long before the industrial tribunal. Hazel comes and takes Gigha out for me and feeds the hens: I daren't risk being that far from the loo.

I crave fizzy lemonade. Granny Vogan sends some up for me. When I am better I take her a silly picture of someone with a wild hairdo: Granny Vogan is always laughing about her 'Bad Hair Days'. I am upset because a villager cold-shouldered me today. 'That's why you must go from here, Love. Not very far away, so we can still visit you, but you need to go,' Granny Vogan soothes.

The next morning Hazel comes running to my door in a great to-do. 'Mrs Vogan's DEAD! At least, I *think* she's dead. Come quickly!' I run down to Granny Vogan's, through the back door and upstairs to her bedroom. There is no doubt. It is difficult to believe that someone so full of warmth can feel so cold. She is half-dressed. It must have been mercifully sudden but that does not lessen the shock for Hazel and me.

I offer to help the undertaker lay out the shell of a woman whose goodness touched me. Our corner in Kilry will not be the same again. It has lost part of its heart.

Granny Vogan's daughter Genny comes up from Dorset with her family to make arrangements for the funeral and the clearing of the house. Genny is wonderful to us all. She has lost her mother but she thinks of everyone except herself. Two of Granny Vogan's friends from England stay in my cottage and Genny cooks us all a meal – in between seeing lawyers, collecting cremation papers, and deciding what to do with her mother's belongings.

The minister from Alyth takes the funeral. Genny realises how difficult it is for me to go into the Kirk alongside the Nicolls and others who've slandered me and sit beneath a man in my own pulpit. She asks me to say prayers at the scattering of her mother's ashes. I feel privileged beyond imagining. We climb Balduff Hill on their final morning in Kilry and let the wind carry the last remains across the heather-clad slopes.

Genny dies less than a year later, leaving a legacy to me from her and her mother and a letter stating that they believed me to have been treated unjustly. I weep.

It is eighteen months after Granny Vogan's funeral that Hazel finds the old woman from up on the hill dead. She passed away in her sleep, just as she wished. I saw her yesterday. She was bright and cheerful.

I buried one of her sons, in tragic circumstances, when I was the 'real' minister in the parish. The family are not church-goers and so Ramsay had permitted me to perform the obsequies. I knew many non-church parishioners better than he did. Now the remaining sons want me to commit their mother's body in the burial ground at Lintrathen, alongside their father and brothers. I've washed her and dressed her. This is the last honour I can perform.

The woman has written in her Will that she doesn't want a

church service but just a simple graveside ceremony. The interim minister in the parish – Leslie Barrett, the one who trained with me but was instructed not to speak to me – is informed by the woman's sons, out of courtesy, of their mother's wish to have me preside. As the burial ground is the property of the Council he cannot refuse permission. I do not expect, however, that he will be present. He doesn't know the family and the ceremony is to be brief. I imagine he will leave me to do my job.

The morning dawns, sunny and windless. Many of my former parishioners gather at the gate of the burial ground and I am talking with them. The undertaker comes across and I am completely taken aback when he says, 'The Minister is here. They're just going into the church.'

'But that isn't what she wanted!'

'No, but the Minister has arranged for everyone to go inside first.'

The Minister is standing at the church entrance, waiting for me. 'Ah, Good morning,' he greets me in public school tones. 'I'll start the service and recite the 23rd Psalm and lead the congregation in the Lord's Prayer. Then we'll go outside. Perhaps you would do the Committal?' I thought that was what I'd been asked to do by the relatives but I've never been good at making sarcastic remarks. I acquiesce, like the five year-old I still so easily become in the face of control-freaks.

He asks if I'll join him in the vestry (my vestry) or sit in a pew. At least I have the wit to choose the first option. He would have been more comfortable if I'd stayed as a meek sheep mingled in with the crowd. I sit in the vestry with my head lowered until Leslie announces authoritatively, 'That's the congregation seated.'

Leslie processes in. I am knocked back a subservient five paces behind him, just like the times I shared services with Ramsay. Already tense, it being the first public service I have taken in my former parishes since the allegations, this unexpected situation throws

283

me. But the pettiness of his ploy does not escape the congregation.

My nervousness shows, but my ex-parishioners are encouraging. Mrs Anstice takes my arm at the tea afterwards saying, 'I wasn't the only one who thought you should be back in that pulpit.' I feel a bit better.

Relationships change and deepen. My most senior elder used to make me feel uncomfortable when he put an arm around me in greeting. He is eighty and a prayerful man, but somehow he used to unnerve me. Now when I go to see him I sense that his affection is genuine and unclouded by any of the condemnation I might have expected from a churchman of his generation. It is as if he sees my requirement of Christ's compassion and forgiveness and recognises his own broken humanity reflected in mine.

I begin to see what lies inside people as they open themselves to me in a way they have not always done. A woman I sometimes found bitter and prickly learns to trust me with the secret of her barrenness. Miniature miracles of transformation begin to occur in folk because we share an awareness of our vulnerability.

I am no longer officially their minister but my former parishioners now react to me as the kind of pastor I always aspired to be. They understand what I always tried to tell them of my own need of the Cross. I never preached morality, never set myself up as an example, but expectations that the Minister should be aloof from ordinary folk formerly hindered me from reaching those folk. Exiled, I am a better priest.

The Industrial Tribunal

'Thou art the daftest fuill that ever I saw!
Trows thou, man, by the law to get remeid
Of men of kirk? No, nocht till thou be deid!'

Sir David Lindsay: *The Thrie Estaitis*

September 1998

It's not that my lawyers are pushing me to pursue legal action. They are never in any doubt of the justice of my cause, but they remind me of Dickens's tale of *Bleak House*. They think I'll win, eventually, but by the time that happens it could be a Pyrrhic victory.

I am not seeking any financial compensation. Not one penny. I only want recognition of my concerns about the justice of the procedures that were used against me. ACAS, the free arbitration service, contacts both parties. I am willing to withdraw my application. All I ask is for the church to negotiate a short press statement – and, this time, not to renege on it. It would cost them nothing! Not even a great deal of pride, since I'm not dictating the wording. The press is not going to be very interested anyway. It won't be worth the printing ink: no cash, no sex, no sleaze. It seems so little to ask of an organisation whose very mission is to offer

Christ's healing and reconciliation. But they will not have it. The Church lawyer, Jeanette Wilson, spurns the assistance of ACAS. Never, says my Advocate, has he encountered such arrogance – employers frequently pay out thousands to avoid the embarrassment and further cost of being shown up in court.

The Kirk can afford to be so entrenched because of a unique and extraordinary Act of Parliament – the 1921 'Church of Scotland' Act – that grants the Church of Scotland exclusive jurisdiction over 'matters spiritual'. No civil court has the right to intervene in questions of worship, doctrine, appointment or discipline. That rule has never, so far, been challenged successfully. It is a principle of immense historic significance and goes back through centuries of bitter wrangling between Church and State, from the days of the Covenanters. Today, Parliament has a hand in the appointment of Bishops in England, but the Kirk of Scotland is independent of the Crown. The wording and form of her prayers are 'subject to no civil authority'.

When I was ordained, I declared my acceptance of the Constitution of the Church and I vowed obedience to her Courts. In making this pledge, however, I did not envisage the Church breaking its *own* laws. Had I been tried fairly and convicted, I'd have accepted the punishment. As it was, I could be 'disciplined', because I was not tried and I was not found guilty of any sin, despite what was assumed in the media. I was tricked into giving up my status and I lost my livelihood. Basic human rights – including the right to a fair trial – do not, surely, come under 'matters spiritual'?

There can be no industrial tribunal until the 'jurisdiction' question is settled. A date is set for these preliminaries in September 1998, at the Tribunal Office in Dundee. The Church has hired the services of the Right Honourable Lord Mackay of Drumadoon, until recently the 'Lord Advocate' (the Senior Law Officer for Scotland). Lord Mackay must argue for the Church that the civil court has no right to hear my case.

It is the first time my local small-town lawyer has been matched against a 'bigwig' like this. He comes into the waiting room looking somewhat flustered, not having expected such a weighty opponent. This is, after all, merely a pre-hearing. The unfair dismissal claim itself is not yet under discussion. 'Lord Mackay must be costing the Church at least £2,000 just to put in an appearance!' he exclaims.

The courtroom is packed with reporters. A couple of other ministers who have experienced 'rough justice' at the hands of the Church are in the gallery.

There's been an interesting development since I lodged my appeal, in that devolution of government has come into effect and the new Scottish Parliament is about to be sworn in. At the same time, European Human Rights legislation is being incorporated into domestic law. The Church authorities have been in consultation with the Government for many months about this legislation. They assumed they'd be granted an exemption clause as far as Human Rights are concerned but things are not looking good for them. There's been a debate in the House of Lords. The majority of the English peers were not in favour of an ecclesiastical exemption. This angered some of Scottish peers, however, who expressed fear for the constitutional implications: the Church should be answerable to no-one but God, they maintained, even where Human Rights are concerned. In any case, there will never be problem, they argue: 'A situation could not be imagined in which the Church could be guilty of human rights abuses.' Indeed, I could not have imagined such a situation until a couple of years ago. Now I know anything is possible.

In the end a clause was inserted that was meant to satisfy the Church but has not allayed her fears entirely. In this clause, the civil courts are urged to note the separate right, under Article Nine, to 'freedom of thought, conscience and religion'. They are asked to respect the preponderant view within denominations on 'matters of doctrine'.

But is the right to fairness and justice really a 'matter of doctrine'?

Not unexpectedly, Lord Mackay of Drumadoon refers to this clause in his defence of the Kirk's position. Then he says something that shocks me, because I don't think it can be true, and I am in possession of evidence to the contrary: Lord Mackay asserts that the Secretary of State for Scotland, Donald Dewar (the 'First Minister' since devolution), has 'given his assurance' that the Government had 'no intention' of the 1921 'Church of Scotland' Act being affected by the Human Rights legislation. Of course, I recall, it was Donald Dewar who nominated Lord Mackay to that exulted position of Lord Advocate which, as a political appointment, he retained as long as the Tories were in power. Lord Mackay, of all people, would surely be privy to the thoughts of Donald Dewar. The pair must have discussed the issue at length. I would believe Lord Mackay, therefore, if I did not have in my hand a copy of a statement made by the very same Secretary of State for Scotland. This copy was provided by my M.P., John Swinney. In it, Donald Dewar appears to say the exact opposite of what Lord Mackay of Drumadoon just led the court to think. I push across the document to my lawyer and whisper to him that there seems to be a contradiction . . .

My lawyer rises to his feet and begins, 'I have a letter here from. . . err. . .' [The hesitation for dramatic effect is splendid.] 'Oh! It's from Donald Dewar! In May of this year, the Scottish Secretary made it quite plain that the Church cannot be excused from the requirements of the Law:

> '"We see insuperable problems amending the Bill in
> the way that the Church would like to introduce a
> specific safeguard for the 1921 Act. We have looked
> very carefully at whether the Human Rights Bill might
> be amended in a way that would meet the Church's

particular concerns without undermining the integrity
of the Bill. We have not been able to identify such a
specific amendment." '

It's so well done that I'm tempted to laugh.

My lawyer then argues that as both the European Human Rights
Act and the Sex Discrimination Act (1975) postdate the Church of
Scotland Act (1921), they must supersede them.

The Chairman announces that he will deliberate on the
submissions. Parties will be notified in due course.

Inexplicably (except that there is so much more going on here
than simple truth and justice) the Chairman finds in favour of the
Church. The 1921 'Church of Scotland' Act is upheld. The civil
courts have no jurisdiction to hear my complaint.

The next step is to approach the Employment Appeals Tribunal
in Edinburgh.

Even lodging an appeal is fraught with difficulties. At first I'm
told I have no right of appeal because this would only be permissible
if the dispute was over a 'point of law'. But what is this if not a
'point of law'? To me, it seems obvious. Eventually an appeal is
allowed but there have been months of delay.

The next struggle is to obtain funding. Merely seeking an
'Opinion' from Counsel costs £200. I'm offered the money by the
family of another individual who has had to go all the way to the
High Court to defend himself against bureaucracy. Humphrey
Errington has a little artisan cheese-making business in Lanarkshire.
Not long ago, South Lanarkshire Council claimed to have found
listeria in the 'Lanark Blue' cheese, closed down the sheds and
blockaded the narrow road out of the farm. Humphrey pointed
out that there are many types of listeria, certain ones being necessary
to make blue cheese and only a few, other, types being harmful.
The Council refused to make available the laboratory reports. Lanark
Blue was withdrawn from the market for many months, during

which the family had no income and could not pay their handful of employees. The story attracted public interest and, putting together small donations from a number of well-wishers, Humphrey took his case all the way to the top – and proved the cheese was safe.

Tenacity. That is what is required. And the courage to stand up to the big boys.

A Highland Clearance and Porcine Obstinacy

' "It is their land, Mrs Scott, and the law is on their side. . .
Nevertheless, I'm sure you will be helped to remove your
furniture and. . . er. . . impedimenta. I'm sure that Mr
Sellar will see to that." '

Iain Crichton Smith: *Consider The Lilies*

December 1998

The time comes when I have to leave my tied cottage. Fortunately
Major Gibb, one of my ex-parishioners, has offered me a cottage
way at the top of the glen. It will be a mere twenty minutes' drive
from Kilry in summer but the hill road is frequently un-negotiable
in winter because of snowdrifts or thick mist.

The worst part is the distress caused to my animals and I dread
moving the pigs. Hazel's husband, Eck, is lending me his trailer,
but I don't expect the hefty girls to co-operate. If it suits Grace
she'll roll over on her back with her trotters in the air to have her
toenails trimmed, or grunt contentedly while I wipe the stour from
within the deep wrinkles and folds of her black face. If she isn't in
the mood she can be a crabbit midden. I know her. Eck doesn't
listen. He is convinced the pigs will simply meander into the trailer,

lie down compliantly, and allow themselves to be driven to their new abode, snoring and oblivious.

It takes six of us an hour to load Grace. The men sneak out while I am scrubbing the final patch of kitchen floor, thinking they'll have the ramp up in a trice. But the squeals have to be heard to be believed and I run out to see Eck kick my beloved sow in the face in an attempt to turn her as she heads for the trees. I grab a pail and hood her with it. She stands still when she can't see but reversing a pig any distance with a bucket over its head is easier in theory than in practice. Each time we have her cornered she barges past the strapping lads, heaving their corrugated sheets aside. There's not much on a pig that's gripable. Even the legs are difficult to grab, being somewhat stumpy and hidden beneath much belly. Chick ropes around her copious waist and she has a man hauling on each lug and two at the rear before she sinks to the ground three feet from the ramp. Her flanks heave with the effort of running and screaming.

The others are all for bullying and half-carrying her the last few feet, but I stretch across her whale-like form and, in tears, refuse permission to continue until she's rested. Pigs can die from heart failure under stress. 'It's all right, lass,' I keep soothing her. 'I'll never forgive the Church if you die.'

Eck calls her an 'ill-natur'd brute'. I remind him that for all her cussedness she hasn't bitten any of them, even under provocation. We heave her into the trailer where, with an almighty fart, she collapses into the snoring heap Eck originally envisaged.

Meanwhile, hearing the din, the smaller gilt has disappeared deep into the nettles. It is by now pitch dark, nobody has a torch, and she is black. . . and silent.

The hens have flown up into trees, or are dim shapes in the woodshed. Several hours later, still without a torch, I've found all but the cockerel. They are stowed behind my car seat, wedged between a clothes-airer and a gas cylinder. There is no room for

Stanley Turkey, who is the size of an average Labrador. I cart him in my arms and plump him on the passenger seat of Eck's truck. He doesn't flap on the journey and gazes out of the window with mild interest.

The first week in the glen sees snow and ice and the temperature at night falling to −11°. The cockerel, left behind in Kilry, escapes capture for a day or two before deciding life as a bachelor has little to commend it. He is reunited with his girlfriends, but one of them, the Spotty bantam, does not last long after that. She squats in the snow one morning, shoulders hunched and giving me a sideways and bleary-eyed look which, when I imitate it in my neighbours' kitchen, has them roaring with laughter. 'How do you know if a hen looks *cold*?' Well, they did ask! There is no mistaking her pinched-up demeanour. I remove her to the comparative warmth of the loo, with an oven rack over the top of her box in case she revives and tries to flap her way out. She looks much perkier the next day, but I should not have put her outside again so soon. Another dawn and she is a stiffened, lifeless form on the henhouse floor.

I torture myself for weeks over the thought that the little spotty hen might have lived had I been more careful of her. Solicitous by nature of the tiniest of living things, the occasions when I have been cruel or neglectful of my pets have lived with me for years. I still remember Fred the Three-Legged Tortoise, when I was six or seven, devouring dandelions like a wolf at meat after I'd forgotten to feed him for a day.

The move to the keeper's cottage is not a success for my menagerie. The wood at the back is dark and wet and harbours vermin. By mid-December my prize-winning duck, resplendent in black and green and purple, has been nipped at the back of the neck by a pine marten and is paralysed. On Christmas morning her equally famed spouse is in the same condition. After several weeks of being carried to the burn and fished out and wrapped in a towel each day, the drake begins to walk again, sitting back on his hunkers. Then he gives up the ghost. Only a few months ago both the drake and I swelled with pride when my former university lecturer, Steven Mackie, visited us at the District Agricultural Show and exclaimed over our red ticket.

Grace Pig remains in hibernation in her straw-filled shed for almost five weeks before summoning the enthusiasm to explore the policies, on an unusual bright morning in January. It rains by midday and she takes to her bed again.

I am not permitted to keep my cat. Major Gibb detests felines. I miss her sorely, fierce as she is. No place is home without a warm ball of vibrating fur curled up on a chair and a daily offering of gall-bladder-of-mouse left strategically beside the bed for unslippered toes to find in the morning.

I am homesick for Kilry.

Vipers' Tongues

'O ye wha are sae guid yoursel,
Sae pious and sae holy,
Ye've nought to do but mark and tell
Your Neebours' fauts and folly!
Ye high, exalted, virtuous Dames,
Ty'd up in godly laces
Before ye gie poor
Frailty names,
Suppose a change o'cases;
A dear-lov'd lad, convenience snug,
A treacherous inclination –
But, let me whisper i' your lug,
Ye're aiblins nae temptation.
Who made the heart, 'tis He alone
Decidedly can try us.'
    Robert Burns: 'Address To The Unco Guid'

1999

Christmas is miserable, the beginning of January worse, and I need to go away. Ken, a fellow minister recovering from a heart attack, offers to take care of my little darlings for a few days so that I can go through to Paisley to visit friends from my first parish. He will benefit from the quietness of the cottage, with no traffic and no television.

I am glad of Ken's help: in Kilry I'd had a dozen neighbours I could have asked to feed animals for me, but up the top of the glen I am isolated and have come face to face with open hostility for the first time in the eighteen months since being accused.

What do any of them think I've done to deserve their scorn? The forester lends me a mell to hammer in stakes for a hen run and furnishes me with a list of the crimes of the parish: gamekeepers who torture pets and poison eagles; farmers who beat up their kids when they are drunk; Christian ladies whose charms are enjoyed not only by their husbands. I am not to heed, therefore, anything I hear said about myself. They've no right to speak, he assures me.

They have no right to speak, but they do. 'They *kill* ministers in Angus,' Freya and Douglas Murray warned me when I came to these parishes. Were capital punishment still legal I believe some of them would indeed execute me. It matters not that the stocks are out of use. They are vituperous in their condemnation and their words sting harder than rotting vegetables.

'Personally I think she should be locked up!' proclaims the wifey from Buchail. And even those who purport to be my friends jeer and laugh once the drink is flowing at a party at Crandart, speculating what the 'Lady Minister' must have been like in bed.

I am friendly with the local vet, who relays how she did not let on she knew me to one of the cattlemen in Kilry who was enjoying giving her the details of my prowess: 'Aye, she's been with every man in Kilry!'

She'd wanted to tease, 'You too? You live in Kilry: what was she like?'

I'd dearly love to have seen his face.

Sandy Nicoll's brother Richard puts in his tuppence-worth. He deliberately puts round a tale. 'She made a play for Richard too,' says his mother, 'and he had to make a hasty exit.'

The only time I ever spoke to Richard Nicoll alone was outside the gate when he delivered a henhouse to The Faulds for me. I offered him a mug of tea. For goodness sake, I gave tea to everyone who came to my door! Folk let themselves in and made their own if I wasn't there. For Richard Nicoll, two years on, suddenly to make out I'd offered him more than just tea is sheer wickedness. But the story spreads and some folk add more arms and legs to it. Ken Jackson accepts coffee one morning (bravely!) and relays what the folk at Kilry Lodge have been saying of my exploits. Ken Jackson says that he and his neighbour drove past my house afterwards chortling, 'We two must be the ugliest bastards in the whole district: we're the only ones that lass hasn't slept with!'

I don't suppose I've heard half the things the Nicoll family said about me. One week I am reputed to have written off my car, drink-driving, and one of my male 'clients' is supposed to have bought me a new one. It's daft: people must wonder why I'm still driving around in the original vehicle without any sign of so much as a dent in it. Most of the stories contain some reference to my nympho-mania. If only they knew how frightened I am they'd realise I'm as likely to fly to the moon as jump into bed with someone.

Every day for five years I've woken up feeling sick, my grief so heavy I can't lift myself out of it. Heather was conceived without my consent. Her legacy to me is lifelong regret and hurt.

A neighbour asks me to look after her children when she is at work. I love them but dread taking the bigger ones to school because some parents and teachers turn their backs on me.

There are folk who hear the tales but see that they don't fit the image of the quiet young woman they know. One of my elders in Paisley tells me that her dad, a respected senior police officer, was in tears over what he read in the *Scotsman*. He begged her, 'Tell Helen I'm praying for her. She doesn't deserve this.'

It's my loyal friends I don't deserve. I am so lucky in having them.

When I return from my visit to Paisley, Ken is obviously enjoying from his own holiday in my cottage, so I stay with Dennis in his Manse at Cortachy for two nights. I don't want to give the gossip-mongers any food by staying under the same roof as Ken. They can hardly create a story about me with eighty-four year-old Dennis, can they?

Oh, but they do! With the spitefulness of their tongues some of them actually begin to say the veteran is foolish and fond. Dennis hears it from one of his elders. He treats it with the contempt it warrants. Someone even swears to him with the assurance of the Gospel that men were lining up at my door when I lived at Kilry, parking their cars at a distance and skulking under the hedge to avoid detection as they made their way to the young Lady Minister's gate – and thence one is to suppose to the delights of her bedchamber.

Very often, these rumours are embellished with such fine detail as could only seem to have come from eye-witnesses and this lends them a modicum of credibility. The occasion on which I was 'bathing naked in Forfar Loch', for example, was apparently testified by four elderly farmers – one of them named as Moyra Nicoll's father. They were enjoying a picnic, of brown bread with cheese and green tomato chutney, apparently, and ginger cake and apples, when I arose stark naked as a Nereid from the water, arms outstretched and breasts dripping like fruits from a tree, and asked if they had a towel! Not only did Moyra's dad never go on 'picnics' but the A90 Dundee–Aberdeen trunk-route runs right along the edge of that polluted pond, providing full vista!

Whence was spawned the idea about my tendency to hit the bottle? Rev Peter Youngson visits Dennis. Discussing me, his parting shot is, '*And* she goes to bed inebriated every night, you know!' Dennis is so angry that he says he'll never again allow Peter

Youngson across his threshold. I just laugh. Dennis scolds me for treating it so lightly. 'No colleague should speak so of another, my dear. It is heinous that he did so.'

'But Dennis,' I defend my levity, 'how would he *know*? He'd have to *be* there when I go to bed every night! He'd have to be peering through my curtains! Does he know that I wear 'Winnie-the-Pooh' pyjamas? It *is* funny when it isn't true. I've never once been drunk in my whole life but Youngson's neighbours say *he* spews in their flower beds on his way home from the pub, he's so drunk some nights. I havn't seen him do it and what I do not see with my own eyes I will not believe. Dennis, surely you must have read Lewis Grassic Gibbons' *Sunset Song* and *Cloud Howe*? Grassic Gibbon said gossip was the most rife and most poisonous sin of the people of Angus and The Mearns. Didn't he say there were people here who 'knew everything that happened. . . and a lot that didn't'? It's here in this very district that he lived! It's these small minds he observed. I could say that people in glass houses are always the first to throw stones, but if people say things about me that aren't true, I try not to let it bother me.'

Dennis is hurt by these things as if they'd been said about his own child. He is disillusioned with the Kirk most dreadfully because of how I was treated. He fought so hard for me. 'When I started to ask questions about what they were doing to you and championed you, men I thought were my friends stopped speaking to me. But I'm old and it doesn't worry me. At the beginning of my career perhaps it would have done. But Our Lord was never afraid to be in a minority of one, my dear, and neither must we be. No, we must never be afraid to be in a minority of one.'

I go over and hug him. Darling, darling man. What would I have done without him?

I love Dennis, with the purest fondness. He cherished me and held me up from falling, through the worst episode in my life.

Rooney, who stands to annex the Dennis's parish to his existing fiefdom, goes to visit Dennis and seeks to persuade him to retire. 'People are saying you should go, Dennis. I'm telling you this as your friend.'

'As my friend?' muses Dennis. 'He always says he's my friend! But ever since he told the Presbytery what they did to you was done "in compassion and love", I've never trusted him.'

Eventually Dennis does decide to retire to the Borders. I'll miss him sorely. He has seemed so fragile since his illness the summer after the Inquiry; so wasted physically. I cannot express how hard I find that to watch. Moreover, he's been wounded on my account and that causes me pain. During his illness he said I should take his funeral – 'I want you to see to my obsequies, my dear' – but he also voiced the fear that the Presbytery might disallow this and keep me out of the kirk.

Some people were vicious behind my back but none has been cruel to my face until I meet young Trevor Davison.

Trevor's wife Lorraine is ages with me. I like her. When I sat my lorry test she left me heather for luck and she visited me when I was first suspended. Now that we are neighbours I take something for their new baby.

Trevor is in the yard at Dounie but seeing me he slinks behind the sheds. He emerges carrying a rifle as I reach the back door and makes it clear I am unwelcome. 'I've read the newspapers. I know what you've done. People don't forgive in this glen.' I am stunned. I say I'll leave the gift on the step if Lorraine doesn't want to see me. 'I'm not speaking for my wife. I don't know if she'll speak to you or not.' He strides into the house still holding the firearm. Lorraine comes out, baby in her arms.

'I'm sorry, I don't want to make things difficult between you,' I say, struggling to fight back tears. 'I'll not come back. Please take this,' I put the package into her free hand.

Lorraine is lovely. She asks how I am settling in the glen and tells me she has a new bicycle. Perhaps in the Spring she'll bike up to see me.

I go home and sob my heart out. Whatever is it Trevor thinks I've done that is so terrible?

I have been living up the glen for almost a year when word has it that Trevor Davison of Dounie has been admitted to hospital with a severe psychiatric disorder. This news affects me strangely. Instead of thinking Trevor has received his just deserts for the way he frightened and upset me, I feel a surge of pity for him. When I meet his sister in a car park in the town, I am on the verge of tears. Trevor told me his whole family was set against me, so it takes some courage for me to speak to her and ask her how Trevor is. It's obvious from her answer that she is worried about her brother and the effect of his illness on their father who has little understanding of mental illness. Then, to my amazement, she touches *my* hand and asks how *I* am getting on.

Even in the glen, just as happened in Kilry, something is changing. It is subtle, and soft.

I've so much to learn about brokenness, and forgiveness.

The Readmissions Committee

'They were, doubtless, good men, just, and sage. But,
out of the whole human family, it would not have been
easy to select the same number of wise and virtuous
persons who should be less capable of sitting in
judgement on an erring woman's heart, and disentangl-
ing its mesh, on whom Hester now turned her face.'

Nathaniel Hawthorne: *The Scarlet Letter*

February 1999

Whenever a minister quits, a Presbytery is supposed to let his
resignation lie on the table until a delegation meets with him and
ascertains that he stands by his decision, is of sound mind, and has
had no pressure brought to bear on him. This is so whether he is
ninety years old and desirous of drawing his pension, or whether
he's been offered an attractive stipend in a cushier parish. There is
a loophole, however, under yet another piece of recent legislation
of which they chose not to inform me, whereby in the case of
demission of status – leaving the ministry altogether, rather than
just a particular appointment – the Presbytery can accept a resignation on the spot, without any 'cooling off period'.

So there is a legal requirement of pastoral concern in all cases except this, the most drastic step of all. Very Rev Andrew Herron, in his book on Church Law, explains the anomaly thus: 'only a man [sic] who has utterly lost his faith would demit status, so it is pointless talking to him.'

I haven't lost my faith – at least not in God; though I am convinced the Church has precious little to do with God.

There's only one way to seek restoration of my status. I have had to wait at least a year to apply to the General Assembly, initially *via* the new 'Committee on Admissions and Readmissions'. On the form I am asked to give reasons for reapplying. I write that I should never have left in the first place and gave only verbal assent to a resignation extracted from me under pressure. I want my status returned so I can be tried and be exonerated. At no time have I lost my call to ministry. Surely I shall be a better pastor for my experience of suffering and humiliation? In particular I want to be allowed to resume my care of prisoners: I can now identify with those who've been condemned.

Several people suggest leaving a longer time-gap, of several years. I'll then stand a greater chance of success. But the sense of injustice bites deep. I received punishment without the dignity of a Trial, and only the indignity of a very public examination. I've had to live in a community where I've been tarred a slut and a liar. I seek acquittal. I don't see why I should be deprived of the ministry I loved any longer than I have already. I haven't been convicted; and yet I'm serving a sentence.

By the time the General Assembly takes place I'll have been unemployed for two years. It could be several more years before I find a post. My former parishioners are surprised at the length of my sentence and the rigmarole attached to obtaining 'parole'.

I ask permission to delay payment of the fee to the Readmissions Committee. I wasn't told I'd have to pay a penalty at the time I resigned and am struggling to manage on £49.15 dole per week, especially in the coldest months.

There are other obstacles. The chief of these is the fact that the Convener of the Committee on Readmissions turns out to be a minister of musteline mien from Paisley. I came across him during my time in that district but only spoke to him on two or three occasions and was therefore shocked when he libelled me in the press during the Inquiry. He may have regarded me with disdain because I didn't sport ministerial garb in Paisley, but his comments about my wearing 'hotpants' at Presbytery meetings were uncalled for: brightly coloured trousers, yes, but they came right down to my ankles. They weren't revealing or indecent. They were nothing like 'hotpants'! It grew worse.

The *Daily Mail* printed: 'Rev David Kay remembers Helen as living in a "Walter Mitty world". He says: "A lot of parishioners found her less than truthful. She was unreliable about turning up at meetings and simply didn't conduct herself as a minister should." '

I wouldn't have been so livid if there'd been any justification for these defamatory remarks, but there was none. Nobody ever had reason to question my integrity in Paisley and I never failed to attend meetings if my presence was required.

So now I write to the Committee on Readmissions, objecting to David Kay's participation. A reply is put into my hands in the waiting room immediately prior to the interview: Kay will not assume the chair but will remain present. If I raise objections to any other member of the Committee, these will be considered.

Had I been given time to consider, I should have objected to half of them! Kay should have been removed altogether and so should his counterpart from Paisley. Furthermore Rev John Chalmers is here, despite having been a party to my dismissal and having already put in writing that he considers me 'unfit' for ministry. It smacks of nepotism, moreover, that his wife is the secretary to this Committee and is present. So is Chalmers's best buddy.

When Mrs Chalmers shows me into the room I hand her the

fee and take my seat. The presence of David Kay unnerves me badly. His stoaty eyes are on me. I want to accost him, to ask what reasons he had for his libel. I have to remain demure. Not for the first time in such a situation my thought processes freeze, like the rabbit transfixed by the sharp-featured ermine. I fumble over answering questions and come across poorly.

The odds are stacked against me. The Committee wants to see evidence of my meek acceptance of what the Church has done to me, whereas I feel aggrieved. I am supposed to keep quiet about flaws in the Inquiry. It is held against me that I am recalcitrant. 'You continue to plead your cause,' accuses Chalmers.

Chalmers gives me a hard time. He needles me. He expresses his displeasure at my having dared to speak up against iniquity. Then he adds, 'Of course, the Church can take it. The Church is bigger than the front page of the *Daily Record.*'

I want to say, yes, that's all right for the Church, but what about me? I am not so big. I cannot hide behind the anonymity of an organisation. My life was destroyed. The Principal Clerk leapt to defend the Church whenever there was criticism of the institution in the papers. He penned tart academic letters saying, 'Those who fall foul cry, "Foul!" ' He didn't correct the inaccuracies in the press that damned me! I was thrown to the lions.

It is said that the Church will forgive anything except publicity. Naughty ministers escape media attention and so they also escape censure, invariably. I was penalised for leaks from the Church judiciary to the press.

I cannot take Chalmers to task. That would be another black mark against me. I take his next jibe on the chin, too, though the injustice of it smarts: 'Do you not think,' he asks rhetorically, 'that out of consideration for the Nicoll family, to allow them time to heal – and for your colleagues who may well feel let down by you – you should leave more time before applying for reinstatement?' *My* hurt at the hands of the Nicolls, *my* feelings of being let down by my *colleagues*, are of no consequence. It is all skewed.

I am prepared to take part of the blame for my own destruction, but only part.

There are other objections to my being readmitted. What about the Excommunication Party I held? Was this not somewhat 'unministerial'? Chalmers completely fails to understand that my so-called 'celebration' only served to mask an inexpressibly deep pain. My apparent flippancy was an inverse reflection of the seriousness with which I regarded my exclusion from the Sacrament. It was the only way I knew of dealing with immense shame and hurt.

The last question concerns my church membership. I've never actually joined the Church of Scotland! This causes some consternation. At the time that I sought ordination, when living at Boarhills near St Andrews, neither Peter the Minister nor Herbert the Session Clerk were particularly bothered about rules and regulations. The Session only met once a year, with a bottle of whisky and a large fruit cake, in front of a log fire in the Manse. Hence nowhere is my name recorded in its annals.

'Where do you attend worship, then?' they ask. Where do they expect me to go? Where *can* I go? The new Minister of Boarhills was reluctant to allow me to take part in Herbert's funeral service, despite that having been Herb's express wish. Herb had never treated me like a leper but Mr Sinclair seemed to think I would contaminate his vestry. Dear Herb, who proclaimed it a 'damned cheek' when the Church sent me for counselling after treating me so badly.

I hardly have to wait for the letter of rejection to arrive in Saturday's post. I said not one thing during the interview to deliver myself. Why, then, does seeing the expected result in black and white trigger such distress? Probably the discussion about communicant membership brought to a head all my suppressed emotions surrounding exclusion from Holy Communion. I've borne that disgrace for a year and a half and never mentioned it to anyone. Yet of all the deprivations I've endured it is the most cruel.

Suddenly I need to tell someone what Caskie said to me about taking Communion all that time ago. It is to Robin MacKenzie that I turn. Robin was also much beleaguered as a minister in Angus Presbytery before moving to Argyll. Unlike me, he withstood their kangaroo courts. His appeal to the Judicial Commission was upheld the day after my own appearance in front of the Presbytery on Judgement Night in November 1997. (It was no coincidence that Angus Presbytery was so reluctant to censure me that night: the Clerks, knowing I should also appeal, feared a second loss of face before the Judicial Commission.)

When I tell Robin Mackenzie of Caskie's autocratic decree, the damn bursts. I am stricken. Tears, pent up for eighteen months, flood out. 'Caskie said I'd be able to receive Communion if I admitted guilt,' I sob in anguish. 'I won't confess to something I didn't do, so I haven't had Communion in all this time.'

'Caskie is a clot!' pronounces Robin, with less charity than I've ever heard him speak. 'He had no right to excommunicate you. He was merely the Convener of a Committee of Inquiry. Only the Presbytery has the right to excommunicate someone and there was no Trial.'

'But I'm contumacious,' I sob. 'I won't say I'm guilty. The punishment for contumacy *is* excommunication. It says so in the *Practice and Procedure* book. Caskie's right.'

'Caskie is very rarely right, in my experience. He led the Inquiry against me. He made such a mess of it that I can't think why they reappointed him for your case. I was worried from the start about what they were doing to you. There were better ways they could have handled it. They'd no pastoral sensitivity. Look, take no notice of Caskie. You can only be contumacious if you've been found guilty first. You were never found guilty.'

It takes Robin a while to calm me down. 'You mean you'd give me the Sacrament?' I whisper. 'Though I feel so shamed?'

'We shall be celebrating Communion in these parishes next week. You are cordially invited to the Lord's Supper.'

Shame. It is the same word I use when I break down again speaking to Rev Steven Mackie. 'Why ashamed?' he asks. 'You've done nothing of which to be ashamed.'

'*Shamed*. Not *a*shamed.'

'Yes. That's different. They did shame you.'

I relay how I've not made any Communion. He draws in his breath, feeling my pain. 'Have you not? . . . What a pity the Moderator refused to see you!'

Shame. It is destroying my spirit. The 'Scarlet Letter' sewn onto my bodice is not red, but pea-green. I want my ministry restored to me, but more than that I need an end to the disgrace. It is hard enough to hold up my head in public every day. But being cast out beyond the reach of my God is more than I can bear much longer.

Chief Inquisitor Caskie's excommunication, whether or not he had the authority to declare it, has wounded deeply.

It was wicked, using the Sacrament as a bargaining tool.

The Employment Appeals Tribunal

MY lawyer arranges for me to meet Advocate Brian Napier in New Advocates Close, tucked away off Edinburgh's Royal Mile. I warm to Mr Napier at once. Unlike the Big Lawyer in Dundee who might have defended me at the Trial by Libel if it had happened, Mr Napier is not physically intimidating. He shakes my hand enthusiastically and uses my first name. The set of his mouth gives the impression he is trying to bury a smile all the time he is talking.

Mr Napier specialises in employment law. He is confident. He says he'll see me at the Appeals Tribunal in March and that we'll win. He cautions, however, that the Church will not take defeat sitting down. It is well known that Napier is engaged to fight my corner. Another Advocate has already approached him with the rather thinly-veiled threat, 'Does Miss Percy realise it won't end here?'

Even Lord Penrose – albeit in jest – referred to the impunity of the Kirk recently, during an unrelated case that Mr Napier was defending. Many of the Lawlords are elders of the Kirk and will be at pains to defend the Establishment.

March 1999

Advocate Napier is impressive, if not magnificent, at the Appeals Tribunal. He takes each point the Church's lawyers make and counters it, 'But I say. . .' or 'The Appellant's position is. . .' I sit behind him, finding various documents as he requires them.

The Judge, Lord Johnston, while admitting that he is a Church of Scotland man, appears sympathetic. 'Do you mean to tell me,' he asks of Lord Mackay of Drumadoon, who is back again acting for the Kirk, 'that this woman has no rights?' That is indeed what they are saying: had I been a Church of England priest, or a Free Church minister, I should perhaps have some recourse to the civil courts. The Kirk, however, is in the unique position of being protected by that 1921 'Church of Scotland' Act. It is invincible. Lord Johnston feigns surprise.

As he did at the Office of Industrial Tribunals, Lord Mackay says something that shocks me, because I know it to be incorrect: he argues that my appeal through the civil courts is an unnecessary exercise. 'She already has a right of appeal through the Church courts; through the General Assembly,' he proclaims.

I have no such right! I don't! When my resignation was penned for me, my right of appeal was forfeited. The Principal Clerk had made that abundantly clear to me, in writing. I was no longer a minister. I had reached the end of the road. I should not have turned to the civil authorities if I'd had any other avenue left to me within the Church's own system. Whether or not Lord Mackay of Drumadoon knew that, the Kirk's lawyer, Jeanette Wilson, seated at his left elbow, most certainly did know it.

'Surely he can't say things that aren't true?' I put in to Advocate Napier. 'Surely he has to tell the truth in the Court?'

'No, he doesn't,' explains my Advocate. 'He can say whatever he likes. It's up to the Judge to ascertain whether or not it's actually true.'

After the hearing is over and we are packing up our papers, Lord Mackay slides across to Mr Napier and asks for a word in private. Brian Napier rejoins my lawyer and me in the basement room five minutes later, grinning. 'Lord Mackay says the Church would be willing to settle out of court,' he informs me. 'You should discuss with Mr Baxter what you would like out of this.'

I am elated. What do I want? Most of all, to reclaim some dignity. Originally, I asked for a simple press statement. My lawyer thinks that after all the hassle the Church has put me through in its arrogance, I should not now agree to so little. So, my pension contributions? A donation to Rape Crisis? Funding for a course to enable me to work again?

We are stunned when Lord Johnston writes that he has found in favour of the Church. It seems I have no right to be heard in the civil courts, nor in the ecclesiastical courts either.

I must apply for leave to appeal to the Court of Session, the highest court in Scotland. Another year. More costs.

The Church will not consider a settlement now it appears to be winning.

A Chink in the Armour

I CAN make neither head nor tail of the various ecclesiastical Acts and Regulations, and when I seek clarification from the Church headquarters they rarely reply.

The Readmissions Committee having refused to 'transmit' my application to the General Assembly, I am apparently entitled to 'modify' my petition. No-one in Church HQ will tell me what 'modify' means. They simply do not answer.

I had asked the Readmissions Committee to regard the irregular circumstances surrounding my demission, particularly the Presbytery's precipitate acceptance of a resignation that was penned for me when I was in a highly distressed state. The Principal Clerk had ruled that any right of appeal was forfeited by that same resignation.

Now I am informed that examination of this matter is not within the remit of the Readmissions Committee.

So in whose 'remit' is it? Where *can* I have my complaint heard? No answer.

There is no route left for me to clear my name.

By chance, I come to meet the minister and lawyer from Dundee who, earlier, had written to the *Scotsman* about the unfairness of Church procedures. Alan MacKay and Maggie Morton know their way around Church Law and have clarity of mind. They couch things expertly. They achieve a breakthrough where I have failed. Suddenly, the Principal Clerk is embarrassed into offering a way forward. I am to be allowed to petition the General Assembly. [*Appendix II*]

There are still hurdles to clear. I've no actual *right* of appeal. I can only ask that the Assembly consider using its *nobile officium* – the discretionary power of the highest court to grant an appeal where no such right exists under strict law. There is no guarantee, firstly that the Assembly will even agree to hear me speak, and secondly that it will choose to exercise its power to allow the appeal.

The General Assembly

'Groping knee-deep in technicalities. . . and making a
pretence of equity with serious faces, as players might.'

Charles Dickens: *Bleak House*

7 May 1999

Rhona, the friend I met through the Rape Crisis Centre, has
promised to cut my hair on Friday night, hoping that this will boost
my confidence for Saturday at the General Assembly. Rhona's flat
is above a chip shop in one of Edinburgh's less salubrious districts.
There's no light on the stair and the bell at the graffitied entrance
has been disconnected. It's necessary to stand in the street outside
the chippy yelling for admittance.

I have huge admiration for Rhona. When I met her, her self-
esteem was so badly damaged by her experience that she barely
spoke. She wore dark clothes and hid herself in the corner of the
room, too timid to look up. Fragile and afraid myself, I felt robust
beside her. But she put herself through college, feeding her children
by working at a superstore checkout every evening.

Having dutifully inspected each one of her daughter's nineteen
hamsters, I am shown Rhona's wardrobe and choose a skirt smart
enough to borrow for Saturday. Then she sits me in the kitchen

and pulls out the scissors. She is tentative, afraid of making a mistake. Her daughter doesn't help: she keeps pulling faces and grimacing! With one half of my hair short and one half still long, I go to meet Mike, another friend who has offered to be there for me, at Waverley Station. We go back to Rhona's for the rest of the haircut and I give the troublesome youngster money to go away for pizza.

Mike has caught the train straight from work. He is the former Leader of Sheffield Council and is wearing a suit and tie. We met on a work fortnight on the remote western isle of St Kilda, so I've only ever seen him in waterproofs and old jumpers. He shifts into jeans in Rhona's loo and then the English politician is immediately at home eating pizza in a dimly lit kitchen above a fry bar.

8 May 1999, morning

1999 is the only year the Assembly is not housed on The Mound, because that building is on loan to the new Scottish Parliament. The International Conference Centre is a plush, modern venue.

The first major obstacle to clear on Saturday morning is the Report of the Committee on Bills and Overtures. Some individual could move that it is incompetent for my Petition to be heard, and then my presence will not be required this evening. I have to be on hand to 'argue competence', whatever that means. (The Principal Clerk is typically unforthcoming on this when I seek guidance, and only sends me the barest of details regarding proceedings – not even a copy of the Standing Orders to help me understand.)

Steven Mackie, Mike and I arrive at the vast new International Conference Centre about half past ten. Lyndsey meets us there. She was on St Kilda with us.

Sleek limousines are rowed up outside the glass entrance and police guard the doors because The Lord High Commissioner is in the building.

We find a table and wait to be told when to go upstairs. Gowned and robed officials swoop in and out of the auditorium. Marjory

MacLean spies us and briefly puts a cloaked arm around my shoulders. She thinks I am unlikely to have to 'argue competence' during the morning session, but the same situation could arise tonight if someone moves not to receive my Petition then.

Douglas Galbraith sweeps down on us next, black bat-wings of his Precentor's robe enveloping me. Douglas always looks incongruous swathed in ecclesiastical cloth. He's far too human to carry off the clerical guise. He was the University Chaplain at St Andrews but now has a senior position in the Church, in the administrative headquarters. He has remained unaffected by his rank, and occasionally sends me facetious, and very funny, observations on the internal goings on at HQ. He has always said it was the Church's loss, not mine, when I left the ministry.

We sit up in the gallery for over two hours. The Report of the Board of Practice and Procedure is received. Concern is expressed regarding the Church of Scotland's position with regard to the Human Rights Act, to be incorporated into domestic law by the new Scottish Parliament. Fervent reassurances are given that Human Rights legislation will not affect the Church. But, 'for the sake of public confidence' they intend to review the Kirk's judicial process:

'. . . to ensure a judicial procedure of integrity. . . an
effective tribunal of first instance which is untainted . . .and
the opportunity to appeal on a point of law to an impartial
body if dissatisfied with the decision at first instance.'

That chance to appeal to an impartial body is precisely what I am requesting in my Petition. Will the Assembly recall this in six hours' time when I stand before the bar?

The Report on Bills and Overtures goes through on the nod at five past one. The first session is over.

We walk to the West End. As we enter the café a smallish bearded minister with poppy-out eyes and prominent front teeth addresses me. The city is full of ministers during Church of Scotland General Assembly week (though, so the standing joke goes, there's not a prostitute to be found in Dundee!) This man's features are familiar, but I cannot recall his name. Then I remember: 'The Rat' is what a colleague from the Presbytery of Dundee had called him. I had always assumed his nickname had physical origins, rather than characteristic ones. He seems most genial – almost gushingly so – and wishes me well for the evening session.

'Well, that's one person you have on your side,' says Mike chirpily.

'I wouldn't be so sure,' I answer. The rodent grin has given me the creeps.

8 May 1999, evening

> 'It had come to his knowledge, he said, that a foolish and
> wicked rumour had been circulated at the time of
> Boxer's removal. Some of the animals had noticed that
> the van which took Boxer away was marked "Horse
> Slaughterer", and had actually jumped to the conclusion
> that Boxer was being sent to the knacker's. It was almost
> unbelievable, said Squealer, that any animal could be so
> stupid. Surely, he cried indignantly, whisking his tail and
> skipping from side to side, surely they knew their
> beloved Leader, Comrade Napoleon, better than that?'
>
> George Orwell: *Animal Farm*

The foyer is much busier in the evening. Annebeth and Steven Mackie are both here at this session, and Dr Lesley MacDonald, from Scottish Christian Women Against Abuse, has promised to sit with me at the bar when I go up. Rhona is coming independently. I am afraid if Mike misses her she'll be sitting alone; if indeed she finds out where to go in this vast emporium. The Assembly is such an overawing convention.

Annebeth points out Professor Shaw. I've received his permission to refer to his support for me at the Judgement Night during my speech. Just a word from someone like him gives me strength.

A couple of friends who went through university with me pass through the foyer on the way to take their seats. Donald and Roderick are cheery enough, but I have the impression they are embarrassed to acknowledge me and they hurry past. Perhaps they've already decided how they will vote. It must be impossible for anyone who has read newspapers to maintain impartiality.

I am to make myself known to an official who will direct me, but the uniformed Senior Janitor finds me first. Again, there is a hand on my shoulder, unexpected kindness, and an attempt to put me as at ease as possible in the circumstances. He describes where the 'bar' is. Even being 'at the bar' is intimidating: I don't know the meaning of the phrase. I am expecting, literally, a solid metal barrier at chest height, like the ones that prevent the bulls from jumping out of the ring at the livestock markets. I've little prior experience of how courts work.

The hour comes to move upstairs. I am guided to a seat in the staging of the packed auditorium with Lesley MacDonald and Steven Mackie. The session opens with a rousing hymn I cannot sing. I feel faint. I put my head between my knees, on the verge of passing out with terror. I feel Lesley rest a hand on my back.

The Committee on Readmissions reports and the musteline Rev David Kay is in his element presenting his candidates. There are six: most of them transferring from other denominations. They sit dumb on the platform, side on to the horde. All except one passes without inquisition. It is clear that the sixth candidate is returning to ministry following voluntary time out because of some misdemeanour. When his name is spoken, a dog-collared delegate calls out, 'Moderator!' and moves forward to the rostrum. He phrases his question in such a way that no malice can be inferred, and yet it is hardly innocuous:

'Moderator, I assure you I believe wholeheartedly in the gospel of forgiveness in the Lord Jesus. . . but I was in a neighbouring parish to Mr X and what I want to know is whether he is penitent for his sins?'

The unfortunate petitioner is required to face the throng and make an act of public contrition. I bleed for him. He draws himself to his feet and, with a heaviness in his voice which tears up those of us who witness it, says slowly, 'There is not a day that I do not feel remorse . . . my wife . . . my family . . .' I don't know the nature of his misdoing. It may have been heinous; but this is awful.

The Court moves on. There is something about a continuing vacancy for a minister on the Isle of Jura. Then they come for me.

The Steward leads me down towards the big platform, where the phalanx of Angus Presbytery is making itself comfortable. I was told I'd be stationed on the far side of the Procurator's 'playpen' and so am alarmed at being indicated a seat right beside my adversary the Presbytery Clerk. He isn't too amused either! Rooney's expression is that of the haughty pupil forced to share his desk with the class outcast; the one the other kids say has fleas. I look from Rooney's turned-up nose to the Steward's ushering hands and decide it behoves me to sit. Several officials begin making disapproving noises, the Steward realises his mistake and I am transported to the opposite side, in front of the Moderator's Chaplains and other dignitaries. I sense Rooney's birse subside and whisper to the Steward that I need a glass of water. I still feel faint.

There is no table at my side. Proceedings are stalled until one is brought. It takes ages. I feel exposed, transparent, held there in front of them. The Moderator apologises for the delay and we sit still longer. Eventually a table is placed in front of me, draped in royal blue. It seems pea-green.

The Moderator bellows for parties to identify themselves. I step up to the microphone and, not knowing the form, say, 'My name is Helen Percy, and I am representing myself.' I do not know that a curt, surname only, 'Smith, representing the Defendant,' is usual.

Rooney mimics me when it is his turn. 'My name is Malcolm Rooney,' he enunciates the initial words in mocking tones, 'Clerk of the Presbytery of Angus. I am representing the Presbytery. And on my right . . .' he continues to introduce with a gesture encompassing the serried ranks at his flank, 'Mrs Helen McLeod, Deputy Clerk of the Presbytery of Angus . . . Dr William Kinnes, Vice Convener of the Board of Practice and Procedure, and Assessor to the Presbytery of Angus. . . The Very Reverend Dr James Weatherhead, former Principal Clerk of the General Assembly of the Church of Scotland and member of the Presbytery of Angus.' (He doesn't let on that Weatherhead was not actually a member of the Presbytery of Angus at the time the Trial against me was instituted.)

A goodly number of henchmen are bunched together in the block. Among them I notice my friend Rev Brian of Aberlemno, and wince at his treason. Their numbers and the stature of the noblemen Rooney has highlighted are meant to convey the rightness of the Presbytery's cause. Neither Kinnes nor Weatherhead is to be called upon to speak: their sole purpose is to impress upon the Assembly that the figureheads are on the Presbytery's side. Who would defy such men? Weatherhead's *The Constitution and Laws of the Church of Scotland* is the authority on that subject. If *he* is stationing himself beside the Presbytery then the rules *must* have been followed. That is what is being 'said' when they put him in the front line and announce him.

The Principal Clerk reads some Standing Order regarding 'contentious cases', reminding commissioners that only those who remain present throughout the case may vote. No-one can go out to the coffee room and come back in to cast their vote. And they must base their judgement solely on what is heard in the court this evening. (It will be difficult for any, however, to set aside the phenomenal volume of media coverage to my detriment.)

Five hundred pairs of eyes are on me. When I stand, I am surprised I can find my voice:

'Moderator,' I begin, 'when I lost my status as a minister, I lost also the right to have my name cleared. I shall never be free of the unproven allegations and rumours attached to my name, unless this Petition is granted. . .

'I have no wish to enter here, Moderator, into an adversarial debate, which would damage the Church. It seems to me that if I reply to all to the points in the Presbytery's written response, one by one, the Assembly will in fact be holding precisely that kind of public and acrimonious inquisition that your Petitioner has sought to avoid for the Church by asking for an independent enquiry. May it suffice simply for me to show that there is reasonable question. . .'

[full text, *Appendix IV*]

Throughout my speech I am aware of holding the Assembly in a silence so absolute I think they'll cease to breathe. Once or twice from the pulpit, similarly, I've been scared by the spell I could cast. I conclude. . .

'. . . I believe that it is in the interests of the Church and of all concerned that justice should be seen to be done and I therefore ask that an independent enquiry should be permitted as an appropriate forum.

'Thank you, Moderator.'

I am not even seated before a man in the centre floor is haranguing, 'Moderator!' and being told this is not yet time for questioning. 'Point of order, Moderator!' he insists. 'All the time Miss Percy has been speaking . . .' (I am convinced he is going to say that the microphones hadn't worked and I'll have to start again, or that it is transparent I am a whore and should be banished before bringing any further disgrace on their godly Assembly) but he continues, '. . . someone has been flashing photograph after photograph from the gallery. No-one has attempted to remove him.

In view of the sensitive nature of this case, would it not be appropriate to make a ruling?'

Now my opponent, Rooney, jumps to the microphone unbidden. 'I would have thought, Moderator,' he begins sarcastically, 'that in view of the number of photographs she has already had taken it is a little late for that.'

'Thank you, Mr Rooney,' intercepts the Moderator most firmly. '*I* shall decide whether to make a ruling. I do not need your assistance.'

Had I been put down by the Moderator like that I should have felt ashamed of my behaviour but Rooney is totally unabashed and begins his prepared retort in ebullient manner.

He protests loudly for almost twenty minutes, emphasising and reiterating the printed replies that the commissioners already have in front of them. [Text, *Appendix III*] He is theatrical, disparaging, and full of righteous indignation.

He dramatises each of the Presbytery's points in turn. These are cunning, detailed, and make reference to many a legal loophole that I have no means of checking. Clearly the Presbytery has been resourced by experts in ecclesiastical law, including Weatherhead (who had, however, looked somewhat embarrassed when I quoted from his book to the detriment of the Presbytery). No such resource was available to me.

Rooney swears he never said I'd be found guilty of adultery even if I hadn't consented. 'Figments of her imagination become facts in her mind!' he declares. Then, denying that anyone from Presbytery ever commented to the Press, he alleges that I first invited the reporters to my own front door. How anyone could believe that astounds me.

Having passed off as 'pastoral advice' Ramsay's threatening Sandy Nicoll with a jail sentence if he didn't withdraw his evidence – 'This visit was one of pastoral care and concern! Sandy Nicoll was one of his parishioners! He was advising him, not threatening him!' – Rooney goes on to read to the Assembly a letter from Ramsay himself, in which Ramsay 'absolutely and categorically' denies that the alleged conversation ever took place!

Rooney has begun to sound so much like Ramsay, his predecessor as Clerk, with his whining and stressing of key words.

'The Presbytery submits that it had, and has, the competence and integrity to conduct a fair Trial,' pontificates Rooney, still quoting the text of the Presbytery's response to my Petition.

The destruction of my credibility completed to his satisfaction, the conclusion is thus:

> 'The Presbytery of Angus submits that it has acted fairly, and in accordance with the law of the Church, throughout this case. . . That, far from showing any grounds for questioning the honesty, integrity, or legality of any of the Presbytery's actions, the allegations in the Petition are found, on examination, to be variously groundless or inaccurate, revealing ignorance and misunderstanding. . . There is no case at all for reviewing the Presbytery's decision.'

Well! The Assembly listened to me attentively, but Rooney's subsequent performance has been long, loud, angry, tub-thumping, and filled with rhetorical tricks and histrionic oratory. They have forgotten everything I said. The effect is lost.

After Rooney is seated, Rev John Chalmers is asked to give his version of what took place at the meeting of 30th November 1997, at which my demission of status was arranged.

He's dyed his hair boot-polish black since then.

Chalmers also speaks at unnecessary length, though not quite with Rooney's drama. He gives the impression of pained incredulity that I could have misrepresented events so. The meeting arranged had been 'a difficult meeting . . . an emotional meeting . . . but how can she stand there and speak as if she had been shanghai'd into something?' He sounds querulous.

He goes on to list all the things the Board of Ministry has done for me since I demitted status: 'She's had no end of pastoral care. We paid for her to see a professional counsellor. We allowed her to stay on in the cottage in which she was residing for a year – a whole year.' He all but says, 'And this is the thanks we get!'

I wonder whom he is kidding about the pastoral care. I want to remind him that Dr Treliving saw me at the expense of the NHS, not of the Church, that I had tried to pay rent for the cottage, that they'd let the *Daily Express* hound me over its evacuation. . . that none of these things would have been necessary if I hadn't had my job taken away from me in the first place. Everything he says, however, is irrelevant: whatever they have or have not done for me *since* I demitted status doesn't change the fact that my demission was procured unfairly. It is all beside the point. It is not competent for the court to take subsequent events into account: I presume the jury will see all this for the red herring it is and so I don't rise to the bait.

It is difficult for commissioners to appreciate the shift in the Assembly's role from Conference to Court of Appeal. I was mistaken in believing they'd take no account of Chalmers' irrelevant remarks. One commissioner tells me afterwards that these were in fact the points that swayed the vote against me. 'One always looks at the whole picture in these situations,' she says, sounding sagacious. But in a proper tribunal almost everything Chalmers said would have been dismissed. The Principal Clerk had read a Standing Order explaining that judgement must be made on the facts of the case alone, not on subsequent events.

Steven Mackie will write to me afterwards, 'Chalmers gave an explanation which, had it been true, would have been quite reasonable. But of course it was *not* true. The Assembly had no way of knowing that it was untrue. The Secretary of a major Church department will always be believed.'

The General Assembly is a bizarre court in that no-one exists whose role is to guide the jurors as to what they should and should not hear as 'admissable evidence'. There's no-one to 'sum up'. The role of Moderator is not the same as that of Judge. Also, a jury of four or five hundred people must make the Assembly the most unwieldy court on earth.

The Moderator now turns to me and invites me to the rostrum to reply to Rev Malcolm Rooney and to Rev John Chalmers.

But the Principal Clerks had told me to spend all my ammunition in my first speech.

They had advised me that I would not be permitted to counter my opponents' arguments afterwards. I was not prepared for the chance to speak again, unless either one of them brought up new material.

In fact Rooney has hardly deviated at all from the Presbytery's written submissions, which are printed out for the commissioners in the Order of Proceedings. I've taken no notes, because I've been concentrating on picking up anything he should add – to which they told me it *would* be competent for me to respond. For all his histrionics Rooney has in fact introduced little that is new.

'Moderator,' I begin, turning towards his 'throne', 'I am advised that I can only reply to anything new that Mr Rooney has said. . .'

'No, no,' the Moderator butts in. 'You may say anything you like, as long as you haven't said it already.'

Shock. I feel sick and my head is light. I have been given the wrong set of rules. As a result I've blown everything. Here I am being given the chance to lay down my trumps and win all the tricks but I've already played them. I've shot my bolt. The sense of frustration and despair is inestimable. They are expecting me to speak, and standing there at the microphone, I am feeling very, very stupid. . .

Of course, what I should have said is, 'Moderator, I have been misadvised by the Principal Clerks. I require the court to adjourn.'

Then I should have had time to re-gather my power. I do not say that and there is no Advocate to prompt me. Instead, I make an unsuccessful attempt to unscramble my brain and make an intelligible response, trying to remember what I would have said if only I'd known I'd have the chance to say it. . . Then I sit down again. Rooney is invited to reply. He shrugs his shoulders. I've added nothing to which it is worth replying in any case.

The Moderator throws the floor open for questions. I have lost the place. I am reeling from the misery of the realisation of the opportunity lost to me because I've been misinformed of the procedures. I don't even really hear the questions properly because my mind has gone blank. I am fighting to concentrate but I've glazed over. I have to ask a couple of people to repeat their questions. One man asks if I understood the difference between 'demission of status' and 'demission of charge.' I say I did. I should have elaborated that I'd understood the meaning but hadn't been given time to consider the consequences.

The same man then asks the Principal Clerk if there is another mechanism within the Church by which I might be readmitted to the ministry in the future. The Clerk replies in the affirmative. This must have an effect on the Assembly's decision – yet it is missing the point entirely: I am not asking to be readmitted, but for the chance to clear my name through an independent enquiry. That chance will never be given to me if I am readmitted through the ordinary channels. The Readmissions Committee has already declared itself incompetent to carry out a judicial review. In a decade's time, perhaps, when David Kay and John Chalmers have both moved on, I should stand a chance of being readmitted. But I shall always have to live with the presumption of guilt without having been proven innocent.

One of the few questions put to the Presbytery, rather than to me, is posed by Dr Robin MacKenzie who, unlike Weatherhead, *was* a member of Angus Presbytery throughout the Trial (but who had effectively been silenced at the time because the Presbytery was trying to oust him). 'Moderator, I should like to ask if the Presbytery paid any regard to the issue of gender while handling this case?'

It is a pertinent question and less likely to raise hackles coming from a male. Of course Robin knows that the Presbytery's standards in this area have been abominable, but the Presbytery Clerk believes otherwise: he puffs out his chest with pride as he lists the many considerations and concessions that have been in the name of gender awareness: 'Moderator, when Miss Percy was informed of the allegations, Mrs Helen McLeod – a lady – was present. When the Presbytery appointed a Committee of Inquiry, two male members and a lady were chosen. When the Presbytery appointed a solicitor it was quite deliberately – quite deliberately – a lady. The Presbytery was indeed very aware of the issue of gender, Moderator!'

Quite apart from his politically insensitive use of the word 'lady', which makes manifest his total ignorance of women's issues, Rooney seems ignorant that in any equitable organisation no male would have been present in the room where a female was being questioned on matters of an intimate nature. It is not sufficient simply to have a token female as a witness. As in many of the things he avers, however, his assertive protestations are convincing. If a lie is told often enough or loudly enough it can seem akin to truth.

The questioning ends, parties are 'removed', and the Moderator calls for motions. Only one is made and it is by the grinning 'Rat' who was so smarmy and friendly towards me in the café earlier. The real reason for his nickname suddenly becomes apparent. 'Moderator,' he makes bold to say, 'it is quite clear that the Presbytery has acted in accordance with the rules. I move that the Crave of the Petition be not granted.'

The extreme discomfiture of the Assembly, palpable, appears to dissolve. It cannot be at all clear to anyone that the Presbytery acted according to the rules. One man is saying it was clear, however, and so it seems that the rest of the Assembly breathes a sigh of relief and can now vote with him.

His seconder is a minister whom I've never met. She has bleached-blond hair and identifies herself as 'Drake 107': 'Moderator, I have seen Helen over the years, at a number of Assemblies – and she knows what demission of status means!' screeches Commissioner Number 107, by the name of 'Drake'.

Nonplussed, I turn and whisper to Lesley, 'What's she getting at? I've already said I know what demission of status is. Who is she anyway?' 'Drake 107' has implied a level of acquaintance, using my Christian name, that she could be relied upon to know my mind; and yet I don't recall ever having spoken to her or being introduced to her. I'd remember a surname like 'Drake' if I had, surely.

The treachery is done. Those supporting the motion are asked to stand. The majority is overwhelming. A card count is hardly necessary. 342 for: 41 against. The Moderator 'recalls the parties' and informs the Assembly formally of the result. He then turns to address me, acknowledging the 'disappointment' I must be feeling, and congratulating me on the manner in which I've carried myself and the dignity with which I've spoken.

I am determined not to show any emotion while the cameras are full on my face. I am just able to muster the words, 'Thank you, Moderator.'

The Assembly, having moved this very morning to update the Church's judicial process and 'to offer the opportunity to appeal on a point of law to an impartial body', has just denied me exactly that. The quixotic nature of this decision cannot have escaped either the Moderator himself, or a number of others who are concerned for the integrity of the Church. They must have realised that such blatant disregard for the principles enshrined in the Human Rights Act will have historic and serious ramifications for the Constitution of the Church if it comes to a clash between Church and State. It will no longer be possible for the Church to claim impunity from temporal safeguards for justice. It has always been the assumption that the Church will, by very dint of her Divine Appointment, practice jurisprudence. It is now patently clear that she has not done so.

The Presbytery Clerk of Lothian, whose relative I cared for in prison, is unafraid to be seen grasping my hand and expressing his regret at the result as I am shown out. Once through the side door, a young woman immediately takes me from the Steward's care and informs me the press are waiting: do I want to speak to them or will she find me an escape route? I beg her to spirit me away but it suddenly occurs to me that perhaps she *is* press, that this is an ambush, and that I have fallen right into their booby trap on stepping through the door. 'You ARE press, aren't you?' I cry out.

'No, I'm not – I'm from the Church Press Office but I'm not press.' Convincing me she is not from the enemy camp she instructs me to wait in the unlit passageway until she can guide me through the basement to a back door. In the middle of all this, Dr Robin McKenzie comes towards me in the gloaming to offer consolation. He must have found his way quickly through several tunnels from the far side of the auditorium. Seeing Robin triggers the tears I've kept under control until now; tears of disappointment in myself. I reach out and he clasps me to him for the few seconds it takes for me to right myself. It sticks in my memory because he was given a name by some in Angus Presbytery for coldness and yet this is the second time poor Robin has been drowned with my tears. On both occasions he has been quick to console.

Lesley and Robin are holding a discourse on what has just transpired, in which I am too dazed to take part, when Rev Marjory McLean enters the passageway. She's slipped out of her prestigious place in the Procurator's playpen to assure me that the Moderator meant what he said in his closing words. I acquitted myself well, notwithstanding the outcome.

The woman from the Press Office returns to tell us that the getaway car has arrived. She'll go ahead of us to make sure the coast is clear. Annebeth has ascertained the plot and is outside with the taxi. Mike has gone back in to look for Rhona. Annebeth is incensed by the hideous performance of my counterparts but Rhona, she says, is desperately upset.

Rhona is weeping because she cannot bear what they are doing to me. Our tears have been mingled before, Rhona's and mine, through the aftermath of rape and sexual abuse. She knows, more than anyone else can know, my experience of shame and humiliation at the hands of men. She doesn't go to church but she cannot believe she's just witnessed several hundred Christians tearing one of their number limb from limb in an arena.

Lord Mackay of Drumadoon has been present and he descends from the gods, storming into the foyer. He pauses to pass bitter comment to some churchmen he knows, that the Assembly's vote to deny me a fair trial amounts to blind foolishness. When I learn of Lord Mackay's remarks from Douglas Murray, I realise that Lord Mackay of Drumadoon is perhaps not, after all, the 'bad guy' who told the civil courts I had rights within the Church, when it was clear I had no such rights. This man has in all likelihood been advising the Church leaders all along that it would be wiser to talk with me, and not to put their precious Constitution to the test. The 1921 Act of Parliament has prevailed against several aggrieved ministers in the past, but never in the context of European Human Rights legislation and the 'right to a fair trial'. Almost eighty years have passed since the 1921 'Church of Scotland' Act. Times they are a-changing. The Church bigwigs refused to heed Lord Mackay's warnings. They instructed him to fight to deny me a voice in the civil courts and now they have refused to accord me a hearing within the ecclesiastical courts. We are running out of courts! This case could now very well end up in the European Court of Human Rights, and the Church is likely to find herself short of allies there.

Mike observes afterwards, 'The Presbytery Clerk had to prove he was right, even if it meant lying. He did it with relish and in a bullying manner that worsened his case. It puts me in mind of that bit in Orwell's *Animal Farm*, where one of the pigs jumps up and down and blusters – just in the way yon Presbytery Clerk bluffed and blustered. The pig convinces the other animals that Boxer, the old cart-horse, hasn't *really* been sent away in a knacker's van: how can they be so stupid as to think that their leaders would do such a thing? Of course, there's a perfectly feasible explanation: the veterinary surgeon had bought the lorry off the knacker and hadn't had time to paint out the name on the side of the lorry! Then the pig goes on to list all the things that were done for the poor horse, all the expensive medicines they'd given him, all the veterinary care, and the soft bed of straw he'd been given, no expense spared. . . Oh, I can just hear that Chalmers bloke all over again, making out you'd been given "no end of pastoral care" and how they'd sent you for counselling, and bent over backwards to support you. . . Like Hell they had! Then there was the 'Rat' – that Judas who was all over you in the café– and his female accomplice, who pretended to be your friends, then stuck in the knife by saying it was "clear" the Church had acted properly, though it was anything *but* clear. . . Anyway, that's just it: because Orwell's farm animals *want* to believe their leaders are virtuous, they breathe a communal sigh of relief when they're fed a pack of lies. . . Helen, those commissioners at the Assembly tonight did not want to find the Church guilty. It was so much easier to find *you* guilty; though only a heart of stone could have remained unmoved, and most were not really convinced they had done right.'

The Death of Grace

'"Thank God!" Jude said. "He's dead."
'"What's God to do with such a messy job as pig killing, I
should like to know!" she said scornfully . . .
'The white snow, stained with the blood of his fellow-
mortal, wore an illogical look to him as a lover of justice,
not to say a Christian; but he could not see how the
matter was to be mended. No doubt he was, as his wife
had called him, a tender-hearted fool.'

Thomas Hardy: *Jude The Obscure*

9th May 1999

I return home to the glen from the General Assembly to find Grace
Pig skulking in the back of her sty refusing to emerge even for a
jammie dodger biscuit. She is often disgruntled if I desert her for a
day or two, but this time when I crawl in beside her she shrieks in
fury and, I realise, in pain. She attempts to clamber to her feet but
collapses in paroxysmal distress. She appears to have broken a
foreleg. I call the vet, who agrees that the animal should not be
hauled about for proper diagnosis. She has never seen a creature
in such agony. I beg her to put the sow out of her misery at once.

The vet has neither a captive bolt nor a needle long enough to inject straight into the heart. It is impossible to hold Grace's head still for a vein to be raised in her ear or under her tongue, as she writhes and screams. An injection into her side sufficient to kill a cow is metabolised by her fat. I run to the Big House to fetch my landlord, Major Gibb, from his dinner. He brings his butchery knife to slit the sow's throat. Thankfully she is already virtually unconscious.

An hour after the vet has left, Mrs Gibb comes across to the cottage to say she has cleared out the bloody sty and that Robin the forester has already forklifted out the carcass. I could kiss her for sparing me this awful necessity.

The smaller pig is so traumatised she will not let me near her and runs away. At dusk I find her in a miserable heap, squeezed into the henhouse.

I do not shed a single tear over the death of Grace. Bit by bit I have distanced myself from things that mattered to me, lessening the potential for further grief. My beloved pig saw me through many troubles over the years but in the most distressing time of all I had not dared turn to her. I'd spent little time with her, deliberately. She could have comforted me but I'd suffered so much loss that I could not risk being attached to anyone or anything else that could possibly be wrenched from me by fate or human cruelty.

I've been surviving by shutting myself off from all feeling. It is as if the events of my life are happening round about me. I am a spectator, not a participant. This dream-state has become my normal sphere of existence. I am wasting the precious gift of breath. Each day is a step nearer the oblivion of death and yet I cannot kick myself into sentient appreciation of life.

July 1999

Borrowing Catriona's ghost grey mare, I ride up onto the purple hill above the fish-silver loch. It is a glorious day, such as to make every gully, every leaf, stand out for miles. I am at one with the horse, without a saddle, and my own legs bare, so that I feel Sorrel's warmth beneath me as we canter across Craighead Ridge. A blackcock chirrs in alarm. The sun glints on the quartzite.

I think how happy I ought to be, but am not.

As a child I stood in the hornbeam wood, entranced by the sunlight dappling the carpet of wild hyacinths with shades of mauve and indigo; and was moved to tears by the beauty of it . . . and because innocence was lost. 'I saw but could not reach what had been stolen from me,' I wrote in a poem then. My trust in the essential goodness of creation was broken.

Now it is my spirit and not only my body, which has been raped. It is not the hyacinths alone that have been 'torn up by the whites of their stems,' never to bloom another year.

I steady Sorrel to a walk at the bare patch where the heather-burning took place in spring. I feel the shudder along her flank as an insect bites. I hear the whited bones of the heather crack under her hooves.

PART IV
LIBERATION

A Surprising Result

Sex perverts 'got off' on the press hype. That was one of the reasons for my agreeing to quit, rather than face Trial by Libel under the media spotlight.

Even after my resignation, they don't stop. Used condoms, anonymous threats of rape and volumes of pornographic material drop through my letter box on a daily basis, delivered by Royal Mail. These are from men who've never met me; no-brains who read the *Daily Record* and are titillated. Far worse is attention from men who *do* know me, to whom I've never paid the slightest heed nor given any flirtatious encouragement – who now regard me as some kind of challenge. 'Surely she will not be able to resist *me*, with *my* potency!' they seem to think. They have such incredibly inflated egos.

Sidney, Drusilla's husband, who's put the world to rights over many a mug of coffee in my kitchen, telephones me. Fine, but it's at three o'clock in the morning! 'Can I come down and see you?' he asks suggestively. I am enraged. He *knows* me. He *knows* I'm not like that.

Salt is rubbed into the wound when 'Slimeball Sid' is made an elder in the parish where I'm living.

Sexually explicit letters, written in many different hands, could have originated anywhere the *Daily Record* or the *Sunday Mail* are circulated. Semen, however, can be DNA tested and perhaps matched with existing computer records. I take the most recent batch of used condoms to the police station.

'Any idea who could be responsible?' asks Constable Houston.

336

'No.'

'Anyone who has a vendetta against you?'

'Well, only Robert Ramsay. You've heard the things he's said about me on the telly. He wouldn't do something like this, though.'

'We'll send someone to see him anyway.'

They do and a patronising officer calls on me the next morning. It's obvious Sergeant Duncan Cunningham has been converted to Robert Ramsay. 'It wasn't Mr *Ram*say who sent these things to you,' he sneers. 'Mr *Ram*say's a Minister of the Cloth!' (Cunningham forgets that I, too, was a 'minister of the cloth' until very recently.) He emphasises certain syllables, like a teacher who relishes making a child feel small: 'I spent a *long time* with Mr Ramsay yesterday afternoon. Mr Ramsay was most co-*op*erative. And he's very con*cern*ed about you. Yes, very concerned for your *wel*fare. . .' There goes Ramsay, implying that I have psychiatric problems again. Cunningham has been well and truly taken in by him.

Dorothy, the Clerk to the Congregational Board, is helping me pack china and is in the next room during Sergeant Cunningham's visitation. I haven't told her about the condoms but she overhears Sergeant Cunningham impressing on me the lily-white nature of my former colleague. After I have seen out my guest, I find Dorothy hooting with laughter. 'Mr *Ram*say was very con*cern*ed about you,' she mocks Cunningham's intonation. 'Oh, pull the other one! Mr *Ram*say was so con*cern*ed that he de*lib*erately set out to destroy your career and ruin your life, and *lib*elled you in the national media!'

It is true. As Presbytery Clerk and the initial recipient of the complaint against me, it would have been within Ramsay's power to have sent me to another place, quietly, without disturbance to our parish and without further distress to the Nicoll family. He could have promoted healing and reconciliation. He chose, instead, to wreak havoc. There was something hideous about what he did. Yet the Moderator of the Presbytery thanked him most profusely for his work and wished him well in his future career as a 'representative of our Lord Jesus Christ'.

The contents of the condoms are never identified but, coincidentally, it is the last time I receive such unsavoury material in the post. To this day I shake when the mail arrives through the letterbox. I am filled with dread, not only if I don't recognise the handwriting on the envelope but also if the address is typed and it appears to be official. This fear is irrational: what more can they do to me now?

The prurient interest of the press has left its mark on me. I was made out to be a whore, publicly. I feel cheapened and filthy. One stupid comment can cut me and bring it all back.

The 'phone rings after midnight. It's a man, an older man, whose house I passed not long ago on my way back up the glen from work. His wife is a good friend to me and I often have my tea with them.

The fact that it's so late isn't an immediate indicator of how the conversation will go. If he's tried to 'phone earlier and I didn't answer, he'll have realised I'm on a back shift at the care home where I'm earning a few pounds. He may have heard my car, if he was outside shutting up the dog for the night when I drove past their house.

He starts off being chatty. . . They haven't seen me for a while . . . the wet weather. . . the price of hay. . . a neighbour whose marriage has ended because there's Someone Else. . . 'Do you think I should get a girlfriend, hey?' A natural enough progression, for a joke. Then, 'WHAT WOULD YOU SAY IF I CAME UP NOW?'

He mustn't be serious. Or can he be? I choose a flippant rebuff that won't be out of place, either way: 'I'd lock you out.'

'Nah. The Minister's door's always open.'

'No it isn't.' . . .Suspicion he may not be jesting.

'Yours is. You wouldn't lock me out.' I don't believe he's saying this. The very thought of him – of any man – creeping round my door at night sickens me. 'What do you say, Helen? I wouldn't hurt you.'

You just have, you bastard. You've just undone all the good your family ever did me. The injury you have done will last forever.

'You've insulted me.' It is not nearly strong enough.

'No, I haven't. You should be flattered!'

Flattered? I put down the 'phone on him, lock all the doors and pull the curtains shut. Rev Dennis Leadbeatter would be proud of me. He's always saying, 'Now, is your door locked? Go and lock it, Love. I worry about you. . .'

YOU SHOULD BE FLATTERED. . . I'd be more flattered if his mongrel widdled against my leg. Hell, where do men like him get this conceit of themselves?

I don't sleep; my stomach full of undigested anger and self-disgust. Why *self*-disgust? How do such men make *us* feel dirty when *they* are the dirt? I've neither done nor thought anything to my shame. He has. Yet does he feel disgusted at himself?

I wonder if I hate all men. Except Steven. Except Dennis. Jock. Alan. Mike. . . No, I can think of a list of males who don't think filth every minute of their tiny lives.

If I admit this happened, the Church will say it's My Fault. They'll say I'm 'Not Suitable' for the Ministry. I have 'Deeper Issues' which I need to resolve. . . *Is* it my fault? *Did* I do anything to bring this on myself? I did not. My only crime was to be a Woman-Who-Lives-On-Her-Own.

It isn't just me. In this case there's another Woman-Who-Lives-On-Her-Own. He pawed her on two occasions some years earlier and I happened to be her confidante.

I 'phone her. She's just going to work but promises to come up in the evening.

The two of us sit on the front step of the cottage for a couple of hours after it has grown dark. She smokes and keeps the midges at bay. It has been hard for her to cope with her work that day. What I told her this morning brought back everything that happened to her at the hands of this same man. 'You must confront him,' she says. 'I didn't and I regret it. I've carried this around with me for three years.'

We realise that, for both of us, the betrayal of trust is worse because the man used to do for us the kind of things he would have done for a daughter – lifting things and fixing things. His moves were calculated. There was a stealth about the way he cultivated his wife's friends and spun a web of good turns for women who didn't have a husband to rearrange his face for him outside the pub. Women-Who-Lived-On-Their-Own.

This time, we'll force him to deal with his own behaviour. This time, we are not prepared to carry the loathing he should feel for himself. This time, she will take the opportunity to face him with what he did to her in the past. We'll both confront him.

We decide what we'll say and rehearse the lines over and over in our heads. When the time comes I find myself shaking as I approach his house. He should be shaking, not me! Why should *I* be the one who is so upset by his suggestion? How will he react to what I am going to say to him? He will, both of us women are certain, try to deny everything and say we are mistaken. Perhaps he'll become violent.

I reach the door – and he is out.

He happens to telephone me later. It's not ideal over the telephone, but I don't want to miss my chance. I launch into my spiel about knowing what he's done to other women, about how his family will get to know if he ever puts another foot wrong, about him better never coming to my house again in his puff. . . I finish with the punch-line we agreed, 'And I think you should apologise!'

To my total amazement, he says sorry.

A Wise Woman

Two conversations in the ensuing year affirm my decision not to return to the Church for further humiliation. . .

September 1999

Four months after the General Assembly I summon enough courage to visit a minister. I've never met her but I crave pastoral care.

Her husband shows me through a dim passageway to a cluttered room where a plump but pretty woman of about sixty sits swathed in patchwork, a needle in one hand and a cigarette in the other. She doesn't rise.

'You won't know me,' I hesitate.

'I know your face . . . Ah! Your friend spoke about you outside Tesco's. Do you mind if I carry on sewing? I listen better if I've something to do . . .'

'You told my friend I'd be allowed back into the ministry eventually if I kept quiet.'

'Yes. If you *want* to. . . I did more ministering before I was ordained than in these fifteen years since. I wouldn't choose Ordination if I had my time again . . You committed the cardinal sin: you made a fuss! But you could still go back in a few years if you're prepared to say, "I'm dreadfully sorry. I've sorted myself out now and I'm sane. I've gone through the menopause. I'm not a woman any more." Have you met anyone else who's been treated abominably by the Church?'

'A deaconess contacted me. She was pregnant. They said they'd overlook it if she had an abortion. She refused, but then she miscarried. She had to read out a confession in front of her presbytery. No-one went with her to the meeting. She had to walk in alone. They humiliated her, then decided not to actually 'punish' her. But National Mission sacked her anyway. No-one ever went to see her afterwards. The man who impregnated her's still a minister, of course.'

'Men!' she chuckles. 'They're on a testosterone high from age twelve!'

I laugh. If only more ministers were as real as she. 'Male ministers don't get away with some things,' I reason. 'I've met one man who made himself unpopular by being too outspoken about land reform, in a presbytery that was predominantly Tory. So they found some loophole for refusing his presbyterial certificate. Then there was the man in Fife who had his pastoral tie dissolved. They did a census of congregational attendance in the depths of February and sabotaged the church heating boiler so no-one would come because the building was freezing. The subsequent Trial started at 9.30 am, and by 2.00 am the next night they abandoned business because the witnesses were no longer fit to stand! He appealed and the Judicial Commission found against him – but it was inquorate!'

'You must learn that all people are shit,' she responds philosophically, drawing on another cigarette. 'Then be pleasantly surprised when you find a kind side to some of them. You've been too trusting and too naive. That was your crime. Your openness, your ability to relate to people, is a gift. You must learn not to use it! Reserve it for those simple souls: children, very old people, those who are dying. Use it then. Otherwise, don't cast your pearls before swine.'

'I was wrong to resign,' I muse. 'If I'd been a Catholic priest they'd have banished me to some remote island. The irony is I'd have *loved* some wild place no-one else wanted to serve. I'd have cared earnestly for the folk.'

'Ah, but Catholics know how to handle these things. They know about original sin. They expect shit and they deal with it. . . Why do you say you were you wrong to resign? Surely at the time you couldn't take any more.'

'But I wouldn't have done it three days later! They didn't give me a chance to think. They cornered me in a weak moment.'

'Of course! They did what they had to do. They set a trap and they hoped you'd walk in.'

'They do that.'

'It's like putting sheep in a pen. You open the gate and if you choose the right moment to shoo them, hopefully you can shut the gate before they go past. Trust ministers? Don't.'

A Wise Man

1st January 2000

It is the first day of the year and of the new millennium. Some of my friends in Edinburgh have persuaded me to go to a special evening service in Edinburgh. They are both singing in the choir. It's nothing to do with the Church of Scotland and they tell me it will not be like the normal dull event. It's being organised by the Most Reverend Richard Holloway, Bishop of Edinburgh and Primus of the Episcopal Church in Scotland. I've enjoyed reading some of this senior cleric's books and I've heard him speak on the radio. He's a respected scholar and thinker, though the conservative wing cannot thole his liberal theology.

My friends could not have known that the reading the Bishop has chosen for tonight will be a modern soliloquy, told in the first person and based on the Gospel story of the woman caught in adultery. In this alternative version of her condemnation and intended execution, the indignant mob ready to hurl the stones at her is made up of newspaper reporters and television cameramen.

There is an army of them standing in the young woman's garden, baying for blood. The self-righteous horde is bashing on the doors and windows of the downstairs flat where she has gone to earth. I am crying by now. They are haranguing her, shouting for her to come out of her den and face them and explain herself. In this rendition of the event, the rocks her accusers hold in their hands as ammunition are notepads, cameras and microphones. Then, to flush her out, one of them bends down to pick up a stone from the path and lifts his arm to lob it at the window behind which she sits, terrified. My heart leaps to my mouth.

The Bishop preaches about abuse of power in institutions: the media and the Church. He is cutting close to the bone.

Next, baskets of broken bread are being passed among the people.

'No more shame,' he says, as he invites everyone to partake of the Body of Christ.

I yearn for that Bread, of which I have so long been deprived.

The tears are streaming down my face.

When the service ends, the Bishop cannot help but see my distress and he comes across to me. He asks if I would like to tell him why I am so upset.

I want to answer but I am mute. My jaw moves but no sound comes out. I am winded with emotion. Air enters my stricken windpipe but it doesn't pass out again. The Bishop waits patiently, for a minute or perhaps longer. I gaze at him helplessly, willing him to pull words out of me like a line from a fish's gullet. Eventually, realising that I cannot overcome my disability, he turns his attention to someone else.

People are milling around, talking and exchanging New Year greetings. I am too shaken to stand up and walk out. My friends are still up in the organ loft. A woman who's known me since the time I lived in Edinburgh comes over to me, but I am still dumbstruck. She asks if she may tell the Bishop who I am and I nod assent. At once, he knows why I am so distraught. He frees himself and returns to me.

'What they did to you was quite, quite dreadful,' he says. He gives me time to speak, but still not one word will come. I am a river-trout pulled out of the loch, left gasping on the water's edge. Unblinking, mouth agape, the unhelpful breeze flows over my gills. The barbed fishing hook has lacerated my throat. I am maimed.

'Well, if you ever want a cup of coffee and a blether. . .'

March 2000

Three successive Moderators of the Church of Scotland have refused to give me pastoral care, even when my university lecturers pleaded with them to speak to me. Now here is the Primus – the Chief of the Episcopal Church – offering to see me. This pastoral leader is not frightened off by the intensity of my grief. This Most Reverend holy father does not fear moral contagion.

For the best part of four years the majority of my colleagues have avoided me like effluent from a blocked sewer. I have been judged and I have internalised their judgement. I know myself to be a ragged and stinking example of an 'untouchable' caste. So it is several months before I dare accept the Bishop's coffee.

Bishop Richard Holloway poses all the right questions: obvious questions, but which nobody else has thought to ask: 'What about theology? God, Jesus, and all that stuff? What's all this done to you?'

'God's all right. It's just the Church.' I am already crying, as always when I speak of the loss of my ministry.

'Mmm. That's what God thinks, too! The way they handled it was atrocious. Even if you'd *wanted* to go to bed with the man, there are ways of dealing with human frailties. Why did it happen this way?'

'I worked with a threatened man.'

'Ah, yes: Robert Ramsay; the Presbytery Clerk who libelled you in the national media. I can see it all. . .'

'They made out I'd lied, denied everything, changed my story. But I'd never denied what happened. They just couldn't grasp that I hadn't desired him. There was one article that made Sandy out to be an evil sex fiend, but that wasn't any closer to the truth than the rest of the stories, that had me for a whore and a trollop. Then there were the "stripped to her undergarments in the pulpit " type tales. Do you want to know where all that came from? It was an illustration for a children's sermon about what's in our hearts being more important than the show we put on for people. I didn't 'strip' at all!'

'The truth is, though,' he comments, 'most of them would have *liked* to see you in your bra and knickers. Most of the churchmen who judged you were having lurid thoughts about you. It was their own fantasies, their own guilt, they projected onto you.'

'Even if I'd been tried and acquitted it would have been impossible for me to return to my pulpit,' I explain. 'Six of my own ruling elders were members of the Presbytery, my jurors, including bosom pals of the accusing family. The details of my private life were revealed to the people among whom I lived. The Church dealt with the matter in a juridical fashion when that was inappropriate. And they didn't protect me – from the press besieging the house, nor from the sex perverts targeting me afterwards. The shaming, the humiliation, was awful.'

'What about your family?'

'I left. Escaped sexual abuse. They didn't protect me, either.'

'So you've nobody who's really close to you. Unless you're in a relationship?'

'No. I'm not. I'm too scared to have a boyfriend. Despite all they said about me being "hot for the boys", I can't. I'm scared. I don't want anyone to touch me or kiss me, or anything.'

'Sex isn't a bad thing anyway, Love . . . And you should stop going to church.'

He says extraordinary things, for a bishop: things I need to be told.

Easter 2001

This week the Court of Session ruled that, despite the Church having broken its own rules, the civil courts have no jurisdiction to hear my case.

I have exhausted all the legal remedies that may have been available to me within Scotland. The Court of Session was the last resort, after the preliminary hearing at the Office of Industrial Tribunals in Dundee and the Employment Appeals Tribunal in Edinburgh. It has taken several years already.

The trouble is, impartial as perhaps the Lawlords may be, the National Church does wield remarkable unseen power in the circles that count in this country. With the exception of the token Roman Catholic or a Jew, a Lawlord is most likely to be an elder in the Church of Scotland. At the very least he will be a member of the same Edinburgh Club as a former Moderator. He will wield a golf iron on the same green, have sons at the same private school, imbibe in the same haunt, or luncheon in the same eatery on the Royal Mile.

My self-respect, and concern for others I know who have been cast aside by the Church, demand that I continue to seek justice. The process may take a couple of years longer than it has already taken but at least in London the verdict will lie with Judges from south of the English border. My case will be before the highest court in the United Kingdom. I am going to appeal to the House of Lords.

Meanwhile, I am still finding it hard to find a proper job. I'm given occasional work by former parishioners, dosing sheep with worming medicine, trimming hooves, or clipping the shit away from ewes' tail-ends to discourage flies from laying eggs there. Blow-fly larvae, sometimes in their thousands, eat into the flesh of the animal, causing immense distress and death. I do some childminding and, one day a week, care for someone who has dementia. This keeps me from being dependent on state benefits. I may not be paid for all of these tasks, but it matters more to me that I do not feel entirely useless. I have even spent several days walking behind a tractor and plough picking up worms for the mole-catcher. I don't have the confidence to go to places where people may recognise me. I don't want to have to wear pea green. At least my neighbours know I do not fit the picture the newspapers paint consistently, with computer-imaging lipstick added. I struggle with anxiety even answering the phone or opening letters: I'm sure the contents will be bad.

A friend who has just returned from South Africa visits me in my eyrie, where only sheep have kept me company for some time. She envisages me in another remote setting; somewhere I never dreamed of going. She has the details of the volunteer position sent to me. I read through them, and I *know* the job is meant for me. The interview is in central London. I'm nervous but I'm so certain I shall be chosen. I pack up my cottage, and head off to work with children who have been raped, in the villages on the fringe of the African Kalahari. It is a region that is notorious; rife with this crime.

The years in Africa will have to fill another volume.

London

September 2005

The House of Lords Hearing: Percy v Church of Scotland.

My first visit to London since returning from Africa. With me is my trusted lawyer, Jamie Baxter, his colleague Mr Elliot, and my Queen's

Counsels Brian Napier and Susan O'Brien, for whom I have enormous respect. Jamie Baxter and his colleague sit with me in the grandest room I have ever entered, with tall leaded windows, leather-upholstered benches, and oil paintings of distinguished members of the court, larger than life, in gilded frames that would smash your head in if they fell off the oak-panelled wall. Jamie and his colleague stand guard outside the toilets in case newspaper reporters are sniffing around. They treat me to pie and chips in a pub round the corner from the Houses of Parliament at lunch times, and escort me to the tube station at the end of each afternoon, making sure that I'm through the ticket barrier without being pursued back to Finsbury Park, where I am sleeping on a friend's floor.

Blairgowrie, Scotland
December 2005

Jamie Baxter telephones me and asks me to come into his little office over the chip shop in Blairgowrie High Street. He wants me to be sitting down and for him to be able to watch my expression, when he tells me that word has come up from London, from the House of Lords. . .

We won!

England
May 2006

I am flying south to meet my father for the first time in twenty years. He is very sick with cancer. He has expressed a wish to see me – a message relayed through my godmother. I have no desire to see him but I could not live with myself if I denied a dying human being such a request.

My godmother has made the arrangements for this meeting,

easing some of the stress on me. I have not spoken to my father even on the telephone. He assured my godmother he was well enough to drive to the airport. I shall spend two or three hours with him and then he will drop me at a train station so that I can go on to my godmother's.

We sit on the tarmac in Edinburgh, already safety-briefed and seat-belted, when the announcement is made that the Easyjet flight will be forty minutes late taking off. My father will be anxious. He will not know if I really did board the flight until it lands at the other end. My survival strategy is to pretend to myself that this meeting is an everyday occurrence. I allow no emotion. I convince myself that I am dispassionate.

When I emerge into the arrivals hall I know at once that the wraith steadying itself on the metal barrier is the father I saw two decades ago. He is half the girth he was then; a skeleton with cellophane skin drawn over it, eyes ringed red. He struggles to speak and fails. He is a rabbit; disease-ridden, crouched at the road-side, swollen eyes unseeing, ears turning to hear how and from which direction death will come.

I have no words. I would have picked up a rabbit by its hind legs, whacked its head against a fence post, put it out of its misery. I cannot bring death's mercy to my father. I take his fragile arm. What else can I do? Pity and compassion flood me. There is no crevice left for any other feeling to hide.

The walk to the short-stay car park is interminable. Airport staff keep stopping us to ask if they can bring a wheelchair. He is so frail! He assures each one that he has no need of assistance. I wish he would give in. He cannot remember where he has parked, although it is not far from the forecourt. He fumbles with the ticket. The machine won't work because his time has expired. I have to find someone in a uniform to raise the barrier and find myself apologising for my father's condition. My father, who always pitted his wits against traffic wardens and officials. My father, who could find a route through the one-way systems of any vast city. My father, whose self-assurance verged on pomposity at times. My father, whom I am helping to find his way out of a car park.

He unwraps the sandwiches he has made us. I am not hungry, but I eat them because I know it is a matter of small pride that he is still able to make a loaf of bread. He eats no more than a wren.

He talks now. He speaks of subjects to which I am antipathetic: the house he has built, his army career, his idolisation of 'Lady Thatcher'. He speaks, also, of several injustices in his life that have left him raw with hurt.

He knows of my success in the House of Lords. I guess he has read only the hideous and skewed version portrayed in the *Daily Express* and it is clear that he has no insight as to how my childhood under his roof was at the root of all that ensued. Nonetheless, it is apparent that he is proud of me. He is proud that I 'desired the right'. He quotes from the Falklands War repeatedly. He would like it to be said at his funeral that he also 'desired the right'.

I see something of my father in me. Politically we are poles apart – but we share a stubborn determination to pursue justice and truth, each in our different ways. Both of us have had to deal with bitterness and disillusionment as a result of the battles we have fought so doggedly.

I am surprised that my father's pride in me means so much to me.

Ardfenaig, Scotland
November 2007
I am squatting behind a lichen-encrusted slab of rock, hoping they will go away soon. Strangers. Snooping around the wagon in which I now live. Walkers with rucksacks, intrigued by the simplicity of my primitive habitation. They have dogs and my own collie is keen to bound forth and greet them, giving away our presence. I whisper

a threat to him and he flattens himself down in the bracken; but nose, eyes and ears are intent on the intruders and he is all of a quiver.

I wait and watch. One man mounts the steps, tries the handle, and shoves at the door. The wood is swollen with wet. There is a knack to opening it. Even in the distance I hear as the fragile frame splinters.

They even go inside, one by one, ducking down to negotiate the small doorway, taking it in turns to squeeze into my minute private space and to comment on the paraffin lanterns, the miniature wood-burning stove, the wooden box seats and the narrow bed that takes up the entirety of the back wall.

I feel immense sadness. My refuge, remote as it is, has been discovered and invaded. My existence is still pea-green, after all these years.

They are picnicking under my hazel tree. I need them to leave. I have crossed the inlet at low tide, sliding through mustard-coloured bladder-rack without enough clothes to sit them out for any length of time on a cold day. Clambering up the face of the quarry, the clatter of loose stones will attract their attention. I stay where I am, shivering, aware that the rising tide will flood the saltmarsh and my return journey will take far longer than my slithering escape.

A reel of pea-green thread is running back to the years of my childhood. Here I am, still trying to hide away: from impertinent hillwalkers, from paparazzi, and from a tractor-man who cannot help but see my gaudy coat as I huddle in the bottom of a ditch. I trace back the confounded gleaming thread all the way to the first time my abuser pulls me towards him and forces me to kiss him. I think that there it will stop, with the tiny pieces of something unidentifiable but distinctly green floating in the pile of my vomit.

I am ten years old. I have spewed up my revulsion and my self-disgust into the bathroom sink and the volume of the contents of my stomach is choking the plug-hole. It won't go away. I see my own ashen face in the mirror; the grey around my eyes. The sweat turns cold. My nightdress, the one with the elephant embroidered on the front, has bits of sick spattered on it, including the remains of green vegetable. The adulterated nightdress is lifted over my head and I am put into a pair of my big sister's spare pyjamas. Both taps are running hard. The vomit is reducing. There, it's all gone. All washed away. The last of it. Gone.

Only, I spy it now, for the first time: there is a frayed end of the pea-green twine in the drain.

There is more. It goes back further than I realised. It loses its verdure now. It is muddied. But strong. And it goes back through a whole century.

Malaya

1951

My father, at eighteen years of age.

My father is hiding, not behind a rock, but under banana leaves, close to a stink-tree. The stench of rotting meat that derives from its fist-sized fruits turn his stomach. He is hiding, not from hill-walkers, but from Chinese bandits. If he trembles, the leaves will give him away.

They know he is in the vicinity. He shot dead one of their number, not ten minutes ago – before his own head could be sliced off. He has killed a man. They are hunting him now. He evacuates his bowels in terror. The fruit of the stink-tree hides his smell from his pursuers.

England

1940

Three little boys – the middle one is my father – arrive home to present their spoils: mangolds. They were stolen from a cart left at the side of a farmer's field and stuffed under the boys' winter coats. They anticipate the vegetables mashed up and steamy hot for their tea. This is the time of black-outs, ration-books, air-raid sirens and watery porridge. Mangolds are a treat. Their mother will be pleased.

Their mother sees only the muddy coats and shorts and bog-coloured socks. She berates the boys and pours boiling water from the giant kettles into the tin bath in the kitchen. She strips the clothes off her three sons roughly and lifts them into the bath.

She does not heed their screams. She makes them sit down in that water. She does not notice the blazing red legs and bottoms when, finally, they are allowed to climb out.

My mother told us this story about my father's childhood. It is the only story I know. He left school to go to work when he was twelve, but I don't know where he was employed, or where he was brought up. He never spoke about any of it, nor of what happened in Malaya.

Norfolk

1906

The tail end of the thread goes back to a pig-farm in Norfolk.

This time, the little boy is my paternal grandfather. Ted is picking up wind-fallen apples in the orchard. He must not go near the piggery on Sunday, because the pigs are not fed that day and if they

354

hear anyone in the yard they will scream their rage. Ted's foster-father says starving them on the Sabbath means they eat better on Monday and they grow fat quicker. Ted suspects this may not be true. Pigs are always keen to shove their snouts in swill, even if they have breakfasted recently.

This is all I know of my father's lineage: my great grandmother was a Percy, of the Dukedom of Alnwick in Northumberland. It was the Percy name that she gave her son, but she kept his existence a secret from her family. She paid for him to be reared by a couple on a pig farm in Norfolk and he became a pig-man like his foster-father.

At one time my father attempted to trace his forebears. My great grandmother was deceased by then, but her sister was shocked, terribly, when she learned that my great grandmother had 'issue'. Whether my great grandfather was her lover or rapist no-one else will ever know. Either way, the social disgrace of pregnancy out of wedlock was of pea-green shame to my great grandmother. My father was haunted by the illegitimacy of his father. His rage when my teenaged sister called him 'bastard' was out of all proportion. My sister called him many names in her rebel years, but that one epithet struck home hard.

'The sins of the fathers,' as the Old Testament says, were indeed 'visited unto the third and fourth generation.'

Ardfenaig, Scotland

November 2007

My father has been dead for over a year. I am in my rocky hideout, avoiding the hillwalkers. Today, stunned by the juxtaposed shining patches of bright green and blood-red sphagnum moss, I have realised the connection between my life and my father's, and his father's, and his grandmother's. Today, I realise that I have forgiven him for everything that happened, wholeheartedly.

Kilry

Autumn 2006

It is a year since the House of Lords overruled the Court of Session's earlier decision, permitting my case to be referred back to the industrial tribunal. The case is settled out of court at the time of my father's death. Even then the Church is sly and wangles it so that I can only claim damages for the small part the Board of National Mission played in suspending me prematurely, and not for all the rules the Presbytery broke. The Church says the Board of National Mission was my employer, but the Presbytery, although it was responsible for disciplining me, is an agent of God. This is ludicrous: how can a Board of the Church have a separate legal identity from the rest of the Church, when it is the Church that creates and dissolves the Board and appoints its members and decides on its remit? Nevertheless they swing it.

A snide remark in the press made by the Church of Scotland's lawyer, Jeannette Wilson, infuriates me. She says as I have agreed to settle for such a small sum I cannot have thought I had much of a case. How twisted can someone be? She knew that, years back at the Employment Appeals Tribunal, by changing the name of the Respondents to 'The Board of National Mission' rather than 'The Church of Scotland', the Church was planning ahead for damage limitation, should a final judgement be in my favour. It was sleekit, and I had not wanted my Advocate to accept the change at the time. I knew what the Church was scheming. Advocate Brian Napier, and later Queen's Counsel Susan O'Brien, had both been adamant that it would make no difference – that the name used was just a name, that it could be changed back again, and that in any case the umbrella organisation would be held responsible for the actions of its subsidiary boards and committees. I had been uncomfortable with this and was to be proved right. The Church was devious through and through.

The House of Lords decision had been in my favour, but Lord Hope was careful in his written judgement to leave the Presbytery an 'out', by saying that I was the legal employee of an insignificant committee, while the Presbytery itself was an agent of God and free to act independently of any human law. . .

I'm given a fraction of the compensation I'd have gained if the Presbytery's actions had been taken into account.

I refuse to collect the cheque for £10,000 from my lawyer's office for a long time and the day I do, frowning, I put it straight into a separate account. I send it to a charity for survivors of rape in South Africa. I don't want it.

Autumn 2010

Front page of the *Daily Record* again. My photograph in at least half a dozen other papers. National television. Radio. Wrong address, though. (Not surprising then, the obligatory comments from neighbours: 'We don't see her very often, she keeps herself to herself.') Wrong age. (I don't look that haggard, do I?) Wrong amount of council tax benefit that I'm accused of having obtained fraudulently.

Wrong dates. . . Most of that time I was either a volunteer in Africa or living in a wooden wagon like a tink. A mad cat lady. With sheepdogs, not cats. I'd struggle to keep two dogs, eight puppies, chickens, and graze a flock of sheep on a tiny bit of mowed lawn in the town where the newspapers maintain I'm living. Yes, I did once keep a pig in a back garden, but there is a limit! It is a waste of time writing to the toothless Press Complaints Commission. Besides, the more ludicrous the articles are, the safer I am from unwanted visitors. They won't be looking for me in my lair in the glen. I work as a shepherd back in Kilry these days, although the hot sun of the Kalahari and its children have also become part of my soul over the intervening years.

The fact that all those years ago the Presbytery left out one crucial sentence of an agreed press statement – that sex happened on one *'single occasion, without consent'* – means that each time my name appears in print I am tarred as a slut.

It seems I am guilty of giving away too much money – of impoverishing myself deliberately, and then claiming benefit. The scale of the media coverage is completely disproportionate to my 'crime': it's hardly as if I'm the Moors Murderer or Bible John.

I choose to live an eremetical life on top of a hill. I'm one of a handful of people who doesn't have a television, and it's only recently that I've rented somewhere that has electricity. I drive a clapped-out two-seater Skoda that doesn't start reliably and needs new tyres. It's hardly as if I swan around in a fancy limo! Work is difficult to find, especially when I've been so maligned by the media and have become reclusive. Based on my actual income, there is no doubt that I would qualify for the council tax discount. I do have some savings, and I do own a ramshackle building on a boggy patch of land – but it's not some mansion with gold door-knobs, as the press would have readers believe.

The absurdity of criminal law is almost as Kafkaesque as the ecclesiastical set-up. All the court officials will tell me is that I have to plead 'guilty' or 'not guilty', but they won't send me a copy of the charge against me – except to an address where I don't live – so how can I decide? I receive a missive regaling me for not appearing in court, but I was never told about the hearing in the first place. All they will say is that I should engage a lawyer – and this should not be Jamie Baxter, more's the pity, because he is a potential witness. He knows why I gave away that money. He knows

I was disgusted with the way the Kirk's lawyer behaved. He knows that that I deemed the Church of Scotland's cash to be from an 'unethical source'. I had wanted justice, not some begrudged compensation.

So I pick up the phone directory and dial the number of a firm of solicitors, randomly. The receptionist puts me through to a young man who says he will take on my case. He avers that there are 'certain procedures that must be followed' and that I should not make any plea at all. He does not seem to find an appropriate juncture to defend me within the rigid system, but only to trot along to the court building every now and then, arrange a postponement, write to tell me a new date, and bill me for writing to tell me the new date. I'm not allowed to see the evidence against me – but the press is given access to everything, even my medical certificates.

Exasperated, after months of legal dilly-dallying, and the day before yet another court appointment, I contact Jamie Baxter. I need advice on procedure, even if he cannot act for me.

'Can you prove you sent that money to Africa?'

'Yes. The bank will have copies of the transactions in its archives.'

'Then don't plead guilty. You *didn't* do it in order to qualify for a state benefit. You gave it away because it was 'dirty' money. Look, I'm going to be at court tomorrow morning anyway. I won't have long, but I'll have a word with someone who is competent, and ask them to speak for you. Drop the papers through my door and I'll take them along for you.'

I would trust Jamie with my life. He brought me through a long ordeal in the past. I know that I am in safe hands now.

They alter the charge against me at this juncture. Now they are saying I didn't have too much capital. They are more interested in my boggy bit of land, which I did declare, but the Council has mislaid the documentation.

Strathnaver and Brora

Spring 2011

Sarah is from Highland Council Criminal Justice Services. She will be my 'probation officer'. I'm thankful that she agrees to meet me in the village so I don't have to go into the town. I am virtually agoraphobic these days, partly because I still feel shamed – branded – by what happened to me all those years ago, and partly because I've spent most of the intervening years either in the Kalahari Desert or up on a hill in the company of sheep, curlews, and eagles.

Sarah is the same size as me, which is useful as she kits me out in her own clothes to attend court. She drives two hundred miles to stand beside me in front of the Sheriff down in Perth. She does her damnedest to persuade me to go to the Council and ask for help with housing. She's certain I'd qualify to have my rent and council tax paid. I won't do it, so she insists on giving me £20 of her own money and buying me some food which, equally, I insist is not necessary. My clothing is ragged and dirty because I have been working with sheep. I am not as poor as I look.

I won't go to the Council because my name was used fraudulently by the 'friend' who looked after my sheepdog, Roy, when I was in Africa. This woman and her partner have warned me not to seek repayment and not to expose them at a tribunal. I've received dozens of abusive text messages and phone calls from them and I know they have been looking for me up the glen. My former neighbours are protective of me and won't let on where I am. The police are aware of the difficulty, but they can hardly provide a twenty-four hour body-guard: I'm not royalty! I know the couple have a close relative working in the Housing and Council Tax office, so I don't want to give an official address where I could be flushed out by them.

Oddly, a death-threat finally breaks the tension for me: it is so ridiculous that I find myself laughing about it, and no longer shaking with fright.

A threat to my animals I treat less lightly. I am afraid they will harm my dog.

I love that dog more than I have ever loved any creature and he makes it clear he's mad about me, too. He leans against my shin and gazes into my eyes. He would go to the moon for me, and back, if I asked. I've only to whisper and he drops to the ground, or flies to the ridge of the hill to fetch sheep. He does not blame me for going to Africa, though it's clear he had a hard time in my long absence. Roy is at my side day and night. He is so intuitive that he knows the thoughts of my heart.

Then Roy is killed in a road accident.

It is Sarah who offers to help me lift the dog's bloodied body into the back of my rusting Skoda. It is Sarah who assesses me for suicide risk (I'm off the scale) but puts her neck on the line professionally and does not cart me to a psychiatric unit for my own protection. She recognises that I'll be safest left alone in the mountains with the herds of red deer, to mourn.

The man for whom I'm working meets me at the footbridge and carries Roy across the Brora River and up the hill to the shed. He is concerned about the degree of my distress but, like Sarah, he respects my need to be left alone. He helps me dig a hole for the burial, but goes away so that I can fill it in myself, with earth and with tears.

My noble dog lies on a crag between the Pictish fort and the loch. If I should crawl beneath the carcasses of sheep in the dead hole on the low strath, and die, he would be above me, guarding my rotting body, as he watched over me in life.

361

Why do I plead guilty in the end? The reasons are many, as they were when I admitted *'improper'* conduct to the Church – but not to being *'scandalous'* or *'immoral'*. History is repeating itself. This has already cost me so much in time, in health, and in cash – the lawyers' fees will soon exceed the amount of council tax I owed in the first place! The Council has still not found my documents, so I can't prove what I declared. I'm working in such an isolated place that I cannot reach the city within the day's notice I'm given to plead 'not guilty' in person. I've hardly seen another human being for weeks and I know I'd collapse in fear if I had to face a crowded courtroom at trial, whereas sentencing will take place when the court is less busy. And now my dog has been killed. Nothing else matters. I don't care what they do to me any more.

The Sheriff's decision itself doesn't worry me. I'm stuck within the system now and he'll have to impose a penalty of some sort because a pleasant soul has tipped off the press as to my identity. It's been a fantastic excuse for the newspapers to reel out all their favourite headlines: 'SEX SCANDAL MINISTER' and 'MISSIONARY POSITION FOR RANDY REV'. Otherwise, the matter of my council tax would have been dropped last July when I paid it. But Sarah says it's a minor offence and the worst the Sheriff can do is order me to see her for a few months – which would be a pleasure for both of us. We've already decided we'll be friends for life.

No, what terrifies me is walking into the court building in Perth and facing the press photographers – even dressed in Sarah's suit and wearing her dark glasses.

But the street is quiet. It's lunch time. No cars pass us. There's nobody else at the columned entrance to the imposing court house when we mount the stone steps. I need not have worried. There's no-one around. The place is almost eerily deserted. . .

The following day there is a big picture of me on the front page of the newspaper, in Sarah's outfit, and film footage of me on the television news. The shots were taken right there where I stood on the steps outside the court. I cannot think where the snipers can have been lying in wait for me. They were using a long-range device. I didn't see anyone. I didn't know they were there.

From now on, nowhere feels safe. This is the invasion of my privacy that I dreaded. They have stripped me naked and put me on public view. This is a rape repeated.

I wake around four o'clock in the morning with the clearest vision of Roy. My dog is standing on the pavement in front of the court steps, twelve yards away, facing me. He just stands there, looking at me, waiting for me to tell him what to do. He is unable to protect me from the cameramen because he doesn't know where they are, either.

I burst into tears, calling out to my dead dog.

Would I give away that tainted money all over again? I've seen children in Africa eat sand mixed with water just to fill their bellies before bed-time. Would I 're-offend' in order to feed them if I had the opportunity? In all probability, I would.

The Strength of Gossamer
Kilry
June 2011

'Never again would she go to that church. . . Sundays
here were for ever her own.
'The victories last only a short time while the defeats last for
ever. . . But, just the same, things came in on the high tide
which you could keep when the tide was going out again.'

Iain Crichton Smith: *Consider The Lilies*

ON the side of the hill behind the village church, I am coaxing a
late lamb to breathe after a difficult birth. Tickling the inside of its
nostrils with tufts of dry grass brings it sneezing into life. I pull the
ewe round to sniff her offspring. A field away, cars are arriving and
upright fur-coated figures are making their procession into church,
but I am absorbed in persuading the young ewe to take to
motherhood after the trauma of an assisted birth. I slip the lamb's
wet tail between her teeth, making her taste what she must lick.
Eventually she mutters a deep-throated purring and begins to sup
up the yellow mucous, a sign that she will stay to tend to the lamb,
rather than bolt the minute I let go of her. I creep away slowly.
Sitting up, I hear the organ lurch into sound. *'Now the green blade
riseth from the buried grain; seed that in dark earth many days
hath lain. . . Back from the grave, that with the dead has been. . .'*

I still believe that life is stronger than death, that love is stronger
than hate. But I weep, hearing the hymn, because I am excluded
from God's people. I am denied communion.

At least grief no longer consumes me completely and, though

364

I feel no joy in life, my ability to feel compassion has increased. Though I still carry with me a sense of injustice, at last the truth will be told. I hope that as a result of publishing this book there will be fewer victims of a callous and intransigent ecclesiastical system in the future.

Last night there was an eclipse of the full moon. She had barely risen in Scotland by eleven o' clock, but in Southern Africa she had been blood red for almost an hour, the sky was strewn with stars, and it seemed like a dark prayer. I know this because friends around the globe who had met my dog offered to watch the moon at the same time, and weave a loving web around me into which I might fall when I need it.

Now I know the strength of gossamer strands.

I intend staying in this glen, which was the bed both of curse and of blessing.

In the woods the wild hyacinths, indigo blue, are finally going to seed. But they'll flower again.

∽◉◡

Turning out documents in the impossibly small living space of my wagon, I come across the poem I wrote in the hornbeam wood when I was fourteen years old:

Hornbeam Wood

It was the strong scent of nettles and dog's mercury
crushed underfoot
that brought me back to Norwood End.
I had pressed from my mind
the pain of its beauty
since the blackbird's swollen-throated singing after rain
seared through me
and I saw but could not reach
what had been stolen from me.
The yellow wych-elm in the corner of the wood
may still stand
against a bruise-hued sky
and the faint wine fragrance of thrum-eyed primroses
yet mingle with violets on the edge.
Its heart should daze with the intensity of wild hyacinth
indigo
and the odd milky flower-head still be cherished among them.
I shall not know this:
robbed prematurely of innocence
I dare not go back
lest I find my childhood haven also
raped
and the hyacinths torn up by the whites of their stems.

APPENDIX 1

1. CATHERINE DEVENEY: SCOTLAND ON SUNDAY, November 9 1997

For the first time in public Nicoll has described the incident that led to Percy's downfall. 'As soon as it was over I remember thinking that this was not what the lassie had wanted,' he said.

The day they had sex was in December 1995, when he took soup made by his wife to her home. She was ill in bed with flu. He says he knew she would not resist sex because of her background. Percy claims she 'froze' and was unable to respond at all. Afterwards, Nicoll says there was immediate regret. 'I said to her: "That was rape, wasn't it?" . . . I betrayed her trust. I've probably ruined her life.'

Nicoll says he wrote to the Presbytery confirming that Percy had not consented to sex but was accused of covering up for her.

2. JAMES ROUGVIE: THE SCOTSMAN, November 10 1997

. . . Another minister claimed Nicoll's confession was part of a plot to 'save her neck'. The Rev Robert Ramsay said: 'There's a lot more to come yet. She now seems to be saying that she has never denied having sex with him. But she's denied it all along, until last week. Her story changes with the wind quite honestly. He's just come along now to back up her story, but that's just what I expected. The woman doesn't have the slightest idea what the truth is and she never has had. The two of them have concocted this. Reading this, it makes her look like little Miss Innocent when that is clearly not the case.' He added that the whole affair had ripped apart the Kirk community in Angus.

The letter, found in Nicoll's farmhouse, showed that there had been collusion between the two of them:

'Dear Sandy, I don't know how to get out of this s✱✱✱.

'Your family knows that I faxed you through EDA and that you have vowed to stand witness for me that you raped me, though that does not seem to impress them. They think you are so besotted you'd say anything. You must insist that you did indeed rape me when I was ill in bed and you brought soup from Moyra, and you took advantage of my extremely vulnerable state. . . We both needed to talk about the resulting pregnancy, loss and shared grief. You asked for me to meet you in Perth on your last return from Bosnia. You were so pissed that you can't remember why. The fact that I met you is part of their allegations.

'I cannot in any way have contact with you when you come back, but using Drusilla who would meet you if necessary, we have to keep in touch to know what is going on in each other's situations. . .

'I still don't want to be with you unless you are divorced. (If that's what you choose. You could still choose to stay with your family.) If you want you could divorce and have your name changed by deed poll! But Sandy, however much I love you, there are other people who love me and whom I would be letting down. . . All this is very heavy, but very important. I have lost everything that matters to me through this but I still love you. Don't forget that because I may not have the chance to tell it to you again. Who knows where each of us will be, what will happen. I shan't stop loving you, or forget the pain and the tenderness we have shared. . . Don't leave any more bits of paper and incriminating evidence lying around.'

3. CATHERINE DEVENEY: SCOTLAND ON SUNDAY, November 16 1997

The small clump of snowdrops Percy planted in a wooded lane at the beginning of 1996 were chosen because they are always in bloom in January. . .

No passer by would guess the secret of those fragile flowers but the snowdrop memorial holds the key to the final part of their story and explains the 'shared pain and tenderness' described in the letter.

The letter, it was claimed by her accusers, showed that Percy was coaching Nicoll to say he had raped her. But it could be interpreted in two ways: as a plea to tell lies, or a plea to tell the truth. "You must insist that you did indeed rape me. . .' she wrote.

What was not open to interpretation was that the letter showed a strong emotional relationship between the two. . . Nicoll claims the relationship shifted ground after the 'rape' but it was never again physical.

Percy was terrified to discover she was pregnant...It was a time that she needed to confide in someone. But there was only one person who knew what had happened: Nicoll.

Percy and Nicoll knew more about each other than almost anyone else. But the baby was a new shared secret that affected them as a couple, not just as individuals, and it was to change the way they saw one another. . . At the time, both decided the only answer was an abortion. But neither predicted how profound the emotional effects of that decision would be. 'I thought I would only feel relief, but I felt intense grief and guilt at stealing another life,' said Percy. 'To have to make this public is awful.'

But it has become public. . .

The Kirk has found it impossible to believe that the relationship between the two could be anything other than sexual. . . Percy used the word 'love' in the letter to Nicoll. But however anyone else interpreted it, she did not see it as a declaration of anything other than affection.

Nicoll said, 'I hoped there would be a long term relationship but deep down I didn't really think there would be.' But even if there had been, he knew it would be emotional, not physical. This weekend, Percy's associate minister Robert Ramsay told *Scotland on Sunday* he had been deeply upset by the whole business, that Percy was a consummate liar and there had never been anything wrong with the Nicoll's marriage until she arrived on the scene. He hoped the truth would emerge at the trial.

APPENDIX II

Unto the Venerable the General Assembly of the Church of Scotland
The Petition of HELEN PERCY
Humbly Sheweth:
1. That your Petioner agreed to demit status under pressure to avoid
a Trial by Libel which she had reason to believe would not be
conducted fairly because *inter alia*:

    i)The Convener of the Committee of Inquiry had denied your
Petitioner her right to legal representation at the beginning of
the inquiry.

    ii)Your Petitioner had subsequently been denied the right to be
present at all meetings regarding the Inquiry, and to defend
herself at all times (contrary to Section 6 of Act VII, 1935) both
by the Convener of the Committee of Inquiry and by the
solicitor duly appointed by the Presbytery and Prosecutor
Designate.

    iii) The Convener of the Committee of Inquiry informed the
Presbytery that your Petitioner **had** been 'present with her
Adviser at all meetings of the Committee in accordance with the
Act'.

    iv)Information had been leaked from the Presbytery to the press
throughout the Inquiry, and colleagues libelled your Petitioner
in the national media.

    v)Your Petitioner was informed by the Presbytery Clerk on 30th
November 1997 that she would be found guilty if tried, even if
she had not given consent to the single act with which she was
to be charged.

    vi)The Presbytery had already advertised your Petitioner's post
as Chaplain to Noranside Prison.

vii) The former presbytery Clerk had attempted to influence the main witness, threatening him with a prison sentence if he did not change his story.

2. That demission of Status was presented to your Petitioner as one of three options at a meeting on 30th November 1997 at which there was no-one present whose role was to advise her of her best interests, and that she was given no time to consider her decision but was required to decide by 5 p.m. that same day. The other options were:

 i)A trial in which the presbytery Clerk informed her she would be found guilty.

 ii) Suspension *sine die*, without having been tried.

3. That your Petitioner did not sign her demission. A copy of a statement to which she had, in great distress, given only verbal assent was forwarded to the Presbytery on her behalf and accepted at once.

That the Presbytery did not abide by the terms agreed in the statement regading what was to be released to the press.

That the Presbytery did not appoint a committee to confer with your Petitioner to ensure that she was fully aware of the consequences and implications of her Demission of Status.

That your Petitoner had been informed that having been suspended she was no longer entitled to be present at Presbytery meetings, and neither was she cited to appear at the meeting on 2nd December 1997. Therefore she had no right of appeal.

4. That the Church Medical Officer had, before the Inquiry began in June, advised your Petitioner be given time to seek counselling because she was in no fit state to make a reasoned decision regarding Demission of her Status. This time having been disallowed, and following the intense pressure of the media intrusion over several months, she was in even less fit state to make that decision when she was suddenly presented with that option on 30th November 1997.

5. That the legislation regarding Demission of a Charge (Act V, 1984, section 27, as amended by Act V, 1996) and which Very Rev Dr J. L. Weatherhead identifies in *The Constitution and Laws of the Church of Scotland* as being 'especially' important to follow for Demission of Status 'and even more so in the face of a trial by Libel' were not followed. Had they been followed your Petitioner would not have demitted status.

6. That your Petitioner demitted status 'to receive counselling'. (Minutes of Presbytery, 2nd December 1997) That counselling has now been received to the satisfaction of the Church Medical Officer.

7. That your Petioner is now prepared to face trial if this is in accordance with the Acts of the Church and is the desire of your Venerable Court.

8. That if your Petitioner had been found guilty of the 'single encounter' (Minutes of Presbytery' 2nd December 1997) the mitigating circumstances were such that she would not necessarily have been required to demit status.

9. That approximately two hundred of your petitioner's parishoners signed a petition on Sunday 9th November 1997 asking that the Presbytery **not** remove her status. Their petition was not made known to the Presbytery by the Clerks.

10. That the Presbytery has contributed to the raising of a scandal and that it is incumbent on your Venerable Court to assoilze her. (Act IX 1707)

11. That your Petioner has never lost her sense of vocation and believes that she would now be a far better Minister as a result of her experiences in June 1997.

May it therefore please your Venerable Court to instruct an independent investigation to examine the actions of Angus presbytery from June 1997, with particular regard to its decision to remove your Petioner's Status in December 1997. May it then therefore please your venerable Court, if fault be found with those actions, to revoke the decision of Angus Presbytery to remove your Petitioner's Status.

Or do otherwise as your Venerable Court may seem good.

And your Petitioner will ever pray.

APPENDIX III

THE REPLY OF THE PRESBYTERY (ABBREVIATED)

1. The Presbytery denies that the Petitioner's offer to demit was made under pressure. . . the Presbytery submits that there is a presumption that any Court of the Church will act fairly. . .

i) The general rule is that parties 'may' have legal represent-ation 'unless the Court shall otherwise determine'. . . The Convener of the Committee did 'otherwise determine'. . . **(Could a mere Convener legitimately take such a decision without consulting the Court?)**

ii) and iii) The Petitioner was not entitled to be present at meetings of the committee which were not part of the actual Inquiry, such as a consultation with one of the Assessors about arrangements for the hearings, and a meeting to prepare its report. **(Deviously, emphasis was placed on these 'purely administrative meetings' rather than on those to which my Petition referred. No reference was made to the Convener having misled the Court.)**

iv) The Presbytery denies absolutely that it was responsible for leaking information to the press, or for any defamatory items. . . **(Documents confidential to the inquiry had been published in national newspapers. Presbyters' names appeared beside numerous damaging and misleading quotes. Ramsay had called me a 'consummate liar' on national television.)**

v) The Presbytery Clerk denies that he made the alleged statement or anything like it.

vi) The Presbytery did not advertise the post. This was done by

374

the Board of National Mission. . . **(This was quibbling: who actually paid for the advert to be placed was beside the point.)** This was to take effect on the normal termination of the petitioner's appointment. **(Who ever advertises a job a whole year and nine months before it is intended to become available?)**

vii) The Presbytery has no knowledge of the alleged action of the former Presbytery Clerk. In any event, not being an action of the Presbytery, it is irrelevant. **(The Presbytery subsequently unearthed the letter of complaint from my solicitor and was forced to change its story.)**

2. The conclusion of that mediation meeting was that demission of status would be in the Petitioner's best interests, and those present were satisfied that she was fully aware of the consequences and implications. **(I was not advised, *inter alia*, that the Presbytery would be consulted if I applied for re-entry, nor about pension implications.)**

3. a) The Petitioner's offer to demit status was communicated in a letter signed by her solicitor. **(This evaded the issue of who instructed my solicitor.)** The authorisation to release the statement did not oblige the presbytery to do so. . .

b) The Petitioner had been informed several times that, although her suspension included suspension from membership of the Presbytery, she was entitled to attend open meetings of the Presbytery. If she thought otherwise, the Presbytery accepts no responsibility for her ignorance or misunderstanding. **(Items on the agenda pertaining to my case were taken in private. I was informed that I would be removed from the courtroom during these items.)**

She could have withdrawn her offer of demission, in which case no question of an appeal would have arisen.

(The whole point was that I was given no time to consider this decision.)

4. The Presbytery believed that, by the time the Preliminary Inquiry began, the Petitioner was in a fit state to be subject of that Inquiry, and affirms that at no time did she apply for sick leave, or ask to be excused from a hearing or meeting on medical grounds. **(My employers were in receipt of a medical line. The Convener of the inquiry possessed a letter stating that I was not fit to take part in a hearing.)**

5.It is not reasonable to claim that the option of demission of status was 'suddenly' presented at that meeting, since she had been made aware of that option for five months. **(Throughout those months I had been told that my demission would be accepted only if it included a written confession. The option to demit without acknowledging guilt was sprung on me for the first time that day in November.)**
The statement that procedure for demission of a charge should be followed is no legal obligation, but a moral one. It relates to the fact that the point of conference with a minister offering to demit is 'to ensure that the minister is fully aware of the consequences and implications of demission, especially if it is to be a demission of status.' This moral obligation has already been fulfilled. **(The implications had never been properly explained, and I had not been in a fit state to comprehend them.)**

6. The Presbytery has no knowledge of the Medical Officer's opinion. **(If the presbyters themselves had no knowledge of this it was because the Clerks and members of the Business Committee chose not to tell them.)**

7. Noted

8. Since the trial did not proceed there was no way of knowing what the precise terms of the Libel would have been. . . **(Rooney again denied having stated that the Libel would record my failure to report the assault to the Police. He had said this in the presence of two witnesses.)**

9. Parishioners had no locus in a trial by Libel, and it was therefore irrelevant to the proceedings. Indeed, it was an improper attempt to influence the course of justice. **(Parishioners, as interested parties, have every right to ask to be allowed to keep their minister. Legally, a petition <u>must</u> be lodged. The Presbytery had discarded the petition without record.)**

10. The words apply to a situation in which a judgement of an inferior court has been revoked on appeal to a superior court. They are not relevant to this petition.
11.Subsequent actions of the Petitioner, which are matters of public record, were inconsistent with a vocation to the ministry of the Church of Scotland. . . She made an application to an Employment Tribunal. . . in which she claimed unfair dismissal and made allegations which she has repeated in the present Petition. **(I had**

no other recourse to justice, and no right of appeal through the Church courts.)

She solemnised a marriage, changing her name to 'Douglas'. This action was contrary to Act I 1977. **(I had permission from the Registrar General and did not pretend to act as a Church of Scotland minister, and so did not contravene the Act. I had changed my name by statutory declaration a year prior to the marriage.)**

In view of the foregoing answers, the Presbytery of Angus submits:

I That it has acted fairly, with honesty and integrity and in accordance with the law of the Church throughout this case.

II That far from showing any grounds for questioning the honesty, integrity or legality of any of the Presbytery's actions, the allegation in the Petition are found, on examination, to be variously groundless or inaccurate, revealing ignorance and misunderstanding and containing misrepresentation. They are also largely irrelevant.

III That the Petitioner has not shown a *prima facie* case for an investigation.

IV That there is no case at all for reviewing the Presbytery's decision of 2nd December 1997.

APPENDIX IV

SPEECH BY HELEN PERCY TO THE GENERAL ASSEMBLY 1999

Moderator: When I lost my status as a minister, I also lost the right
to have my name cleared. I shall never be free of the unproven
allegations and rumours attached to my name unless this Petition is
granted. I have continued to be presumed guilty in the media – even
though I was neither tried nor convicted.

Dr Weatherhead writes in *The Constitution and Laws of the
Church*:

> 'An offer to demit should not be taken as tantamount to a
> confession of guilt, because a person who claims to be innocent
> may choose, for a reason other than guilt, to opt out of the
> process of trial by which innocence may be established. . . The
> responsibility of the Presbytery to appoint people to confer with
> anyone who offers to demit is particularly onerous if the offer is
> made in the face of a trial by Libel and, in the absence of
> specific legislation, especially if it is to be a demission of status.'

The Convener of the Committee of Inquiry refused to consider
my demission in July 1997 unless it included a written confession of
guilt, which I declined to make because I was not guilty of adultery.
At this point I was also told by the Convener that he would advertise
in the press for witnesses if I did not confess guilt.

By December 1997, however, the Presbytery agreed to accept
my demission without a confession (and without appointing people
to confer with me).

There were indeed reasons 'other than guilt' why at that
particular point, that afternoon, I opted to avoid the process of Trial
by which, had the Trial been conducted fairly, my innocence would
have been established:

I had been worn down by media intrusion and harassment. One 'phone call would have me shaking with fear for the rest of the day, because they knew where I was and my home was not safe. Sometimes a whole row of reporters' cars remained parked outside all day long so that I could not leave. They would be at the back door and at the front, shoving letters through, threats to write this or that if I did not give my side of the story, and constantly phoning. I crawled to the bathroom below window level to avoid their cameras.

I even had to change my name by statutory declaration as soon as I had demitted status, in order to avoid them. And almost every day, as a result of what appeared in pornographic mail would arrive in the post, and used condoms and anonymous threats of rape.

I also hoped that if I resigned my colleagues would start speaking to me again, once they no longer felt compromised as potentially my judges and jurors, and I longed for my sense of isolation and loneliness to end.

I have no wish to enter here, Moderator, into an adversarial debate which would damage the Church. It seems to me that if I reply to all of the points in the Presbytery's response, one by one, the Assembly will in fact be holding precisely that kind of public and acrimonious inquisition that your Petitioner has sought to avoid for the Church, by asking for an independent inquiry. May it suffice for me simply to show that there is reasonable question. For example:

The Presbytery states that I was entitled to attend open meetings of Presbytery. However this would have been of no help to me since I was told I should be required to leave during those items concerning my case, which would be taken in private.

Secondly, I was denied the right to be present and to defend myself during lengthy meetings and conversations between members of the Committee of Inquiry and the Presbytery's solicitor with my accusers. These were not the simply routine 'administrative' meetings that the Presbytery mentions in its response.

Thirdly, the prejudicial statements to which I referred in my Petition were made in front of witnesses. They are not 'irrelevant', because they had an immediate bearing on my decision to demit.

Again, the Presbytery may not have **placed** the advertisement for my post, but it did ask for the post to be filled – and set a closing date of 17th November 1997. But my own appointment was still effective until June 1999.

The Presbytery claims, 'At no time did the Petitioner apply for sick leave, or ask to be excused from a hearing on medical grounds' and 'By the time the Inquiry began again she was in a fit state to be the subject of that Inquiry.' How can Presbytery say this when the Inquiry began **three days** after the Church Medical Officer had advised that more time be given. I was summoned to the first hearing only **ten** days later. The Church was in receipt of a sick line, and I had written to the Convener begging time on medical grounds. My plea was ignored.

These are examples, Moderator, of the *prima facie* case for further examination.

With regard to interference from the press: with respect, I have not said that information was leaked by the Presbytery – but documents confidential to the inquiry were leaked from it, and individual presbyters were interviewed by the media and prejudicial comments attributed to them. These are specified in the Appendix.

There had been no attempt to preserve my right to the protection of my private life, such as the Board of Practice and procedure is now recommending, in line with Human Rights legislation.

I believed that as a result of media coverage, my case had been hopelessly prejudiced before I had an opportunity to say anything publicly in self-defence. I did not comment to the press until the matter was supposedly no longer *sub judice*. This is not 'irrelevant' to my decision to demit because I was advised that a fair trial would not be possible. All the evidence against me was in the public domain but none of that was in my favour. The out-going Moderator of the Presbytery stated: 'An unbiased jury could not be found in this country.' The evidence was contaminated, the case too seriously prejudiced.

I would submit that the Presbytery was remiss in not thinking of the likely effects of press intrusion, should have taken steps to prevent it, and when it did occur, should not have proceeded. The case would have been abandoned in a criminal court.

I was advised in November 1997 that if I pleaded guilty to part of the charge – having acted 'inappropriately' but not 'immorally', back then in 1995 – I could bring it all to an end, including the interest of the press. The Presbytery moved to judgement without Trial. I was faced with a barrage of forty or fifty people from TV crews on my way into the court.

But what I was prepared to admit and what the Presbytery wanted me to admit turned out to be different things. They wanted me to confess to immorality, which I would not do, because I had never expected any sexual advances from someone I trusted, and was horrified (and indeed traumatised) when he made them. In my statement I used the word 'intimate' to denote an affectionate relationship, but it was not my intention to imply any sexual overtones.

I would almost have admitted anything they said, just to have it over. I thank Professor Shaw for keeping my head up. But the Presbytery was determined to have a trial. And so it all began again. I faced another five or six months at least, of cameras and reporters camping in my front garden. This invasion of my privacy was more than I could bear. I was suffering from post-traumatic shock and depression. This, added to the fact that I would not – indeed could not – be given a fair trial, plus the prospect of having to repay legal expenses, meant that at the meeting on 30th November 1997 I was persuaded against my better judgement to demit my status.

I realised in that instant that I would have to leave my home, the community in which I had invested so much, my vocation and my training. I had never imagined anything else than being a minister. I had no family, nowhere to go, and as a result of all that had happened I wasn't well enough to earn my living. I knew immediately I'd made the wrong decision, but that night I wasn't fit either to cope with the alternative – a Trial that would be protracted and very public, and prejudiced beyond hope.

By the next day the Presbytery had accepted my demission. I was told to collect my books from the Kirk under the supervision of the Session Clerk. Even so I had not been found guilty of any crime.

To conclude, it is my contention that I was put under considerable pressure to demit my status at a time when I was in an unfit state to make a decision. The Presbytery did not give time to ascertain these things, or to establish whether I appreciated the consequences. I believe the procedures were deficient and not handled properly.

This morning you received the report of the Board of Practice and Procedure. It included certain objectives – amongst others; the provision of appropriate legal advice and protection from unfair interference – that do not appear to have been met during the Inquiry.

Even if this Court chooses not to provide a remedy, or deal with that part of my Petition which concerns my status, it could nonetheless instruct an investigation in the terms of my Petition, in accordance with Cox's *Practice and Procedure in the Church of Scotland* (6th ed. p. 87).

I believe that it is in the interest of the Church that justice should be seen to be done and I therefore ask that an independent enquiry should be permitted as an approriate forum.

Thank you, Moderator.

ACKNOWLEDGEMENTS

Thank you for treating me the same way you always did.
Thank you for inviting me to eat at your table, or for speaking to me
at a dance.
Thank you for £5, and for the lettuce seedlings.
Thank you for protecting me from newspaper reporters.
Thank you for writing a letter, a bunch of daffodils, and windfall
apples for the pigs.
Thank you for contributing towards my legal fees.
Thank you for signing a petition. I felt supported, though your voice
was disregarded.
Thank you for a prayer, or a candle lit, in my years of loss of faith.
Thank you for offering to sit with me at a court hearing.
In winter, thank you for thick warm curtains, and firewood.
Thank you for carol-singing at my door that night, even though it
made me cry.
Thank you for giving me a job, however menial. It made me feel I
had a value.
Thank you for being proud of me when I felt only shame.
I cannot name each one of you, but what you said or did is not
forgotten.
Know that your act of kindness gave me a reason not to end my life.

In the making of legal history, I cannot thank enough my lawyers
Andrew Murchison (until his move to Inverness following the
hearing at the Office of Industrial Tribunals in Dundee in 1998)
and thereafter Jamie Baxter of Elliot & Co., Blairgowrie; nor my
formidable Queen's Counsels Brian Napier and Susan O'Brien
who, as well as possessing brilliance of mind and the
determination to fight a great injustice, actually cared about
what happened to me as human being.
In the making of this book I thank Eleanor, Winnie, Tracey and Ann,

as I could not even type when I began and found computers as unworkable as I still do kitchen cookers and vacuum cleaners. Jane Argall and Alan Taylor for inspired suggestions – a tweak of chronology here, a change of tense there – that transformed the manuscript. William Scott, Rosemary Goring and Catherine Deveney for their encouragement. Simon Brown of Anderson Strathearn, Edinburgh, for his expert legal advice and his sensitivity to the content. Judy Moir's cat for tolerating four sheepdogs in the garden while discussions took place. Judy Moir herself for recognising the significance of this book and her determination to find a publisher brave enough to take it on. Derek Rodger of Argyll Publishing for being that man of courage.

I cannot praise highly enough my doctors, Jane Delaney and Alan Weir, who prescribed, respectively, Bread and wine (capitalisation *sic*), and sent me to their seaside cottage. They knew there was nothing wrong with my body or my mind. It was my soul that hurt.

I am so very fortunate in my friends.